T0391612

J.R.R. Tolkien in Central Europe

This volume is a long overdue contribution to the dynamic, but unevenly distributed study of fantasy and J.R.R. Tolkien's legacy in Central Europe. The chapters move between and across theories of cultural and social history, reception, adaptation, and audience studies, and offer methodological reflections on the various cultural perceptions of Tolkien's oeuvre and its impact on twenty-first century manifestations. They analyse how discourses about fantasy are produced and mediated, and how processes of re-mediation shape our understanding of the historical coordinates and local peculiarities of fantasy in general, and Tolkien in particular, all that in Central Europe in an age of global fandom. The collection examines the entanglement of fantasy and Central European political and cultural shifts across the past 50 years and traces the ways in which its haunting legacy permeates and subverts different modes and aesthetics across different domains from communist times through today's media-saturated culture.

Janka Kascakova is Associate Professor in English at the Catholic University of Ružomberok, Slovakia and Palacký University Olomouc, the Czech Republic. Her research centers on modernism and the modernist short story, especially the works of Katherine Mansfield, and fantasy literature, chiefly the works of J.R.R. Tolkien.

David Levente Palatinus is Associate Professor in Media and Cultural Studies at the Catholic University in Ružomberok and the Technical University of Liberec. He recently co-edited *Gothic Metamorphoses across the Centuries* (2020). His book *Human/Non/Human: Technics and Subjectivity across Media* is forthcoming in 2023.

Routledge Studies in Speculative Fiction

Genre and Reception in the Gothic Parody
Framing the Subversive Heroine
Kerstin-Anja Münderlein

Lovecraft in the 21st Century
Dead, But Still Dreaming
Edited by Antonio Alcala Gonzalez and Carl H. Sederholm

Motherless Creations
Fictions of Artificial Life, 1650–1890
Wendy C. Nielsen

Posthuman Subjectivity in the Novels of J.G. Ballard
Carolyn Lau

Dystopia in Arabic Speculative Fiction
A Poetics of Distress
Wessam Elmeligi

Contemporary Pakistani Speculative Fiction and the Global Imaginary
Democratizing Human Futures
Shazia Sadaf and Aroosa Kanwal

J.R.R. Tolkien in Central Europe
Context, Directions, and the Legacy
Edited by Janka Kascakova and David Levente Palatinus

For more information about this series, please visit: https://www.routledge.com/
Routledge-Studies-in-Speculative-Fiction/book-series/RSSF

J.R.R. Tolkien in Central Europe
Context, Directions, and the Legacy

Edited by
Janka Kascakova and
David Levente Palatinus

NEW YORK AND LONDON

First published 2024
by Routledge
605 Third Avenue, New York, NY 10158

and by Routledge
4 Park Square, Milton Park, Abingdon, Oxon, OX14 4RN

Routledge is an imprint of the Taylor & Francis Group, an informa business

© 2024 selection and editorial matter, Janka Kascakova and David Levente Palatinus; individual chapters, the contributors

The right of Janka Kascakova and David Levente Palatinus to be identified as the authors of the editorial material, and of the authors for their individual chapters, has been asserted in accordance with sections 77 and 78 of the Copyright, Designs and Patents Act 1988.

All rights reserved. No part of this book may be reprinted or reproduced or utilised in any form or by any electronic, mechanical, or other means, now known or hereafter invented, including photocopying and recording, or in any information storage or retrieval system, without permission in writing from the publishers.

Trademark notice: Product or corporate names may be trademarks or registered trademarks, and are used only for identification and explanation without intent to infringe.

Library of Congress Cataloging-in-Publication Data
Names: Kaščáková, Janka, editor. | Palatinus, David Levente, 1977– editor.
Title: J.R.R. Tolkien in central Europe : context, directions, and the legacy / edited by Janka Kascakova and David Levente Palatinus.
Description: New York, NY : Routledge, 2024. |
Series: Routledge studies in speculative literature | Includes bibliographical references and index. |
Identifiers: LCCN 2023017562 (print) | LCCN 2023017563 (ebook) |
ISBN 9781032525563 (hardback) | ISBN 9781032525587 (paperback) |
ISBN 9781003407171 (ebook)
Subjects: LCSH: Tolkien, J. R. R. (John Ronald Reuel), 1892-1973—Criticism and interpretation. | Tolkien, J. R. R. (John Ronald Reuel), 1892-1973—Appreciation—Europe, Central. | Fantasy literature, English—History and criticism. | Fantasy literature, English—Appreciation—Europe, Central.
Classification: LCC PR6039.O32 Z6645 2024 (print) | LCC PR6039.O32 (ebook) | DDC 823/.912—dc23/eng/20230614
LC record available at https://lccn.loc.gov/2023017562
LC ebook record available at https://lccn.loc.gov/2023017563

ISBN: 9781032525563 (hbk)
ISBN: 9781032525587 (pbk)
ISBN: 9781003407171 (ebk)

DOI: 10.4324/9781003407171

Typeset in Sabon
by codeMantra

Contents

List of Contributors	*vii*
Acknowledgements	*ix*

Introduction   1
DAVID LEVENTE PALATINUS, JANKA KASCAKOVA

PART I
Reception and Translations of Tolkien in Hungary   11

1   Reading Tolkien in Hungary, Part I: The 20th Century   13
    GERGELY NAGY

2   Reading Tolkien in Hungary, Part II: The 21st Century   34
    GERGELY NAGY

PART II
Reception and Translations of Tolkien in
Czechoslovakia and Its Succeeding Countries   59

3   Mythologia Non Grata: Tolkien and Socialist Czechoslovakia   61
    JANKA KASCAKOVA

4   "Through darkness you have come to your hope":
    The Dynamics of J.R.R. Tolkien's Work Reception in
    the Czech Context   74
    TEREZA DĚDINOVÁ

vi *Contents*

5   **J.R.R. Tolkien in the Slovak Press: Situation After 1990**   93
JOZEFA PEVČÍKOVÁ, EVA URBANOVÁ
TRANSLATED BY JELA KEHOE

6   **Unknotting the Translation Knots in *The Hobbit:***
A Diachronic Analysis of Slovak Translations from
1973 and 2002   117
JELA KEHOE

PART III
Studying Fantasy after Tolkien: Legacies and
Contemporary Perspectives   129

7   Growing Up in Fantasy: Inspecting the Convergences of
Young Adult Literature and Fantastic Fiction   131
MARTINA VRÁNOVÁ

8   One Does Not Simply Teach Fantasy: How Students of
English and American Studies in Hungary View the Genre
and Tolkien's Legacy   150
NIKOLETT SIPOS

9   From Niche to Mainstream? Screen Culture's Impact on
Contemporary Perceptions of Fantasy   161
DAVID LEVENTE PALATINUS

Index   179

Contributors

Tereza Dědinová works at Masaryk University in the Czech Republic and is mainly interested in speculative fiction from a cognitive and ecocritical perspective. Her recent projects include the co-edited monographs *Images of the Anthropocene in Speculative Fiction* (2021) and *Fantasy and Myth in the Anthropocene* (2022).

Janka Kascakova is Associate Professor in English at the Catholic University of Ružomberok, Slovakia and Palacký University Olomouc, the Czech Republic. Her research centers on modernism and the modernist short story, especially the works of Katherine Mansfield, and fantasy literature, chiefly the works of J.R.R. Tolkien.

Jela Kehoe obtained her PhD in translation studies from Constantine the Philosopher University in Nitra. She is a member of the Department of English Language and Literature at the Faculty of Arts and Letters at the Catholic University in Ružomberok, where she teaches a number of linguistic and ELT courses.

Gergely Nagy is a Hungarian independent scholar with an interest in Tolkien (and the 20th-century fantastic), medieval English literature (romance, Chaucer, Malory), and contemporary popular music. He taught at the University of Szeged for 16 years and was instrumental in the founding of the Hungarian Tolkien Society.

David Levente Palatinus is Associate Professor in Media and Cultural Studies at the Catholic University in Ružomberok and the Technical University of Liberec. He recently co-edited *Gothic Metamorphoses across the Centuries* (Peter Lang, 2020). His book *Human / Non / Human: Technics and Subjectivity across Media* is forthcoming in 2023.

viii *Contributors*

Jozefa Pevčíková is a PhD student of aesthetics at the Institute of Literary and Artistic Communication (Department of Aesthetics and Ethics) at Constantine the Philosopher University in Nitra, Slovakia. Her interdisciplinary research includes popular culture, fandom and fan activities, intertextuality, and media studies.

Nikolett Sipos is a PhD candidate at the Doctoral School of Literary Studies at Pázmány Péter Catholic University, Hungary. Her research focuses on transmedia storytelling in the case of speculative fiction universes, currently concentrating on Game of Thrones.

Eva Urbanová is a literary scholar, critic, occasional poet, and author of the children's book *Jeleňatý a Kravatý* (FACE, 2019), which won the Debut of the Year Readers Award of the literary magazine *Knižná revue*. She teaches at the Department of Slovak Language and Literature of the Catholic University in Ružomberok, Slovakia.

Martina Vránová received her PhD in Comparative Literature from Masaryk University, Brno, Czech Republic. She is currently Assistant Professor of English at the Institute of Foreign Languages, Faculty of Mechanical Engineering, Brno University of Technology. Her research interests include academic writing, rhetoric, and contemporary fiction. She has edited volumes on literature and LSP and published two novels in Czech.

Acknowledgements

This monograph was supported by the project VEGA 1/0594/20 – J.R.R. Tolkien's Legacy and the Fantasy Genre in Central Europe.

Introduction

David Levente Palatinus, Janka Kascakova

Even a superficial look at contemporary cultural production shows that fantasy, especially in the aftermath of the adaptations of J.R.R. Tolkien's *Lord of the Rings* trilogy, C.S. Lewis' *Chronicles of Narnia*, or J.K. Rowling's *Harry Potter*, was given a new impetus. This curious genre continues to maintain a pervasive presence in our historic present, whilst keeping the ability to garner an extremely wide and solid fan base. Its popularity and centrality in the cultural domain since the 1930s have been frequently attributed to its ability to channel, among other things, cultural perceptions and imaginaries of transgression, sublimity, instances of escapism and otherness, as well as the intricate relation between politics and power. Whilst maintaining its reliance on curiously formulaic patterns of plot, themes, characters, and, most importantly, a peculiar poetics of worldbuilding, it continues to resists rigid categorisation: demarcating its multiple different variations continues to be a challenge for scholarship – but this quality also allows fantasy to be one of the most versatile and heterogeneous forms: especially in its recent manifestations both in literary fiction and across converging media, it has become more and more conducive to (generic) subversion, transgression, and hybridisation. As is the case with other instances of genre fiction, it is the ability to adapt and to constantly reinvent itself, its ubiquity, and its reliance on participatory fandom that makes fantasy, as a genre as well as a mode, so powerful and capable of mobilising audiences across national and cultural boundaries (see Vránová, Vernyik and Palatinus).

Whilst Tolkien's work and legacy continues to be widely studied in the Western world, scholarly approaches to both fantasy and Tolkien's reception in Central Europe remain relatively underexposed. *The Lord of the Rings* was translated into Czech and Hungarian relatively early, still during communist times, although in the former case only as a samizdat available to few. Tolkien studies in the region saw an upsurge only after the millennium and was mostly driven by the film adaptations, which brought audiences back to the original trilogy, opened up Tolkien's universe to curious

DOI: 10.4324/9781003407171-1

2 *David Levente Palatinus, Janka Kascakova*

would-be fans, and launched a peculiar form of participatory culture and fandom in Central Europe.

When fantasy tackled the unresolved tension between rationality and more volatile, suggestible, mysterious conditions, the genre was infused with political and social significance, becoming a vehicle of escapism (see Hume). Fantasy questioned the nature of power and authority, notably in relation to an oppressive past, and the ways in which gender roles reinforced social norms in contemporary society. Tolkien and the cultural myth around his figure emerged as a major factor within this process as his stories often employed supernatural elements to self-reflexivity and to examine the fundamental conventions of the construction of gender roles.

These phenomena began to be contextualised recently within a broader media landscape, shedding light on the exchanges between literature, the press, the radio, and technologically inflected aesthetics. The focus is on an ever-changing, polymorphous fantasy imagination whose pervasiveness and power even seem able to mould reality into its own shape, as shown by the proliferation of contemporary fan art. The reactions of the contemporaneous press to Tolkien's trilogy provided a framework for the conceptualisation as well as the early iconography of the British high fantasy. Far from being tamed within an increasingly secularised, ideology-driven society, fantasy actually resurfaced within a peculiarly rational form. It retains its transgressive power despite the normative and restrictive theorisation it underwent. This project therefore attempts to add a new facet to the "hauntological" dimension of Tolkien, from literary fiction to cinema and fandom.

Due in part to the success of the film adaptations, Tolkien, and by extension, fantasy has recently been rediscovered as a trending genre paradigm in Western literary and media scholarship. It is perceived as a conduit for underlying cultural ideas about worldbuilding and historical nostalgia (Jameson), transmediality, fandom, and participatory culture as well as media convergence. Tolkien and the fantasy genre have seen an upsurge in post-socialist Central Europe as well, yet while the fandom is increasing, the scholarly study of Tolkien's Central European legacy has lagged behind, with fantasy is still being considered a niche genre situated on the popular end of the literary scale. This volume proposes to analyse the ways in which specific discourses (in academia and in the fandom) about Tolkien's legacy are produced and mediated and examine how processes of re-mediation and re-purposing shape our understanding of both the historical coordinates and local peculiarities of fantasy in Central Europe in an age of global fandom. The chapters in this book focus on Slovakia, the Czech Republic, and Hungary. This is partly due to the geographic distribution of the contributors and their expertise and partly was a result of a conscious decision: although Poland geographically belongs to the region, its own

Introduction 3

burgeoning fantasy tradition prevented us from including it in the volume to avoid disproportionality.

To that end, this study also aspires to be both a historical investigation of the development of fantasy through national literatures of Central Europe and a methodological reflection on the metamorphoses that ensure the survival and dissemination of fantasy works.

The contributors bring together scholarship that explores various interconnected aspects of fantasy and Tolkien's legacy through the lens of converging critical and methodological approaches. We view high fantasy as a dynamic form that exceeds the concept of literary genre, proving able to renovate and adapt through constant processes of hybridisation. Starting from this interdisciplinary approach, the individual chapters focus on the domains of literary, filmic/televisual, and popular-cultural studies and mobilise texts from the second half of the 20th century to the present day in Central Europe that have come to constitute instances of local Tolkien fandom.

We offer this volume as a necessary and long overdue contribution to the dynamic but unevenly distributed field of the study of the fantasy genre in general and J.R.R. Tolkien's oeuvre and legacy in particular. While in the USA, Tolkien's work is respected as a relevant academic objective and scholars have been working on it since the 1960s, systematic and academic studies of the various permutations of fantasy in Central-Eastern Europe are only beginning to gain traction. There seems to be a great deal of reluctance for academics to be associated with the study of Tolkien, if not as a secondary interest, then certainly as the primary one. In the post-socialist Central European countries we are discussing here (Hungary, the Czech Republic, and Slovakia), this trend is even more obvious. For that reason, there has never been an attempt at systematically studying the origins and development of Tolkien's reception as groundwork for future academic discussion of fantasy. This volume's ambition is to redress this oversight by discussing the earliest reception of Tolkien's work in the geographical area indicated while it was still part of the Soviet bloc, demonstrating how the potential of fantasy for manifold interpretations and its appeal to general readers were perceived as a threat to the ideological foundations of the so-called socialist states. As this threat was taken very seriously by the authorities, the history of Tolkien's reception shows the tension between the censors' and publishers' effort to thwart the publications of his work and the individual scholars', translators', and enthusiasts' creative ways of sidestepping their obstacles. This also necessitates discussing the hidden influence of Tolkien on the dissident culture, the status of *The Lord of the Rings* as a manifest of freedom and fight against the regime.

Our collection also aims to investigate the post-socialist era's approach to and reception of Tolkien, arguing that fantasy, and Tolkien's work in particular, became an integral part of the democratisation process in the studied countries, one of the manifestations of freedom of speech and expression. The publications of not only Tolkien but fantasy in general soared right after the change of regimes in the first wave; the second wave came after Peter Jackson's popular film adaptations gained traction globally as well as in a more local context, kick-starting a gradually accelerating process of the proliferation of occurrences of the fantastic (and more broadly, speculative) modes and discourses in literary fiction, screen media (including film, television, and video games) – but more importantly, and also as a necessary result, in scholarship as well. Our research, however, indicates that this immense popularity for the general public created a still existing rift between the "fans" and "serious" academics who were, for a long time, seen as polar opposites. Academic research in the field has, for a long time, been sporadic and very cautious. However, what applies to Tolkien is not entirely the case of fantasy in general, as research in the recent years has increasingly begun to adopt new approaches that dispose of the dismissal of views that popular culture is irrelevant to academic study, and opened new avenues to our understanding of the importance of fantasy – especially in regard to the central position that this mode and form occupies on a number of visual media platforms as well as in their respective scholarly studies, be it from the point of view of the genre, audiences, or that of production cultures within a Central European context.

Combining cultural theory, literary studies, and media studies, we seek to explore (1) the ways Tolkien's work has been perceived, disseminated, studied and, most recently, taught at universities in Central Europe; (2) what the shifting focus of literary scholarship towards popular genres reveals about forms of cultural import from Anglophone contexts; (3) what role Tolkien's legacy plays in perpetuating stereotypical perceptions of Britain's past and present; and (4) how fantasy's worldbuilding helps circulate ideas about racial, political, and geographic otherness, femininity and masculinity, domination and equity, practices of exclusion, and, finally, mythological conceptions of good vs. evil, from communist times through to today's media-saturated culture. To that end, we ask the following questions: (1) What is the relationship between discourses of Tolkien's work, our attempts to depoliticise fantasy, and the pervasiveness of our political, economic, and cultural anxieties in Central Europe, especially in our present historic times? (2) Do conceptualisations of fantasy have a history of their own – especially a Central European one? and (3) What does this history reveal about the ways in which we negotiate local cultural legacies in relation to global ones? In order to trace this multifarious legacy, the contributions in this volume attempt to challenge and expand on previous conceptualisations of fantasy itself by suggesting that it returns in times of cultural crisis. This transgressive, experimental

Introduction 5

mode is actually conducive to alternative experiences of the intricacies of our present historical condition, as shown by the proliferation of Tolkien's paratextual universe, fan art, online communities, and scholarly interest.

(Re-)Conceptualising Fantasy? A Convergence of Perspectives

Although literary-historical, genre-based, popular-cultural, or adaptation studies-focused discourses, as well as research into the various cultural forms and modes of speculative fiction and fantasy are well-established in Slovakia (Nagy; Keserű; Nagy and Keserű), the critical re-assessment of Tolkien's legacy and its centrality in the interrelations of Anglophone cultural import and Central European fantasy writing and the academic study of Tolkien fandom is somewhat underrepresented. Therefore, this volume proposes to fill in a void in critical thinking in four interconnected aspects: (1) it reconfigures problems of demarcation (global and local, national and transnational trends in fandom as part of the history of reception, political allergisation vs. attempts to depoliticise fantasy) and repositions questions of agency and participation from the perspective of global and local trends (Dhoest; Risse; Fraille-Marcos; Roudometof). (2) By combining cultural theory, literary scholarship, and media research, the project maps out the underlying processes and cultural forms through which these concepts are produced and mediated. (3) It calls attention to so far underrepresented literary and media texts and offers new, Central European perspectives on well-known literary and media genres to enrich their reception (Dubs and Kascakova). (4) By identifying political, cultural, and historical factors underlying the perception of Tolkien as a niche author from communist times through to the present, it bridges the gap between fandom-based and scholarly approaches to his legacy (Barker; Duits).

The main strength of the volume lies in its interdisciplinary character which allows for substantial methodological reflections on the various cultural perceptions of both Tolkien and the fantasy genre. The volume charts the generic and political diversity of fantasy across five decades, arguing for the striking proliferation of Tolkien's tropes across a range of different media, whilst accounting for the discrepancies in the reception of his works: as some texts were picked up for adaptation and translation more easily than others. Unearthing reasons beyond political or aesthetic preferences both in scholarship and fandom, the primary purpose is to map out the underlying complexity of the historical legacy of fantasy that warrants attention for its ability to survive and adapt to different cultural contexts and ages. The chapters in this book therefore expand the concept of fantasy beyond a literary genre or a single interpretation. They emphasise the aggressive pervasiveness of fantasy as a mode and trace the ways in

6 David Levente Palatinus, Janka Kascakova

which Tolkien's haunting legacy permeates and subverts different modes and aesthetics across different cultural and national domains.

We admittedly and purposefully appraise fantasy in its range of manifestations. It is not by chance that the chapters of this volume move between and across the fields of genre and reception theories, historiography, literary fiction, and finally film and television. Besides covering a wide range of formats, the volume also offers an overview of the metamorphoses and reception of fantasy from the legacy of Tolkien's oeuvre to 21st-century manifestations in popular media. The main strength of the volume lies in its interdisciplinary character, enhanced by the international scope of its contributors, which allows for substantial methodological reflections on the various cultural perceptions of (Tolkienian) fantasy. Taken as a whole, the chapters chart the generic and political diversity of the fantastic across Central European countries, arguing as they do so for the striking proliferation of fantasy tropes across a range of different forms and media. Whilst accounting for the discrepancies in the reception of fantasy and unearthing reasons beyond political or aesthetic preferences both in scholarship and fandom, our collection seeks to map out the underlying entanglement of fantasy as a mode and Central European political and cultural shifts across the past 50 years. We argue that fantasy warrants attention for its ability to survive and adapt to different cultural contexts and ages.

Methodology and Organising Principle

We opted to consider mixed methods, including qualitative and quantitative research. The volume seeks to explore the ways in which we negotiate fantasy across various media and national contexts – not just from the perspective of our present historical time but also through analyses of the history of Tolkien studies itself. Our method builds on the combination of cultural theory, literary scholarship, and media research in order to map out the processes and practices through which fictional and non-fictional renditions of fantasy are produced and circulated in a Central European milieu. The volume intends to fill in a void in regard to systematic scholarly studies of Tolkien's impact on the literary landscape of popular literature in Central Europe, and the apparent disconnect between contemporary audiences' responses and intense engagement with fantasy across media, and the apparent lag that Central European scholarship needs to work off in regard to the subject matter.

The chapters of the collection are arranged into three sections: the first two adopt a combination of diachronic and synchronic approaches in their discussion of Tolkien's reception and translations of his works in specific Central European cultural (and political) contexts over the past half a century. The third section looks at contemporary formations and opens up

Introduction 7

the discussion to adaptation and transmediality via analyses of cognitive narratology in young adult contexts, the teachability of fantasy in contemporary curricula, and screen culture's impact on fantasy's evolution from niche to mainstream.

Section 1: Reception and Translations of Tolkien in Hungary

In this first section, Gergely Nagy offers a two-chapter comprehensive overview and analysis of the reception of Tolkien in Hungary. The first chapter focuses on pre-2000 translations, and comments on what the author calls the first fantasy boom, that, interestingly, wasn't the product but rather the catalyst for the subsequent interest in the works of Tolkien and instigated a first wave of their translation. The chapter argues that at that time, Tolkien was "comfortably slotted into children's literature and science fiction" (14) – as attested by the author's extensive survey of the Hungarian press and literature that discussed Tolkien in this period.

The second part of Nagy's survey of the reception of Tolkien in Hungary then proceeds to focus on the years between 2000 and today and examines how Peter Jackson's film production energised the already existing, yet somewhat less visible fan base. He traces the gradual shift in the dynamics of fan communities facilitated by the Internet. He then offers a historical overview of the founding and development of the Hungarian Tolkien Society, which played a very important role in organising Tolkien Studies in Hungary and was instrumental in shaping the academic discourse on Tolkien and the fantasy mode in more general terms. The chapter concludes with Tolkien's changing cultural role and the proliferation of ways in which he is now approached. It also offers an overview of the scholarly literature published in Hungarian.

Section 2: Reception and Translations of Tolkien in Czechoslovakia and Its Succeeding Countries

While mainly discussing forms of reception, censorship, and translations within specific political milieus, this section contextualises these phenomena within a broader socio-political landscape, shedding light on the exchanges between literature, (post-)socialist power structures, and political activism and escapism. The focus is on an ever-changing, polymorphous fantasy imagination whose pervasiveness and power seem even able to mould reality into its own shape, as shown by the convoluted and imbalanced reception of Tolkien's specific texts. As convincingly argued here, the discrepancies between the reactions of general readership and the (reluctant) approval of the state apparatus provided a controversial framework for the conceptualisation of the status and cultural logic of fantasy, as well

8 *David Levente Palatinus, Janka Kascakova*

as for early translations of Tolkien's works. Far from being tamed within an increasingly secularised society, fantasy gradually resurfaced after the fall of the Iron Curtain, retaining its transgressive power despite normative and restrictive theorisations and framing as a genre/form of lesser importance. The chapters in this section argue that the past continues to haunt the present in fantasy growing into and remaining a form of political allegory and escape. Janka Kascakova's chapter thus traces the development and particular instances of the reception of *The Hobbit* and *The Lord of the Rings*, uncovering the origins of the important place Tolkien's work would gain behind the Iron Curtain. In the subsequent chapter offering a quantitative analysis of conceptualisations of good and evil, freedom, the representation of otherness, racism, and feminist and environmental themes, Tereza Dědinová focuses on the shifts in the reception of Tolkien's works over time, with particular attention to readers who read the novels as adults or teens in the 1990s and younger readers who only came to reading it in this millennium and in the aftermath of Jackson's adaptations. The third chapter in this section, by Jozefa Pevčíková and Eva Urbanová, examines critical commentaries and ongoing fan discourse published in the Slovak press, academic journals, and pop cultural publications (both official and fan-made) since the 1990s until the present in order to account for the shifting trends in the underlying ideological concerns of reception history that inform Tolkien discourse in contemporary Slovakia. The section is concluded by Jela Kehoe's chapter on the challenges emerging from the (un-)translatability of culturally (and linguistically) specific contents in relation to Tolkien's texts, especially in a situation where, on the one hand, the translator has to navigate a sensitive political context and where the lack of similar literary tradition in the native language creates extra challenge for a successful and relatable translation of elements central to fantasy worldbuilding.

Section 3: Studying Fantasy After Tolkien: Legacies and Contemporary Perspectives

The third section of the collection aims at mapping out specific traits of the manifestation of popular (urban) fantasy in contemporary literary, filmic, and television narratives. In recent years, specific fantasy scenarios have again become central to numerous forms of film and television. The chapters in this section operate on the understanding that the fantasy mode has proved to be particularly conducive to figurations of human and non-human otherness, and instances of worldbuilding. Through textual analyses of specific program texts, Martina Vránová's chapter focuses on YA worldbuilding and the ways in which patterns like the rite of passage facilitate the audience's search for identity. Nikolett Sipos's chapter investigates questions of teachability in relation to fantasy by offering a case study of the ways Hungarian students of English and American studies consume and engage with fantasy via various converging media.

In a similar vein, David Palatinus' chapter comments on the technological shifts in filmmaking, and how the proliferation of streaming platforms played a role in moving fantasy from niche to mainstream, and argues that theories of adaptation, transmediality, and participatory agency have to be repositioned to better situate generic hybridity and the (de)convergence of platforms. The contributions in this section ask questions not only about fears and anxieties, attachment and aberration, repression and abuse, violence and control, and the subconscious and the transcendental, but they also ask questions about the broader political and cultural contexts in which these generic transformations unfold and about the complex ethical dilemmas they unmask. The chapters look at the roots of classic and lesser-known renditions of fantasy tropes by ascertaining the shifting dynamics of filmic and televisual adaptations.

Our findings will interest a large number of researchers whose work moves between and across areas of literary and cultural studies, genre theory, and adaptation as well as those whose scholarship focuses on one or more of the key themes in Tolkien's oeuvre. These themes are rapidly establishing themselves as reference points in ongoing critical discourses on fantasy within and beyond academic circles. These insights will also be of interest to Central European scholars who work on cultural representations in genres and who study the cultural impact and reception of Tolkien's legacy in their own countries. Since fantasy has established itself as a mainstream component of university curricula at all levels, outputs of the project will also be of interest to a variety of students. Undergraduate and MA readers will benefit from the innovative, comprehensive, and updated approach with which this project integrates mainstream approaches to Tolkien's works with their multifaceted re-emergences in a variety of arts and media from the 1950s to the present.

Works Cited

Baker, Daniel. "Why We Need Dragons: The Progressive Potential of Fantasy". *Journal of the Fantastic in the Arts* 23.3 (2012): 437–459.

Barker, Martin. "Envisaging 'Visualization'. Some Challenges from the International Lord of the Rings Project". *Film-Philosophy* 10.3 (2006): 1–25.

Dhoest, Alexander. "The National in Contemporary. European Television Fiction: The Flemish Case". *Critical Studies in Television* 2.2 (2007): 60–76.

Dubs, Kathleen and Janka Kascakova, eds. *Middle-Earth and Beyond*. Newcastle: Cambridge Scholars Publishing, 2010.

Duits, Linda et al, eds. *The Ashgate Research Companion to Fan Cultures*. Burlington: Ashgate Publishing Company, 2009.

10 David Levente Palatinus, Janka Kascakova

Fraile-Marcos, Ana María. *Literature and the Glocal City: Reshaping the English Canadian Imaginary*. New York: Routledge, 2014.

Hume, Kathryn. *Fantasy and Mimesis: Responses to Reality in Western Literature*. New York: Routledge, 2014.

Jackson, Rosemary. *Fantasy: The Literature of Subversion*. New York: Routledge, 1981.

Jameson, Fredric. *The Antinomies of Realism*. New York: Verso, 2013.

Keserű, József. "Brandek a magyar fantasy-irodalomban". *Alföld* 67.12 (2016): 91–97.

Nagy, Péter H. *Alternatívák: A popkultúra kapcsolatrendszerei*. Budapest: Prae, 2016.

Nagy, Péter H. and József Keserű. "The Interaction of Canons: Conflict or Symbiosis?: Rereading and Relativity of Traditions in David Gemmell's 'Troy Series' and Dan Simmons' 'Hyperion Cantos'". *World Literature Studies* 7.3 (2015): 87–99.

Risse, Thomas. A *Community of Europeans? Transnational Identities and Public Spheres*. Ithaca: Cornell UP, 2010.

Roudometof, Victor: *Glocalization: A Critical Introduction*. New York: Routledge, 2016.

Vránová, Martina, Zénó Vernyik and Dávid Levente Palatinus, eds. *Crime and Detection in Contemporary Culture*. Szeged, Americana E-Books, 2019.

Part I

Reception and Translations of Tolkien in Hungary

1 Reading Tolkien in Hungary, Part I

The 20th Century

Gergely Nagy

In October 1971, J.R.R. Tolkien wrote a letter to Péter Szentmihályi Szabó, a Hungarian writer, translator, and then editor at the publishing house Gondolat [Thought]. Evidently in answer to some questions, Tolkien, somewhat exasperatedly, asserts he has "no time to provide bibliographical material concerning criticisms, reviews, or translations", and goes on to say that he has "very little interest in serial literary history, and no interest at all in the history of present situation of the English 'novel'. My work in *not* a 'novel', but an 'heroic romance' a much older and quite different variety of literature" (Carpenter 414).[1] In this, he inadvertently encapsulated how his own works were initially perceived in Hungary: Tolkien was approached (and reproached) in terms he did not care for, measured to standards he had had no intention to fulfil, and lumped together with works and authors with whom he had very little in common.

It seems certain that Tolkien and his work were known to some people in Hungary by the end of the 1960s. His first official appearance was the publication of *The Hobbit* in 1975, and until 1981, when *The Lord of the Rings* was published, he was mentioned more and more often in the press. In Hungary, this was the period of the Kádár regime, named after János Kádár, General Secretary of the Hungarian Socialist Workers' Party, whom the Soviet Union picked to lead the country after Soviet intervention ended the 1956 fight for independence. Kádár's regime eventually became much less repressive than his predecessors', and while the infamous III/III division of the Ministry of the Interior kept a close watch on the cultural sphere especially, Kádár's motto was "whoever isn't against us is with us", and so by the 1970s, Hungary was a relatively liveable country, the "merriest barracks" in the Eastern Bloc. There naturally was an underground culture and samizdat, but Tolkien did not belong there, as in Russia.[2] Both *The Hobbit* and *The Lord of the Rings* were published early and officially, both in excellent (although in some sense problematic) translations. Tolkien was not seen as subversive, but he was not fully approved of or appreciated either.

DOI: 10.4324/9781003407171-3

14 Gergely Nagy

He was, at least in the beginning, not taken very seriously. His work was comfortably slotted into children's literature or science fiction, a branch of contemporary literature most tolerated even in Eastern European countries, and his early reception was bound up with SF and its forums. When the "fantasy boom" of the 1970s trickled down to Hungary, Tolkien was seen as its founding father and in a way responsible for it; but by the 1990s, a curious "classicisation" process started: Tolkien's work, especially after the Hungarian appearance of *The Silmarillion* (1991), was considered both seminal and already outdated, old-fashioned. This was partly due to "genre fantasy" and the appeal of more recent works, but it exemplifies exactly what he warned about in his letter: his work was seen as something it did not purport to be, often judged without any appropriate background in languages, mediaeval literature, cultural and religious history. These judgements were more ideological before the change of regime in 1989, but in a sense remained so later too: Tolkien was now considered hopelessly conservative, out of touch with recent themes and topics, morally simplistic, and stylistically quaint. It was only after Peter Jackson's films focused attention on his work, and the Hungarian Tolkien Society was formed in 2002, that a more organised, academic, well-founded approach could emerge in the Hungarian reception.

But that was far into the future in 1971, when Tolkien answered Szentmihályi Szabó, and it took three decades to change. This chapter, the first part of a survey of the Hungarian reception of Tolkien's work, will take the story up to roughly the turn of the millennium, a good cut-off date: pre- and post-Jackson periods doubtless differ everywhere, and the 2002 establishment of the Hungarian Tolkien Society gave the 21st century a decidedly different direction in Tolkien Studies. The 20th century was mostly taken up by translation and a slow building up of the fan base. The main interpretive concerns were where Tolkien's work fits (children's literature, science fiction, fantasy?) and whether (and how) they are real "literature".

Rumours: Before the First Translations

One of the most important people in Tolkien's early Hungarian reception was Péter Kuczka (1923–1999), poet, writer, translator, editor, and advocate for science fiction.[3] Kuczka had been an enthusiastic communist poet who then became involved in the 1956 revolution, and afterwards could not publish either as punishment, or because his earlier poetry made him embarrassing for Comrade Aczél (György Aczél, 1917–1991, the all-powerful director of cultural life in Kádár's regime). During this period, he became interested in film and science fiction. When he could work again in publishing, he ran two ground-breaking fantastic book series, *Kozmosz*

Reading Tolkien in Hungary, Part I: The 20th Century   15

(started in 1969, and later renamed *Galaktika*) and *Kossuth* (running from 1970 to 1975), which made fantastic literature available in Hungarian. In 1972, he founded *Galaktika*, a science fiction magazine that became a veritable literary workshop by the 1980s (Szentmihályi Szabó also worked there from the beginning; see Sohár, "Anyone" 259–261). Judit Gálvölgyi (1946–), future translator of *The Silmarillion,* read an afterword by Kuczka which mentioned Tolkien[4] and wrote to him offering to translate *The Lord of the Rings.* She had read the book in the summer of 1969, in London, and instantly fell in love with it (personal communication). To her surprise, Kuczka wrote back, suggesting that Gálvölgyi do shorter pieces for *Galaktika* first (her first translation appeared in the magazine in 1976). In 1976, Kuczka became editor-in-chief of the publishing house Móra, where *The Hobbit* had by then appeared (and which published *Galaktika* too).

Another early account is by Mihály Erdei Grünwald (1944–2023), a journalist, film writer, director, and producer, who was the secretary of the Hungarian science fiction fan club in 1972, and attended EuroCon in Trieste (Erdei Grünwald, "Arafat"). Here, an American told him about Tolkien and gave him a copy of *The Lord of the Rings.* Though Erdei Grünwald gives his name as "Jan Fiedler", this was in fact Jan Howard Finder (1939–2013), an important figure in the early American fandom.[5] Finder was invited to give a talk in Budapest, and Erdei Grünwald passed the book to Éva Avarossy, a colleague of his who was working as a translator. In 1973, he wrote an article for *Magyar Ifjúság* [Hungarian Youth] about Finder's Budapest talk and included a short interview with him and with Avarossy, who said she "intends to translate this work too" ("Fantázia" 28–29).[6] But she soon saw the book would require a full-time translator and wrote a detailed, glowing reader's report for Gondolat, where Szentmihályi Szabó, by some called Kuczka's "left (and right) hand man", was editor and who, as we saw, had already corresponded with Tolkien by then and also mentioned him in print ("Rev. of Baxter").[7] It seems this is how *The Lord of the Rings* ended up with Gondolat, where it would be published in 1981.

Tolkien garnered a few other mentions in the Hungarian press before *The Hobbit* was published that made a somewhat wider public than just science fiction fans aware of his existence. In 1974, the periodical *Valóság* [Reality] published a review article about current artistic movements in the world, in which Tolkien was mentioned as "coming into fashion" in the 1960s ("Közelmúlt" 127). In an article by Gisbert Kranz, published in the digest of foreign books and periodicals called *Mérleg* [Scale], Tolkien's trilogy was declared "one of the most compelling and inventive works of our time" (55), and it was also mentioned that he wrote "a few novels in the early 60s too".[8] The clubs and associations devoted to Tolkien's works and languages soon became an often-repeated, frequently slightly scornful topos of these reports.

16 *Gergely Nagy*

The First Wave of Translations: *The Hobbit* and
The Lord of the Rings (1970s–1980s)

It was after such antecedents that Móra (a venerable publishing house of children's literature) brought out *The Hobbit* in late 1975, handsomely promoted in the press. The translator was Tibor Szobotka (1913–1982), a poet, writer, translator, broadcaster, literary historian, who could not publish his own work and made a living by freelancing jobs and translations (he translated Galsworthy, Lewis Carroll, and Joyce's *A Portrait of the Artist as a Young Man*). Szobotka's translation is still controversial among Hungarian fans. He knew nothing about the background of Tolkien's work and *The Lord of the Rings*: he changed "hobbit" to a new word formation, "babó", Gollum to "Nyelem" (a quite appropriate Hungarian onomatopoeic word), but left "Baggins". Generally, however, his text was excellent, inventive, and playful. Objections that it was "too childish" miss the point: in its atmosphere and register, Szobotka's *Babó* was a very good approximation of Tolkien's children's book. The poems were done by István Tótfalusi (1936–2020), linguist and prolific translator both to and from Hungarian and half a dozen other languages. His translations appeared regularly in *Galaktika* from 1975 on, and he would later work on other Tolkien texts. The book was also illustrated by Tamás Szecskó (1925–1987), a graphic artist and painter who illustrated more than 500 books during his career. Many regard his drawings (like the balding Bilbo, wearing striped trousers and suspenders) as not appropriate, but his unique style did place him among the most instantly recognisable of the early *Hobbit* illustrations.[9] Sadly, in later editions, his art was discarded, but at least it was replaced by Tolkien's own illustrations.

The Hobbit was marketed as a children's book and designated "meseregény", a Hungarian genre term meaning "fairy-tale novel", usually used for original works for children not set in the real world. Terming Tolkien "children's literature" slotted him away comfortably as something not to be taken entirely seriously. Indeed, Szentmihályi Szabó used the term for Tolkien's work in an article on fantastic literature ("Irodalom", 96, both for *The Hobbit* and *The Lord of the Rings*), and Tamás Vekerdy (1935–2019), later one of the most noted child psychologists in Hungary, cited Tolkien's "On Fairy-Stories" in an article about fairy tales and their pedagogical value (337).[10] In 1977, a short news item about projected new publications featured *The Lord of the Ring* (sic), a book "difficult to define [...] a fantastic fairy tale for adults, in which the writer created an entirely new and exciting, colourful imaginary world". The article accurately reports Tolkien's creation of a "unique language" and a "strange, private mythology", adding up to a "voluminous, high-standard work of art with a definite cultural historical interest" (Mátyás 6). But by mentioning the Tolkien

Reading Tolkien in Hungary, Part I: The 20th Century   17

clubs, it also casts emphasis on the "strangeness" of the phenomenon in the Western world.

After *The Hobbit* came out, Tolkien's name appeared more frequently in the press. Ferenc Mező's review placed him in the context of Anglo-American "nonsense literature" (exemplified by Lewis Carroll, Edward Lear, and Jonathan Swift) but claimed that he is a "characteristically *American* representative" of the genre (10; earlier he said Tolkien had moved to America). He appreciated the book's style, humour, and interesting characters and added that adult readers are most likely to enjoy "the spot-on satirical representation of the American way of life" (10) – perhaps an example of how, based on wrong information and relating to Tolkien on an ideological basis, the establishment in Hungary was ready to find common points even when there were none. Interestingly, the surprising success of *The Silmarillion* after 1977 was also reported. It was called a "grand conglomerate of Pre-Raphaelite sentiments, Wagneriad, Jugendstil and the legends about the isle of Thule" (iszlai 7). It was also noted, however, that "behind fairy-tale plot twists and mythological symbols, it's not only the condemnation of modern warfare that can be seen, but also a nostalgia for the idyllically conceived past before the industrial and scientific revolutions" ("Legunalmasabb" 8). The periodical *Nagyvilág* [Big World], devoted to world literature, even published a translation of Robert M. Adams's now somewhat infamous article in *The New York Review of Books*, "The Silmarillion and the Hobbit Habit", here titled "Tolkien's Heritage".[11] This memorably called the book "an empty and pompous bore" (169; in the Hungarian, 1209), "not a literary event of any magnitude" (171; in the Hungarian, 1210), but is still the first well-structured, academically inclined summary in Hungarian of *The Lord of the Rings* and its themes, sources, and literary context. The translation itself is interesting: it gets "Middle-earth" entirely wrong ("Tengerköz") and uses a different word for "elves" ("villi", ultimately from Slovakian "víla", meaning "fairy") than what the translators of *The Lord of the Rings* settled on but suggests some knowledge of the translation already under way by then: Szobotka's "Baggins" is here already "Zsákos" (a fairly close Hungarian name formation but not at all one that would be inevitably evident). Adams's piece could have made readers aware of *The Silmarillion* and its contents as far back as 1978 – but there were as yet not many such readers, since *The Lord of the Rings* had not been published yet.

But it was already in the works. In the meantime, Éva Avarossy carried on giving talks about Tolkien to the Science Fiction Club, and already in 1978, an article in the Hungarian press taken from *The Daily Telegraph* pointed attention to the new genre called "fantasy", the success of which seemed strange because it "totally lacks one of the main themes of our age: sex" ("Népszerű" 18. Adams also noted the lack of sex, 1212).

18   *Gergely Nagy*

This was the period when "genre fantasy" started to proliferate, thanks to American paperback publishing (on this and its connection to Tolkien, see Anderson). Suddenly, there was news of other fantasy works before the Hungarian readership had even had a chance to read the "original", and this may have contributed to how Tolkien "classicised" prematurely in the 1990s and came to seem old-fashioned and out of date even before he was properly known.

When *The Lord of the Rings* (*A Gyűrűk Ura*) finally appeared in 1981, this readership could start to take shape. The story of the translation was somewhat complicated. After Éva Avarossy's glowing reader's report to Gondolat, at some point in the 1970s, it was decided to commission a translation.[12] The work was undertaken by Ádám Réz (1926–1978), writer, editor, prolific translator from a great number of languages. Réz was intrigued by the book, especially its complex system of nomenclature and the fiction of translation: he is said to have regarded it as a delightful game and started working out the names first. It is not known whether he knew Tolkien's "Guide to the Names in *The Lord of the Rings*", but his solutions sometimes strongly suggest that he did. In other cases, however, especially with names of Germanic origin that Tolkien wrote to leave untranslated in non-Germanic languages (like Shadowfax or Isengard), he diverged, and evidently arguing that such names are comprehensible to the English reader in much the same way as Shire-names are, he translated them. He completed the first 11 chapters (with the inset poems), but then he fell ill and died in September 1978. The unfinished translation was passed around for a while in the publisher's offices and eventually ended up with Árpád Göncz. Göncz was then working as a translator after having spent five years in prison for his part in the 1956 revolution (1958–1963; his original sentence was life imprisonment), and would go on to be a successful writer and translate (among others) Arthur C. Clarke, Mary Shelley, John Updike, Ernest Hemingway, and Stryon (his translations appeared in *Galaktika* from the beginning). At the change of regime, he took an active political role again, and was the first freely elected president of Hungary, serving from 1990 to 2000. Göncz had to finish the translation in an extremely short time: he often said in interviews that he had only three months, and that by the end, he simply hated it. For the poems, Dezső Tandori was recruited. Tandori (1938–2019) was an extraordinarily original and inventive poet and an incredibly prolific translator of everything, from Tarzan to Hegel – it would be difficult to find a bookshop in Hungary which does not have dozens of his translations. The result was an excellent text which was, however, not without its problems, mainly due to the haste with which it was made.[13] Apart from the inconsistency in the use of some names (at the end of the book, Göncz used different forms of some names than Réz had already established at the beginning), there were

Reading Tolkien in Hungary, Part I: The 20th Century   19

various mistakes and errors in the text, the most notable of which was that, probably due to Göncz's oversight of a pronoun, in the Hungarian, it was in fact Merry who killed the Witch-king, not Éowyn – right up to the revision in 2008.

The book's reception was very much determined by Göncz's afterword: he traced some of the cultural and literary historical context of the book and its themes but also said that it was "the longest fairy tale of all time" (Tolkien, *A király* 552) and drew parallels with 20th century history. Along with the publisher's categorisation of this book too as a "fairy-tale novel",[14] this helped place Tolkien firmly with younger readership, and most early reviews also emphasised this. András Tótisz termed it a "fake fairy novel", still a "modern read", however, since its real heroes are "the peaceful citizens" (2),[15] a possibly ideologically motivated conclusion. Another reviewer called the book an "enormous trifle" and judged that unlike the fictional worlds of "ambitious science fiction writers", Tolkien's world was actually beautiful (Széky 11). Being seen as a "sort of science fiction" made Tolkien seem new and relevant in a different way: András Fazekas argued that fairy tales were definitely needed even in consumer culture and named Tolkien and Asimov among "good", "responsible" science fiction writers (7).[16] In the translation of Sam J. Lundwall's 1978 book *It Happened Tomorrow: The True History of Science Fiction* (published in the *Metagalaktika* series in 1984),[17] made by Szentmihályi Szabó, Tolkien was firmly situated within the "utopian/ dystopian" tradition that informs SF (95–96). Lundwall's is not an especially scholarly or even well-argued book, but it did place the whole genre of science fiction in a (literary) historical context and connected it to its precedents. Kuczka appended an afterword specifically surveying European and Hungarian SF (255–270), so Hungarian readers' perception of Tolkien as "somehow" connected to SF was reinforced not only by articles but a more serious-sounding book too. In 1988, Béla Rigó again emphasised the connection: "today, all fashionable SF writers follow Tolkien, whether they admit it or not" (29).[18]

Approaching Tolkien via the new genre "fantasy" was initially a variant of this, since fantasy was first seen as a subgenre of SF. But in the 1980s, American role-playing game systems appeared in Hungary too and infused the first generation of players who shaped the RPG and fantasy scene in the 1990s. Some of these young people formed clubs, and in 1987, even a Hungarian Fantasy Club was founded (Novák).[19] Others wrote more informed and better contextualised short accounts about fantasy in obscure fanzines than anyone in the press (Kornya, "Képzelet", and "Röviden").[20] In the *Galaktika* issue devoted to fantasy in 1988, Szentmihályi Szabó offered Tolkien and Borges as examples of how "pure fantasy can be infused with intelligence" ("Introduction" 1). Tolkien and the fantasy genre also made

20   Gergely Nagy

an appearance in the review of the then fashionable Fighting Fantasy series (Huszta), and Kuczka even started a short-lived fantasy periodical (titled *Fantasy,* in 1989). But Kuczka regarded fantasy as a minor offshoot of science fiction: his goal was to champion SF as the sort of fantastic literature that is to be regarded as "literature proper". By the end of the 1980s, the term "high fantasy" had gained currency, appearing even in a tabloid piece written by Zsolt Nyulászi and Csanád Novák (two important figures of the scene): "high fantasy" is "the style creating myth, using meticulously made-up worlds" (24).[21] Worldbuilding would indeed be a criterion by which Tolkien would never be judged wanting.

Actually, Tolkien did not *have to be* relegated to children's literature anymore. This was the period of the change of regime in Hungary, when political culture, social structure, the economy, and with it, publishing changed a lot in very little time. In 1988, Móra brought out *Farmer Giles of Ham* (*A sonkádi Egyed gazda*), also in Göncz's translation, which again reinforced the children's literature approach, but the reissue of *The Lord of the Rings* sparked more sensitive reviews and appreciation. Called a "breathtaking fairy-tale epic", its linguistic inventiveness and the translators' excellence was now emphasised (Pósa 11). More timely conclusions were also offered. "If in the period of dictatorship, *The Lord of the Rings* could say something timely, why couldn't we see in it now what is important for us today, in 1990 – that an era is irrevocably ended?" (Bethlenfalvy 30). Gábor Bethlenfalvy's review in *Igen* [Yes], a publication for young Catholics, referred back to Göncz's afterword in relating the book to recent history, showing that "applicability" in fact helped Hungarian readers make sense of the book.

Now with a Hungarian readership of his own, Tolkien was more and more taken as a given of contemporary culture. Some interesting facts show his success with readers. As early as December 1981, the title "*Lord of the Rings*" appeared in the crossword in *Ifjúkommunista* ("Young Communist", the paper of the Hungarian Young Communist League (KISZ), "Keresztrejtvény", 1981, 63. A few years later, Frodo's alias also popped up: "Keresztrejtvény", 1983, 75). Writing about the favourite authors of West German youths, L.H. Knoll connected Tolkien with Michael Ende (127–128), whose *Neverending Story* (published in 1979, in Hungarian in 1985; *Momo* was translated a year later, in 1986, and both went through numerous editions since) was also mentioned alongside Tolkien a few years later by Zoltán Pósa, discussing traditional and modern fairy tales. Pósa concluded that newer proponents of "fairy-tale literature" use their own national tales and "international mythology" in creating new work ("Hagyományos" 14). In an article in *Galaktika*, Pósa further asserted that such works often "aim at the

Reading Tolkien in Hungary, Part I: The 20th Century 21

fullness of great ancient myths and epics" ("Hatalom" 55). By 1988, Tolkien was one of the most frequently mentioned "favourite writers" of high schoolers (Nagy, "...mert keresik" 80), and poet István Kemény in a poem titled "A December Evening: The Second-Hand Bookshop" imagined asking the bookseller if "Tolkien's tales are available" (Kemény 59).[22] Kemény first read Tolkien in 1982 but remembers hearing about him on TV a few years earlier. He says he regarded Tolkien "neither as children's literature nor as high literature" – he simply read *The Hobbit* and *The Lord of the Rings* as an "introduction to Tolkienology" but felt that Göncz's afterword was somehow trying to "mitigate" the book, and he assumed this was because a "fairy-tale novel could simply not be literature proper". He also had no problem with the poems: he says he perceived them to have a "nearly sacral" function and thus just accepted that this is a world whose poems are like this (personal communication). All in all, he was enchanted, hence his search for a copy of his own and its appearance in the poem.

Tolkien found his way into some more academically inclined articles and papers too but not yet as the main focus. Anna Mária Szász mentioned him as a "magical" author (358), László Kéry as "roughly contemporary with the members of Auden's circle [...] right-wing, and somewhat older" (1396), and in a review article about modern approaches to fairy tales, well-known folklorist Vilmos Voigt cited Jack Zipes as disagreeing with Tolkien (104). The most important of these was a translation of Umberto Eco's "Footnotes to *The Name of the Rose*" in *Nagyvilág*, because here Eco names Tolkien as a proponent of "romance", one of the "three ways to talk about the past" (599) – recall that in his 1971 letter to Szentmihályi Szabó, Tolkien called his own work a "heroic romance". Eco doubtless also had in mind Northrop Frye, whose book on romance, *The Secular Scripture*, came out a decade before, but Eco's (and Frye's) influence on Hungarian academics' interpretive practices would only grow strong in another ten years, by which time some of Tolkien's own scholarly writing was also published. The only piece entirely devoted to Tolkien was Anikó Sohár's thesis at the Department of Comparative Literature at Eötvös Loránd University in Budapest, in 1986. She wrote about elements of fairy tales, legends, and myths in Tolkien's work and passed with flying colours (she was even invited to join the department as an assistant professor). Sohár remembers that the Party delegate in the defence committee wanted to fail her, though, because her paper included text in English: an example of what sort of control the Party wished to exercise even at that point (personal communication).[23] We see that by the end of the 1980s, the simple categorisation of Tolkien's work as children's literature was well on its way towards more nuanced approaches.

The Second Wave: The 1990s

The 1990s were different: while socially and culturally a period of transition after the change of regime (with Árpád Göncz as the president), enough time had passed since the translations of the first wave for what Tolkien described as "my deplorable cultus" (Carpenter, *Tolkien* 231) to be going full swing in Hungary too. Tolkien clubs were formed, fantasy was a booming new market, and role-playing games had just arrived. There was even a bookshop named "Tolkien Book House" and a beer garden named "Middle-earth" in my hometown, Szeged. The 1990s saw new fantasy being compared to Tolkien, the centenary of his birth remembered in the press, and by the end of the decade, the Internet had also slowly made it into Hungarian culture. Accurate information about Tolkien and the whole of his work was, however, initially still rather scarce.[24]

The exception was the small but growing subculture of RPG fans, who often developed an interest in fantasy. The press now explicitly named "John Roland (sic) Reuel Tolkien" as the "source" of D&D and AD&D ("Új társasjáték" 13). Though the *Galaktika*-offshoot magazine *Fantasy* folded, another one, *Atlantisz* (from 1990) made it through 13 issues. A group of enterprising young people, many of whom had worked with Kuczka on *Galaktika* or *Fantasy* in the 1980s now took the opportunity offered by the suddenly free atmosphere after the change of regime (see Tick and Sohár, "Cultural Importation" 126, 128–129). They established publishing companies (Cherubion and Walhalla Páholy, 1991),[25] which made some of the fantasy genre available in Hungarian as well as putting out their own books, started magazines that dealt in games, short stories, and occasionally more serious articles. One young, enthusiastic reader was Gábor Koltai (1976–), who made two explicitly Tolkien-themed fanzines with his own translations: *Elanor* (1990, containing a summary of Tolkien's yet untranslated works) and *J.R.R. Tolkien* (1991). Neither made it to a second issue, but Koltai became the "Tolkien go-to person" within the subculture, and so when the magazine *Új Vénusz* started in 1991, András Gáspár and Csanád Novák made him responsible for the Tolkien content. Koltai produced an annotated bibliography of Tolkien-related literature ("High Fantasy") and was also responsible for a well-informed and competent article about the posthumous publications at the Tolkien centenary in 1992 ("Elérhetetlen").[26] The many more or less short-lived fantasy and science fiction magazines in the early 1990s became the framework for the Tolkien fandom taking shape.

But the most important event of the 1990s was undoubtedly the Hungarian publication of *The Silmarillion* in 1991, translated by long-time Tolkien enthusiast Judit Gálvölgyi. She had by this time become a well-known translator in Kuczka's *Galaktika* and the related book series and

Reading Tolkien in Hungary, Part I: The 20th Century   23

had also written articles for the periodical. *The Silmarillion* (*A szilmarilok*) was published by Árkádia, in paperback only, and without the Index of Names (this would be restored only in 2015). It was a beautiful, excellent translation, sensitively preserving the grand and eloquent language of the original. Ferenc Takács, from the English Studies department of Eötvös Loránd University, wrote an appreciative review in *Könyvvilág* [World of Books].[27] While in Hungary, he wrote, Tolkien had not become "as much of a cultural totem and fetish [...] as in the West", and his work, "despite being considered *literature* [...] garnered no serious critical attention" by its association with the fantasy genre, the book should not be read in the same way as *The Lord of the Rings* ("Képzelet"). Another reviewer concurred that while the fantastic was not always a worthwhile genre, "Tolkien's book is real literature" (Adorján 61). Not everyone was so enthusiastic. Zoltán Galántai, a young futurologist and science historian, wrote two rather disparaging short reviews in *Galaktika* and *Élet és Irodalom* [Life and Literature]. The term "high fantasy", derived partly from Tolkien's work, circled back to be a restrictive label on him: Galántai complains that worldbuilding takes precedence over relevance and readability, and is particularly repelled by the proliferation of names and the style reminiscent of mediaeval chronicles: "it is about as readable as a hurried extract of a history lecture or a Sumerian king-list" ("J.R.R. Tolkien", *Élet és Irodalom* 11). *The Silmarillion* never became the most popular of Tolkien's books in Hungary, but it has in time been accepted as a fundamental text of the Middle-earth corpus.

More of Tolkien's shorter fiction also appeared. The publishing house Fátum-ars brought out a retranslation of *Farmer Giles* (entitled *Giles, a sárkány ura*) and *Smith of Wooton Major* (*A wooton-i kovácsmester*) in 1994, both translated by Anikó Németh. At least one reviewer, however, called the retranslation of *Giles* "awkward" (Luthár 9). Németh also translated *Tree and Leaf* in 1996, which, importantly, made available Tolkien's own "On Fairy-Stories" in Hungarian for the first time. Her translations, however, did not survive into the 2000s reprints.

The Middle-earth publications also continued. The Szeged-based publishing house Szukits, on Gábor Koltai's advice, came out with *Unfinished Tales* in 1995, although they somewhat deceptively retitled it *A Gyűrű keresése* [The Search for the Ring], and published it first in two volumes (later they made one-volume editions). The translators were Koltai and Judit Szántó (1932–2016), a decidedly more experienced translator, with a lot of books (Stephen King, Coleen McCullough, Tennessee Williams, among others) behind her, but she did not know Tolkien at all. Poet István Eörsi also had a part with the translation of the Istari poem. The Hungarian readership did not quite know what to do with *Unfinished Tales*. No substantial reviews were written, and the posthumous books only drew

24   Gergely Nagy

real attention one year later, when a little Kaposvár-based publisher, Holló és Társa, suddenly put out *The Book of Lost Tales* (*Az elveszett mesék könyve*), in two volumes, translated by poet Dezső Tandori, who had also worked on the poems in *The Lord of the Rings*. It is not clear how Holló secured the rights to publish only these first two volumes of *The History of Middle-earth*, but since the series' last book, *The Peoples of Middle-earth* only came out in 1996, maybe the estate was more willing to licence separate volumes. Tandori even referred to the job in a poem: "You translate Tolkien, / Tinkering with poems of / Linguist-meticule [...] / horse, sort of wine, Tolkien job, / life, livelihood, / enjoyment, supposedly" ("Közelgő", 20, 23. "Horse" alludes to Tandori's love for horse races). *Lost Tales* certainly made reviewers sing Tandori's praise, although most noted that these texts are more difficult to read and are aimed at researchers and philologists rather than readers of fairy tales (Erdei, 13). The "Introduction" to *Lost Tales* now helped readers (and critics) see much more clearly what the "Tolkien corpus" was. One reviewer said we have here the "chaos" from which the "order" of *The Lord of the Rings* derives and praised Tolkien's "language-creating faculty" (-nyulasi-7). The articles about the mid-1990s *The Lord of the Rings* reissue thus had both a wider and more accurate context to place Tolkien and the benefit of hindsight: "it is clear today that the author didn't just give us a literary masterpiece, but also shaped a new horizon" with his detailed imaginary world (tallai 8). Some of the old parallels were brought up again: *Star Wars* because it creates a mythical foundation (Beregi 15), and Michael Ende, in whose works "fairy tales turn into cult-philosophical novels" (Varga 13).

This "new horizon" that Tolkien drew up was "fantasy". As we saw, the efforts of the RPG community and its authors had already energised the Hungarian fantasy scene, but in the second half of the 1990s, other approaches joined them too. The fantasy authors of the scene were not explicitly Tolkien fans, and when they wrote about him, they often did so somewhat disparagingly: this is where we see that Tolkien "classicised" rather early in Hungary. But it is difficult to escape the conclusion that their criticism of Tolkien in some sense mirrored the evaluations before the change of regime and remained in an interesting sense ideological. For the socialist critic, Tolkien was "decadent, escapist Western literature",[28] but the new generation saw him as old-fashioned, conservative, and attached to literary and cultural models that said little to them. Tolkien's supposed "simplistic morality" always came up, as did the untenability of the happy ending in fantasy: new readers (and authors) were looking for new directions, and did not care much for Tolkien's models, or indeed Tolkien himself, apart from his foundational role.[29]

However, a new fanzine, *Aurin* (taking its name from Ende's *Neverending Story*), took a different approach. *Aurin* grew out of a small literary

Reading Tolkien in Hungary, Part I: The 20th Century 25

circle around historian Iván Uhrman, teaching in a high school at the time. Some of his students showed him newer fantasy novels and then their own writings about Tolkien and other authors, which made up the first issue of the fanzine in 1996. Uhrman offered enthusiastic help, and this circle (Illés Varga, Péter Tick, and József Kazár) went on to produce four more issues (circulated in very small number, in bookshops) before they relocated to the Internet.[30] Uhrman says their main interest was in Tolkien (and other authors like Robert P. Howard and H.P. Lovecraft) as literature, since *The Lord of the Rings* was somewhat divisive in this respect: even fans were not sure about exactly how "literary" Tolkien was, and the *Aurin* circle set out to boost Tolkien's acceptance as literature (personal communication). It did not help that leading Hungarian fantasy authors often referred to fantasy as "not art" – Zsolt Kornya famously called what they were doing "carving chair legs", honest work, but ultimately just artisanry ("Raoul Renier").[31] The articles and short papers that appeared in *Aurin*, mostly by Varga and Uhrman, were intended to counter this by bringing academic and historical context and methodology to Tolkien.

Others did something similar too, if not as seriously, and in the 1990s, more and more treatments of Tolkien appeared in print. In a study in *Magyar Névtani Dolgozatok* (*Papers in Hungarian Onomastics*) in 1991, Judit Rácz examined Tolkien's fictional names, with a hint of interpretation (Rácz), and Henrik Hargitai also claimed that the uniqueness of Tolkien's names derives from his "professional knowledge" (18). Tolkien's larger literary context was also seen more clearly: in a review of a new Hungarian novel, Eszter Tarjányi remarked that the attempt to "make the already free-standing world of the novel even more independent of reality" is a "fantasy characteristic", citing Douglas Adams, Terry Pratchett, and Tolkien as examples (41). In a paper on a completely different segment of subculture, rock music, Péter Apor asserted that he "still [hasn't] read a better and more accurate description of the nature of power than Tolkien's in *The Lord of the Rings*" (32), essentially agreeing with Shippey's treatment in *The Road to Middle-earth* (unknown at the time in Hungary, although included in Koltai's *Új Vénusz* bibliography). Gabriella Komáromi mentioned Tolkien in an article about current Hungarian children's literature as the starting point of the kind of children's novel that includes fairy-tale motifs and larger plots (like, again, Ende's *Neverending Story*: "Hol" 16). In a survey of post-1989 children's literature, Katalin G. Papp declared *The Hobbit* as "doubtless an inspiring piece" (19). In 1999, a whole textbook appeared, edited by Komáromi, about children's literature, in which Tolkien was briefly mentioned in the chapter on "Fairy tales and fairy-tale novels": "He created myth by himself", Komáromi wrote, and again connected him to Ende, whose work was "woven through with mythical symbols" (*Gyermekirodalom* 214). Another article by Andrea Lovász used

26   *Gergely Nagy*

"On Fairy-Stories" for the definition of "Tündérföld" ("Faerie"; 4), and "subcreation" (6) and "eucatastrophe" (14) also make an appearance as terms. Anikó Sohár even taught Tolkien at the Department of Comparative Literature at Eötvös Loránd University, in seminars on fantastic literature (up until 1993; personal communication). But by the end of the 1990s, a lot of online interest groups and forums devoted to fantasy and RPG also provided a place for discussion. Tolkien had broken out from "children's literature" but had not yet broken into "literature proper".

On to the 21st Century

By the end of the 1990s, Hungary was quite a different place than at their beginning. Politically and culturally, a much freer atmosphere had been established, and with more and more news becoming public about Peter Jackson's projected *The Lord of the Rings* movie, fans, publishers, and academics alike were thrilled and expectant. The 2000s marked the real upsurge in everything Tolkien, with the establishment of the Hungarian Tolkien Society and its role in bringing together people and expertise in various activities and for various purposes. But the first part of Tolkien's reception in Hungary, from the beginnings to the turn of the millennium, was, as we saw, mostly concerned with finding his place in contemporary culture. Since what "contemporary culture" itself meant, especially in Central Europe, changed a lot between the 1970s and the 1990s, it is not surprising that it was a difficult place to find. After socialist publishing and criticism slotted Tolkien into children's literature (which is quite understandable for *The Hobbit*) and Kuczka's and others' efforts situated him in the context of science fiction, Tolkien in a sense had already entered Hungarian perception as a "classic" of his genre. Science fiction was seen in the socialist period as the literature of the future, of rationality, and was thus acceptable, but fantasy was a different question; it was only after the change of regime that this "irrational genre" could take a real foothold with readers. It was still seen as juvenile, though, so the change of context only made Tolkien "unserious" in a different way, but he certainly would not have attained such a wide fan base as children's literature. More serious attention came with the realisation that there was much more to his work than *The Hobbit* and *The Lord of the Rings*, and it was partly the availability of more of the corpus that redirected attention, even that of academics, towards integrating him into a sort of canon. What canon that should be was again uncertain. But the other ingredient of a more serious appreciation of Tolkien's work was that his fans have grown up, and the Jackson films after the millennium supplied a new host of fans, to grow up and study him later. These would be the contexts in which the second part of Tolkien's reception in Hungary was situated.

Reading Tolkien in Hungary, Part I: The 20th Century 27

Notes

In researching and writing this survey, I attempted to talk to as many people who make an appearance in the story as possible. I am grateful to Judit Gálvölgyi, István Kemény, Gábor Koltai, Anikó Sohár, Iván Uhrman, and Tamás Füzessy for taking the time to answer questions. In all quotations from Hungarian texts, the translations are mine.

1 The addressee's name is here given as "Péter Szabó Szentmihályi", doubtless because the editors believed "Szabó" to be a middle name, while it is in fact a second surname (unhyphenated).
2 On how Tolkien was seen by the authorities in Soviet Russia, see Markova and Hooker.
3 On the publication policies of the Kádár regime concerning fantastic literature, see Sohár, "Anyone" (252–253 on Kuczka in particular). This very informative paper is an excellent survey of the period until the 1989 change of regime.
4 This must have been Arkady and Boris Strugatky's *Hard to Be a God/Monday Begins on Saturday* (published in the *Kossuth Fantastic Series* in 1971). In the afterword, Kuczka wrote about both Tolkien and C.S. Lewis but did not mention any titles.
5 See his short account of the event in Finder. Kuczka also wrote about EuroCon, mentioning Finder's talk (he calls him "Ian") and referring to Tolkien's book as "*The Lords* [sic] *of the Ring*" (123).
6 In another instalment of his online memoir, Erdei Grünwald relates how he learned that the Ministry of the Interior kept a close surveillance on his correspondence with Finder: see "Ügynökügyek".
7 The literary journal, *Helikon*, where this appeared continues to this day. Szentmihályi Szabó wrote a piece on Baxter for the very first issue of *Galaktika*, also mentioning Tolkien: "Science fiction".
8 Published by expatriate Catholics out of Vienna, *Mérleg* was remarkably politics-free and so available in Hungary (after 1969, the Hungarian Post distributed it officially).
9 The second edition of Douglas A. Anderson's *The Annotated Hobbit* shows no less than five of Szecskó's illustrations.
10 Vekerdy stressed that children were more concerned with the good and bad sides in tales than with their "reality" and mentioned offhand that *The Lord of the Rings* would soon be available in Hungarian (337).
11 Neither the source nor the translator's name was given. The original is reprinted in Neil D. Isaacs and Rose A. Zimbardo's *Tolkien: New Critical Perspectives*, 168–75.
12 As in the case of *The Hobbit*, it is not known who made the decision. Sohár says "in most cases it was the executive director of the publishing house" ("Anyone" 246) that made such decisions.
13 Göncz used an American Ballantine Books edition for work, and thus the first Hungarian edition inherited some unique errors from this, like Frodo's Quenya "omentilmo" (instead of the English edition's "omentielmo" or Tolkien's correction "omentielvo"): see Orthmayr 32.
14 In 1982, István Szerdahelyi used *The Lord of the Rings* and *Winnie-the-Pooh* to exemplify "fairy-tale novel" in the *Encyclopaedia of World Literature*: *Világirodalmi*, vol. 8, 286.
15 A writer himself (also under the pen name T.O. Teas) and a translator, Tótisz (1950–2013) became a meme for arrogant ignorance when he translated the

28   *Gergely Nagy*

band name "Kings of Leon" as "the Lion King" in *Fifty Shades of Grey,* and vehemently refused to admit it was in fact a mistake.

16 This was an article on *The Empire Strikes Back.* Tolkien had been connected with *Star Wars* very early, in 1978, in (iszlai)'s "Mítosz".

17 The series started in 1978 as a yearly digest of the best short stories in *Galaktika.* See Sohár, "Anyone" 260.

18 The *á propos* was the Hungarian publication of Frank Herbert's *Dune.* Rigó (1942–2017) was a noted poet, writer, translator, literary historian with strong ties to children's literature and a great love for Tolkien. When *The Hobbit* was published, he was working at Móra.

19 I have only been able to access this piece online. Novák (1969–) was one of the leaders of the RPG movement, later an author too.

20 Zsolt Kornya (1970–, another important figure; later pen name Raoul Renier) discussed Tolkien in both. I also could only access the online version of these articles.

21 This pared-down definition had been expanded on in previously cited (but more esoteric) publications, like Kornya's.

22 The poem appeared in his first volume, *Csigalépcső az elfelejtett tanszékekhez* [*Spiral Staircase to the Forgotten Departments*], but was also published in *Új Írás* [New Writing] in 1985.

23 Sohár (1962–) is a translator and translation scholar, one of the earliest in Hungary to take a scholarly interest in Tolkien. Her PhD dissertation, defended in 1997, was on the Hungarian translation of fantasy and science fiction and came out as a book too: *Cultural Transfer.*

24 A cultural periodical for university and college students even printed a translation of an online FAQ: "Tolkien és világa", translated by one of the editors, Henrik Hargitai, who later went on to write and teach about Tolkien.

25 The very first book Walhalla published was Henry N. Beard and Douglas C. Kenney's *Bored of the Rings* (in 1991).

26 He mentioned Tom Shippey and Ruth Noel too. In the 2000s, Koltai is better known as a theatre director.

27 Takács earlier wrote a series in *Galaktika* on "SF and high literature", dealing with authors like Doris Lessing, John Barth, Anthony Burgess, Salman Rushdie, or William Burroughs.

28 As Csanád Novák put it in a recent interview: see HalfMoon.

29 Even though Sohár finds a "detailed elaboration of the imaginary worlds" in these authors' work, she also remarks that their "palpably cynical ideology", a "withdrawal from any ethical commitment" might be related to "recent sociopolitical changes" in Hungary: "'Genuine' and 'Fictitious'" 45.

30 Some of this material is still available at https://webzone.ee/aurin/index.html.

31 Kornya is quite possibly referring to the Phalanstery Scene (Scene 12) of Imre Madách's play *The Tragedy of Man,* where in a dystopian commune the artist Michelangelo is made to carve chair legs.

Works Cited

Adams, Robert M. "Tolkien öröksége" [Tolkien's Heritage]. *Nagyvilág* 22.8 (1978): 1208–1213. ("The Hobbit Habit". *Tolkien: New Critical Perspectives.* Ed. Neil D. Isaacs and Rose A. Zimbardo. Lexington: University Press of Kentucky, 1981. 168–175.)

Adorján, Sebestyén. "J.R.R. Tolkien: A szilmarilok" [J.R.R. Tolkien: *The Silmarillion*]. *Igen*. 16 August 1991, 60–61.

"A közelmúlt művészeti áramlatai – angol szemmel" [Recent Artistic Movements – from the English Perspective] *Valóság* 17.6 (1974): 126–128.

Anderson, Douglas A. "The Mainstreaming of Fantasy and the Legacy of *The Lord of the Rings*". The Lord of the Rings, *1954–2004: Scholarship in Honor of Richard E. Blackwelder*. Ed. Wayne G. Hammond and Christina Scull. Milwaukee: Marquette UP, 2006. 301–315.

Apor, Péter. "Századvégi utóirat anarchizmusról és rockzenéről" [End of the Century Postscript on Anarchism and Rock Music]. *Valóság* 37.3 (1994): 30–40.

Beard, Henry N. and Douglas C. Kenney. *Gyűrűkúra* [*Bored of the Rings*]. Transl. András Gáspár. Budapest: Walhalla Páholy, 1991.

Beregi, Tamás. "A mítosz visszatér" [The Return of Myth]. *Magyar Hírlap*. 4 November 1995, 15.

Bethlenfalvy, Gábor. "J.R.R. Tolkien: A Gyűrűk Ura" [J.R.R. Tolkien, *The Lord of the Rings*]. *Igen*. 4 January 1991, 30.

Carpenter, Humphrey. *Tolkien: A Biography*. Boston: Houghton Mifflin, 1977.

Carpenter, Humphrey, ed., with the assistance of Christopher Tolkien. *The Letters of J.R.R. Tolkien*. Boston: Houghton Mifflin, 1981.

Eco, Umberto. "Széljegyzetek a *Rózsa nevé*hez" [Footnotes to *The Name of the Rose*]. Transl. András Schéry. *Nagyvilág* 32.4 (1987): 579–601.

Erdei, Sándor. "Elveszett mesék" [Lost Tales]. *Hajdú-Bihari Napló*. 1 August 1996, 13.

Erdei Grünwald, Mihály [E.G.M.]. "A fantázia új útjai" [New Roads of Fantasy]. *Magyar Ifjúság*. 13 June 1973, 28–29.

———. "Ki az az Arafat, aki Magyarország miniszterelnöke lett? Az 1990-es évek eleje" [Who's That Arafat Guy Who Became PM of Hungary? The Early 1990s] *Karnyújtásnyira a történelemtől* [*At Arm's Length with History: Fragments of a Memoir in Progress*], 3–4. Galamus.hu, May 2012. http://galamus.hu/index.php?option=com_content&view=article&id=1370 40:karnyujtasnyira-a-toertenelemtl-toeredekek-egy-keszuel-memoarbol-iii-iv&catid=9:vendegek&Itemid=66. Accessed 18 June 2022.

———. "Ügynökügyek és ügyetlenségek" [Agents and Their Ineptitudes]. *Karnyújtásnyira a történelemtől* [*At Arm's Length with History: Fragments of a Memoir in Progress*], 10. Galamus.hu, June 2012. http://galamus.hu/index.php?option=com_content&view=article&id=144442:karnyujtasnyira-a-toertenelemtl-toeredekek-egy-keszuel-memoarbol-x&catid=9:vendegek&Itemid=66. Accessed 18 June 2022.

Fazekas, András. "Bájital á la Hollywood" [Hollywood's Magic Potion]. *Egyetemi Lapok*. 6 April 1982, 7.

Finder, Jan Howard. "It Is All Tolkien's Fault!" *Tolkien's Legacy*. Ed. Ernest Lilley. http://www.sfrevu.com/ISSUES/2001/0112/9785%20Tolkien%20Tribute/Tolkien.htm. Accessed 18 June 2022.

G. Papp, Katalin. "Helyzetkép az 1989 utáni gyermekirodalomról" [A Survey of Post-1989 Children's Literature]. *Magyartanítás* 39.3 (1998): 12–19.

Galántai, Zoltán. "J.R.R. Tolkien: A szilmarilok" [J.R.R. Tolkien: *The Silmarillion*]. *Élet és Irodalom*. 15 March 1991, 11.

30 *Gergely Nagy*

———. "J.R.R. Tolkien: A szilmarilok" [J.R.R. Tolkien: *The Silmarillion*]. *Galaktika* 7.5 (1991): 39.

HalfMoon. "Interview with Csanád Novák". *Bíborhold*, 30 May 2020. https:// www.youtube.com/watch?v=CuIRsmdkOFc. Accessed 18 June 2022.

Hargitai, Henrik. "Nevek varázsa, avagy Tolkientől Nemeréig" [The Magic of Names, or from Tolkien to Nemere]. *Kávéházi Tavasz*. 1 April 1994, 18–20.

Huszta, Tibor. "Kaland, játék, kockázat" [Fighting Fantasy]. *Galaktika* 18.12 (1989): 72–73.

(iszlai). "Mítosz minden mennyiségben" [Myths All Around]. *Élet és irodalom*. 15 April 1978, 7.

Kemény, István. "Egy decemberi este – Az antikvárium" [A December Evening: The Second-hand Bookshop]. *Új Írás* 25.8 (1985): 59. Also in *Csigalépcső az elfelejtett tanszékekhez* [*Spiral Staircase to the Forgotten Departments*]. Budapest: ELTE, 1984.

"Keresztrejtvény" [Crossword] *Ifjúkommunista*. 1 January 1983, 75.

"Keresztrejtvény" [Crossword] *Ifjúkommunista*. 11 December 1981, 63.

Kéry, László. "A harmincas évek angol írói" [English Writers of the 30s]. *Nagyvilág* 34.9 (1989): 1396–1400.

"Ki a legunalmasabb író?" [Who Is the Most Boring Writer?]. *Magyar Szó*. 30 May 1978, 8. Reprinted in *Nagyvilág* 23.3 (1978): 459–460.

Knoll, L.H. "Mit olvasnak a nyugatnémet fiatalok?" [What Do West German Youths Read?] *Valóság* 25.3 (1982): 127–128.

Komáromi, Gabriella. "Hol is az érték mostanában? (Az érték, a válság – meg a gyerekkönyvek világa" [Where Actually Is Value Today? Values, Their Crisis – and the World of Children's Books]. *Új Forrás* 26.7 (1994): 1–17.

Komáromi, Gabriella, ed. *Gyermekirodalom* [Children's Literature]. Budapest: Helikon, 1999.

Koltai, Gábor. "Elérhetetlen tájak felé: száz éve született J.R.R. Tolkien" [Towards Unreachable Lands: the Centenary of J.R.R. Tolkien]. *Nulladik Típusú Találkozás*. 1 August 1992, 24–25.

———. "A high fantasy megteremtője, J.R.R. Tolkien" [Creator of High Fantasy, J.R.R. Tolkien]. *Új Vénusz* 2 (1991): 44–45.

Kornya, Zsolt. "A képzelet egy másik világa. Amit a fantasyról tudni illik" [Another World of the Imagination. What You Should Know about Fantasy]. *Metamorf* 3 (1988): 14–18. Also available: http://fantasycentrum.hu/old/VEGYES/fantasy. htm. Accessed 18 June 2022.

———. "Röviden a fantasyről" [A Short Introduction to Fantasy]. *Helios* 1 (1988): 29–30. Also available: https://fantasycentrum.hu/old/VEGYES/KZSrovidenafan-tasyrol.htm. Accessed 18 June 2022.

Kranz, Gisbert. "A keresztény irodalom új hulláma" [The New Wave of Christian Literature]. *Mérleg* 11.1 (1975): 45–62.

Kuczka, Péter. "EuroCon 1: Trieste, 12–16 July 1972". *Galaktika* 1.2 (1972): 121–127.

Lovász, Andrea. "A mesélő ember" [The tale-telling man]. *Új Forrás* 31.8 (1999): 3–17.

Lundwall, Sam J. *Holnap történt. Tanulmányok a science fiction világtörténetéről* [*It Happened Tomorrow: The True History of Science Fiction*]. Transl. Péter Szentmihályi Szabó. *Metagalaktika* 7. Budapest: Kozmosz könyvek, 1984.

Reading Tolkien in Hungary, Part I: The 20th Century 31

Luthár, Péter. "Agyzsugorító szellemek. Gondolatmorzsák J.R.R. Tolkien ügyében" [Brainshrinking spirits. Thoughts on J.R.R. Tolkien]. *Új Magyarország*. 11 August 1995, 9.

Markova, Olga and Mark T. Hooker. "When Philology Becomes Ideology: The Russian Perspective of J.R.R. Tolkien". *Tolkien Studies* 1 (2004): 163–170.

Mátyás, István. "Babits beszélőfüzeteitől a Vizsolyi Bibliáig" [From Babits's Conversation Notebooks to the Vizsoly Bible]. *Népszava*. 23 December 1977, 6.

Mező, Ferenc. "Elkésett híradás a nonszenszirodalomból" [Late News about Nonsense Literature]. *Magyar Hírlap*. 22 January 1978, 10.

Nagy, Attila. "'…mert keresik az életük értelmét?' Helyzetkép a 15–18 évesek olvasási kultúrájáról" [Because They're Looking for the Meaning of their Lives? A Survey of Reading Culture among 15–18-year-olds]. *Kultúra és Közösség* 5 (1988): 78–82.

"Népszerű műfaj: a fantasy" [A Popular Genre: Fantasy]. *Magyarország* 15.18 (1978): 18.

Novák, Csanád. "A magyar fantasy klubról röviden" [A short account of the Hungarian Fantasy Club]. *PC Lemezújság* 8 (1988). Also available: http://adata.hu/_ Kozossegi_Adattar/Lemezuar.Nsf/e865e1dacf38e2818525663b007896c5/2eb4 d0712d0b5b568525663e0052ab15?OpenDocument. Accessed 18 June 2022.

-nyulasi-. "Amiből a rend megszületett" [What Order Derives From]. *Fejér Megyei Hírlap*. 3 July 1996, 7.

Nyulászi, Zsolt and Csanád Novák. "Fantáziáljon nyugodtan!" [Feel Free to Fantasise!] *Reform*. 22 December 1989, 24–25.

Orthmayr, Flóra. "Negyvenéves a *Gyűrűk Ura* első magyar kiadása" [Forty Years Ago: the First Hungarian Edition of *The Lord of the Rings*]. *Lassi Laurië* 18.2 (2021): 32.

Pósa, Zoltán. "Az Európa karácsonya" [Christmas at Európa]. *Pesti Hírlap*. 29 November 1990, 11.

———. "Hatalom és uralkodás a sci-fi világában" [Power and Rule in Sci-Fi Worlds]. *Galaktika* 18.12 (1989): 54–55.

———. "Hagyományos, modern mesék" [Traditional, Modern Tales]. *Mozgó Képek*. 1 October 1987, 14.

Rácz, Judit. "J.R.R. Tolkien: A Gyűrűk Ura" [J.R.R. Tolkien, *The Lord of the Rings*]. *Magyar Névtani Dolgozatok* 93. Ed. Mihály Hajdú. Budapest: ELTE Magyar Nyelvészeti Tanszékcsoport Névkutató Munkaközössége, 1991. 13–19.

"Raoul Renier: Interjú a legkiemelkedőbb honi dark fantasy íróval" [Raoul Renier: An Interview with the Most Exceptional Hungarian Dark Fantasy Author]. Originally in *Scythe*, now in Fantasycentrum.hu. https://fantasycentrum.hu/old/ VEGYES/raoul-renier-interju.pdf. Accessed 10 January 2023.

Rigó, Béla. "Könyvjelző – könyvkiadóknak" [Bookmark – for publishers]. *Könyvvilág*. 1 February 1988, 29.

Sohár, Anikó. "'Anyone Who Isn't Against Us Is for Us': Science Fiction Translated from English During the Kádár Era in Hungary (1956–89)". *Translation Under Communism*. Ed. Christopher Rundle, Anne Lange, and Daniele Monticelli. London: Palgrave Macmillan, 2022. 240–279.

———. *The Cultural Transfer of Science Fiction and Fantasy in Hungary 1989–1995*. Frankfurt am Main: Peter Lang, 1999.

32 *Gergely Nagy*

——. "'Genuine' and 'Fictitious' Translations of Science Fiction and Fantasy in Hungary". *Unity in Diversity? Current Trends in Translation Studies*. Ed. Lynne Bowker, Michael Cronin, Dorothy Kenny, Jennifer Pearson. London and New York: Routledge, 2014. 39–46.

——. "Cultural Importation of Genres: The Case of SF and Fantasy in Hungary". *Translation Studies in Hungary*. Ed. Kinga Klaudy, José Lambert, and Anikó Sohár. Budapest: Scholastica, 1996. 125–133.

Szász, Anna Mária. "Between Tradition and Experiment: A Study in Angus Wilson's Novels". *Acta Litteraria Academiae Scientiarum Hungaricae* 27.3–4 (1985): 343–363.

Szentmihályi Szabó, Péter. Introduction. *Galaktika* 17.3 (1988): 1.

——. "Az irodalom negyedik dimenziója" [The Fourth Dimension of Literature]. *Valóság* 19.8 (1976): 89–98.

——. "Rev. of John Baxter, *Science Fiction in the Cinema*". *Helikon* 17.1 (1972): 133–134.

——. "Science fiction a moziban" [Science Fiction in the Movies]. *Galaktika* 1.1 (1972): 51–57.

Szerdahelyi, István. "Meseregény" [Fairytale-novel]. *Világirodalmi lexikon*. Vol. 8. Budapest: Akadémiai, 1982. 286.

Széky, János. "Hatalmas csekélység" [An Enormous Trifle]. *Élet és irodalom*. 8 August 1981, 11.

Takács, Ferenc. "A képzelet alapvetése" [The Foundation of the Imagination]. *Könyvvilág*. 1 February 1991, 13.

(tallai). "Szauron pillantása" [Sauron's Gaze]. *Új Magyarország*. 29 November 1995, 8.

Tandori, Dezső. "A közelgő 'megint'" ['Again' Approaching]. *Tekintet* 9.1–2 (1996): 19–23.

Tarjányi, Eszter. "Üveggolyóba zárva" [Trapped in a Marble] Review of László Marton's *Átkelés az üvegen* [*Through the Glass*]. *Magyar Napló*. 8 January 1993, 40–41.

Tick, Péter. "A magyar zsáner fantasy története dióhéjban" [A Short History of Hungarian Genre Fantasy]. *Roham* 3 (2006): 30–31.

Tolkien, J.R.R. *The Annotated Hobbit*. Ed. Douglas A. Anderson. Boston: Houghton Mifflin, 2002.

——. *A király visszatér* [*The Return of the King*] Transl. Árpád Göncz, Ádám Réz, and Dezső Tandori. Budapest: Árkádia, 1990.

"Tolkien és világa" [Tolkien and His World], Part II. Transl. Henrik Hargitai. *Kávéházi Tavasz* 2.1 (1995) 22–26.

"Tolkien és világa" [Tolkien and His World], Part I. Transl. Henrik Hargitai. *Kávéházi Nyár* 1.2 (1994): 30–34.

Tótisz, András. "Törpök, tünték, hobbitok" [Dwarves, Elfes [sic], Hobbits]. *Esti Hírlap*. 14 September 1981, 2.

"Új társasjáték-őrület: fantázia végkimerülésig" [New Game Fad: Fantasy to the Death]. *Heti Világgazdaság*. 10 December 1993, 13.

Reading Tolkien in Hungary, Part I: The 20th Century   33

Varga, Lajos Márton. "A szakértelem öröme és biztonsága a könyvkiadásban" [The Joy and Safety of Expertise in Publishing]. *Népszabadság.* 4 December 1993, 13.

Vekerdy, Tamás. "Versek, mesék – gyerekeknek" [Poems, Tales – for Children]. *Élet és Tudomány Kalendáriuma*, 1979, 333–338.

Voigt, Vilmos. "Mesék és értelmezésük" [Fairy Tales and their Interpretation]. *Helikon* 36.1 (1990): 101–109.

2 Reading Tolkien in Hungary, Part II

The 21st Century

Gergely Nagy

There were two things that determined Tolkien's reception in Hungary at the beginning of the new millennium: news of the Peter Jackson film adaptation and the appearance of the Harry Potter phenomenon. Jackson's film catalysed the Tolkien fandom that already had time to grow in the 1990s, and by this time had taken to the Internet. Even though the first Harry Potter novel had been published in Hungarian in 1999 (*Harry Potter és a bölcsek köve*), J.K. Rowling's series only became really big in 2000, when the next three volumes came out, all in one year. Readers and reviewers alike were intrigued, and this resulted in a flood of press coverage and even some scholarly interest. One of the involved fields was of course children's literature, and that supplied the connection to Tolkien. The first Harry Potter film preceded the first part of Jackson's film trilogy in Hungary, being shown first in December 2001 (while *The Fellowship of the Ring* premiered in January 2002), and this caused a certain rivalry between the fandoms. But there were also common points, and in time, these proved to be more important.

Hungary at the beginning of the new millennium was a hopeful place. The change of regime was now more than a decade away: the first freely elected president, the translator of *The Lord of the Rings*, Árpád Göncz, stepped down after ten years, and soon (in 2004) Hungary would join the European Union (after becoming a full member of NATO in 1999). What people associated with Western culture changed too: the suspicious official attitude of the communist era had given way to an enthusiastic acceptance (earlier, this attitude constituted an act of defiance, and people had to be very careful in expressing it at all), and by the 2000s, this upsurge was tempered with some caution too. Voices were heard warning about "globalisation", "over-commercialisation", and the like, and this can be seen clearly in how Jackson's films (and the Harry Potter films) were received in certain quarters, and in the fan reaction too. But with Tolkien, the fandom took a step that allowed them to actively shape the reception.

DOI: 10.4324/9781003407171-4

Reading Tolkien in Hungary, Part II: The 21st Century 35

This was the founding of the Hungarian Tolkien Society (Magyar Tolkien Társaság, MTT) in the summer of 2002, which marked the coming together of the fandom and the interested part of the scholarly/professional community. As defined in their mission statement, the Society took a very active role in organising and coordinating everything Tolkien-related, and apart from allowing fans a sort of control on how Tolkien was perceived by the general public, this also created the opportunities and frameworks of a more serious reception. The Society got involved with the film's distributors, with publishers, with universities, and ran very successful community programmes. Many of these lines of activity are kept up to this day, with Jackson's further movies of *The Hobbit* and recently, Amazon's *Rings of Power* series reinforcing the public interest. The Society also took an active part in publishing, initiating, and offering expertise for the revision of the already existing Tolkien texts, and in the early 2020s managing the translation of the *History of Middle-earth* series.

Already at the beginning of the 2000s, Tolkien was a fact of culture and literature for many. This included different groups of fans (fantasy, RPG, Harry Potter, or specifically Tolkien fans), but also several academic fields (fantastic literature, children's literature, the study of popular culture, and to some extent, literary theory). The two aspects both boosted and hindered each other, since a lot of academics tended to frown upon anything with a large and active fan base, while at the same time, some of those fans went to universities and came out with qualifications and a well-argued interest in Tolkien, which they put to use in shaping the critical reception with insiders' enthusiasm. Thus, one of the greatest achievements in the 2000s was certainly the rise of a kind of systematic Tolkien Studies in Hungary and some kind of (in some cases, maybe grudging) canonisation.

Tolkien as a Reference Point: Approaches in the Early 2000s

As Part I showed, there already had been voices in the 1990s arguing that (unlike some pseudo-scientific science fiction) Tolkien's work is "real literature" (Adorján 61). These were joined by scholars of children's literature who discovered "On Fairy-Stories" (published in Hungarian in 1996) and continued to use it: Andrea Lovász, in particular, mentioned the essay in several articles ("Tizenharmadik", "Meseregény", "Mi egy képes"), declaring that by now Tolkien, Michael Ende, and the *Harry Potter* novels, which "utilise and rework (among other things) a traditional fairy-tale world [...] have become veritable classics" ("Mi egy képes" 75). The terms "eucatastrophe" and "subcreation" were also adapted, contributing to Tolkien's points on the very specific historically layered fiction of the fairy story becoming better known to Hungarian scholars too. Tolkien's work now counted among the favourites of children and youngsters ("despite its

36   *Gergely Nagy*

length and its difficult language": László 14; see also Schlemmer 30) and naturally came up among the sources and parallels when talking about *Harry Potter*. It was always emphasised, however, that Rowling comes nowhere close to Tolkien's worldbuilding complexity (Valastyán 9; "HP Kerekasztal" 10), and that unlike Tolkien, who places his story in "the ancient past", *Harry Potter* is firmly in the present (Lovász, "Harry Potter" 55). Harry Potter was in fact very useful for the Tolkien reception, because it provided both a parallel and a contrast: here was something that was roughly in the same genre, was as popular as Tolkien (if not more so) – but was so clearly *less serious* than his work. Detractors of *Harry Potter* really strengthened Tolkien's position within fantastic literature and its appreciation. Their common source material in Western fairy tales, cultural history, and Norse mythology were nevertheless recognised and acknowledged (Nyilasy 24; Lovász, "Mi egy képes" 75), and thus Tolkien even made it into scholarship about "real literature".

But as in the 1980s (see the previous chapter 21), Tolkien also continued to enchant artists in the new millennium. Most prominently, poet and translator Dániel Varró mentioned his characters in an ingenious, half-parodistic section of his enormously popular fairy-tale novel in verse, *Beyond Mt. Smudge*. Here Varró is utilising a playful "ubi sunt" theme to list the good old characters of good old tales, including Legolas, Tom Bombadil, Gandalf, Glorfindel, Gimli, Gollum, and Nine-Fingered Frodo (84). Varró encountered Tolkien in his childhood, when his father read him *The Hobbit* and *The Lord of the Rings*, and he was very taken with these. In high school, he even translated some poems from *The Hobbit* (which remain unpublished, but were very inventive and extremely well done; personal communication), and it is thus certainly no surprise that he included Tolkien's characters in his personal "canonised" list of good old figures.

There were doubtless many people who discovered Tolkien in the 1990s and saw a chance of engaging with his work professionally once they started academic careers. Fantastic literature and its varieties (fantasy, horror, but also film) and the accompanying cultural phenomena (such as role-playing games) became objects of systematic, serious study (and teaching) in the 2000s. Romanist scholar Judit Maár published a small book on "fantastic literature" in 2001, but while readers and critics understood something very different by this in 2001, Maár only used the term for the kind of 18th- and 19th-century literature Todorov and his French contemporaries were interested in, and followed Todorov in treating the fantastic as a "genre". Thus, Tolkien, or indeed, anyone contemporary readers would probably regard as "fantastic literature" simply did not figure in her treatment.[1] But in a short book on Harry Potter and children, written by child psychologist Hanna Kende B., Tolkien did come up. Kende identified *Harry Potter* as a "crossover book" (10) because (like Tolkien) it appealed to not just one but several audiences (12), and located this common appeal in being set in a "closed world" (12), a "consistent, coherent fictional background" (13). Worldbuilding and the immersive experience of readers seem to be acknowledged as an important factor of the success of both books, then. In an article about the "most important phenomena in contemporary world literature", Zoltán Fónod mentioned *The Lord of the Rings* as a "magical-mythical trilogy of tales" (73) that conformed to the "forms of neosymbolism, magic, and irrationality" surging up in the 1970s (Fónod, for some reason, gave 1978 as the publication date for Tolkien's work). Humphrey Carpenter's authorised biography was published in 2001 (*J.R.R. Tolkien: az ember a mű mögött* [*J.R.R. Tolkien: the man behind the work*], translated by Éva Koncz and István Tótfalusi), making accurate information on Tolkien's life readily available for the Hungarian readers.

The single book that had the most thoughtful, balanced, and interesting approach to Tolkien in Hungarian was without question Tamás Bényei's grand survey of the post-1945 English novel, *Az ártatlan ország* [*The Innocent Country*]. Bényei, a scholar of the contemporary English novel, not only situated Tolkien in the post-World War II literary historical context, but also explained his relationship to what he calls the "tradition of the English novel", which by default included the criteria of realism: "not conforming to the criteria of realism [...] automatically excludes any book from being read and even being readable as a novel" (41). Bényei remarks that both Tolkien's supporters and detractors seem to operate with "extreme gestures and stereotypes" (185), but his chapter on Tolkien (185–194) makes use of some very good Tolkien criticism: Tom Shippey, Patrick Curry, Brian Attebery, and Brian Rosebury (among others) are referred to in a sensitive and sensible reading of *The Lord of the Rings*. Bényei notes Tolkien's affinity with the English pastoral tradition (144) and antiutopian fiction: "the experience of the war", he writes, "seemed to be inaccessible for a lot of writers by the tools of realist prose, and thus some turned towards other modes of writing" (163).[2] When Bényei introduces his chapter on Tolkien, he purposely calls *The Lord of the Rings* a "prose text" (as opposed to "novel", 185) and notes Tolkien's "radical outdatedness" (187), which explains some of the critical and readerly bafflement with its following world models and modes of writing that do not seem timely in the 20th century. This fictional world, Bényei maintains, becomes accessible through the point of view of the hobbits (189), while at the same time the very plot of the book can be read as "the critique of the hobbits' point of view" (190), and shows the process by which the old world and the old models of narration in that world are inevitably lost, leading to the "rise of the novel in Middle-earth" (194). This mirrors how the book, itself a "romance... [is] in continuous negotiation with, and [...] follows many of the conventions of, the traditional bourgeois novel" (Shippey 223, qtd.

38   *Gergely Nagy*

on 189), and thus serves as both a critique of traditional modes of writing and a return to the conventional. Elsewhere, Bényei writes that novel series are essentially "a repetition of the act of the creation of the world: they produce a designed, ordered, coherent alternative [...] world, which is also self-sufficient" (292–293), adding that *The Lord of the Rings* is the "most typical" among these since it creates its own "ancient history and mythology too" (293). Bényei closes the book with a set of remarks on Orwell's *1984* and Tolkien, concluding that both authors "wrote both inside and outside English novelistic tradition [...] both a reinforcement and a critique of the ethos of the English novel" (404). Bényei's interpretation of Tolkien, his placement of his work in a larger, contemporary context, paying attention to its specificities, but at the same time not losing sight of how (and why) his work became and remained extremely popular with readers, is an exemplary critical achievement, not only in Hungarian, but in Tolkien criticism in general.[3]

Another important, if not so exemplary piece in the early 2000s was a short essay by fantasy author and translator Zsolt Kornya, entitled "Why Am I Fed Up with Tolkien?" Kornya published this on the site fantasya. hu, avowedly not as "criticism" but in the hope of starting a debate.[4] This it certainly did, as fans of both sides rushed to attack and defend Kornya's positions. But unlike Bényei, Kornya seems not to have read any Tolkien criticism beyond the very early detractors (Moorcock in particular), and despite priding himself on being an exceptionally well-read author, shows no awareness of the "negotiation" in the Tolkien text between different modes of writing, taking Tolkien to task for not writing a "proper novel" (his individual points show he expects a more or less realistic treatment of character and plot by this). Indeed, his text reads as if he deliberately refused to accept the presuppositions (literary and philosophical) of Tolkien's textual world. That said, he did make some points that come back again and again in criticism: such as the lack of female characters (7)[5] or the supposedly black-and-white morality (2). Like Bényei, he notes the cultish enthusiasm of Tolkien's fans (1), but most of his points derive from his unspoken presuppositions: he reproaches Tolkien for making "autonomous thinking, the striving towards change a damnable and dishonourable thing" (3) but does not show any awareness of what "authority" means in Tolkien's world. His examples are full of oversimplifications and downright disregard for what the text says, his attempts to mitigate Saruman, Sauron, and even Uglúk (4) are merely the function of his refusal to accept the facts of the secondary world. He particularly hates the hobbits, whom he finds "too meek, cute, law-abiding and obedient [...] stupid and petty" (5). Kornya's attitude towards both the hobbits and authority in general, and his whole argument seem purposely exaggerated to provoke a reaction.[6] It might be worth noting that while Kornya found the inset poems "the most

Reading Tolkien in Hungary, Part II: The 21st Century   39

terrible of all" (1–2), we saw that poet István Kemény had no problems accepting them as facts of the fictional world (above 21). Kornya's piece did what it was intended to do: it sparked a heated debate among fans on various online messageboards, where some argued against him much more coherently. In a way, he contributed with it to a more rigorous, text-based approach to Tolkien, capable of supplying an answer: Kornya is probably fed up with Tolkien because he insists on expecting something entirely different from his work than what it is.

Kornya is a fantasy author, and in some sense situated Tolkien within the context of fantasy: other treatments also connected him explicitly to the fantasy genre and role-playing games. In a highly theorised reading of fantasy texts making use of Umberto Eco's and Jean-Francois Lyotard's writings, Annamária Hódosy (of the DeCon Group at the University of Szeged) argued that fantasy worlds "demonstrate the textuality, the intangibleness, 'unreadability' of the world, the uncertainty and plurality of meaning" (312), and mentioned the RPG connection. But she decidedly only used Tolkien as a first reference point. Péter Bokody's article on "RPGs and fantasy" claimed RPG as an "inalienable context of fantasy literature" (1299) and also described Tolkien's work as a "world-founding story", a "pure fantasy" at the beginning of the tradition that could still operate without the RPG context (while later authors had to react to the "virtual communal experience", 1300). Bokody also remarked that Harry Potter's novelty was to infuse "world-founding fantasy with the school novel" (1301). Anikó Sohár's work also situated Tolkien in the context of fantasy, and while not engaging with his work in particular, she provided very good and concise overviews of the situation of SF and fantasy in the previous era ("Importált" 6–7 in Hungarian, "Thy Speech" 58–62 in English). Reviews of Tolkien-related books also appeared in scholarly journals. In 2003, Norbert Gyuris reviewed Jane Chance's *The Lord of the Rings: The Mythology of Power* (the book first came out in 1992, but was reissued by the University of Kentucky Press in 2001), finding it wanting in exactly the sort of theoretical background that Hungarian scholars were using most at the time, even though Chance's book was remarkably theory-oriented within contemporary Anglo-American Tolkien Studies (Gyuris). I published a longer review essay on Tom Shippey's *J.R.R. Tolkien: Author of the Century* in *The AnaChronist*, in which I tried to situate Shippey's book in the larger context of Tolkien criticism ("That Fantastic").

One of the problems one met if one wanted to engage with Tolkien in a scholarly way at the turn of the millennium was that there was very little real, scholarly criticism on his works available. Libraries held very few and randomly selected books on him (or none at all), and the periodicals where anything appeared about him were not available – this was before online access, which made things easier later. People relied on

40 Gergely Nagy

personal connections to get books and photocopies of articles (the MLA Bibliography was available in most university libraries, so scholars could at least form an idea of what was published), and so teaching and courses at universities and colleges that included Tolkien or were even about him became very important for young scholars. Anikó Sohár had already taught Tolkien in a seminar on fantastic literature in the early 1990s at Eötvös Loránd University (ELTE) in Budapest, and after 2000, she continued to do so at Miskolc and Győr, until 2014 (personal communication). In a 2000 paper reporting on a several year-long workshop in cultural anthropology at ELTE on "modern myths", Ágnes and Gábor Kapitány brought up Tolkien (and *Star Wars*) as examples for modern mythologies in the arts (129). Roland Barthes's approaches to contemporary "myths" figured prominently in their work (see 130–131). At the University of Debrecen, American scholar Donald E. Morse taught courses that included Tolkien from 2002 to about 2007. He remembers that students were "eager to contribute, communicated freely and joined in a discussion with one another as well as with the teacher" (personal communication). At the University of Szeged, Sarolta Marinovich's courses on the fantastic also touched upon Tolkien's work, and as a fresh PhD student with a project specifically on Tolkien, I started teaching seminars on *The Silmarillion* in 2000 at Szeged too, and in the following years added another course on *The Lord of the Rings*, which I also taught at ELTE as a guest lecturer in 2005. At Pázmány Péter Catholic University, Kathleen Dubs had courses on Tolkien's Christian symbolism. Vera Benczik has taught courses on fantasy and science fiction regularly since 2010 at ELTE, and Tibor Tarcsay, a graduate student from Pázmány Péter Catholic University, also offered a Tolkien reading course in 2015.

Peter Jackson and the Hungarian Tolkien Society

As is already apparent, the form of community communication of choice in the early 2000s on the Hungarian Internet was messageboards [forum]. It was on online messageboards that fandoms started organising themselves: Harry Potter or *Star Wars* fans alike were excited about the new cinematic releases of their franchises. The same was true of Tolkien fans: the steady stream of news about Peter Jackson's film adaptations of *The Lord of the Rings* brought to life the two most important Tolkien pages of the period, tolkien.hu (run by IT student Zoltán Kiss) and Völgyzugoly (Rivendell; www.extra.hu/volgyzugoly, later volgyzugoly.uw.hu, run by another university student, Bálint Barna).[7] The messageboard topics soon proliferated and fans started to discuss much more than the film news. It was here that people first came up with the idea of forming a Hungarian Tolkien Society, on the model of various other societies in Western Europe. After the first

Reading Tolkien in Hungary, Part II: The 21st Century 41

informal meetings, actual plans were made, and in the summer of 2002, the Hungarian Tolkien Society was officially formed in Szeged. The founding meeting and mini-conference was hosted by my institute, the Institute of English and American Studies (University of Szeged), whose chair, Prof. György E. Szőnyi opened the meeting. This was preceded by meticulous preparations, and Árpád Göncz, translator of *The Lord of the Rings* and former president of Hungary, was invited to accept the title of honorary president. This he graciously did, but could not participate in person. The founding of the Society was widely reported in the press, and the members of the newly founded Society threw themselves into various activities.

Some of these were of the popularising sort, some had to do with Tolkien's texts and their publication, and some were explicitly scholarly. 3 January 2003 marked the "eleventy-first" birthday of the Professor, and the Society organised a full-day programme to commemorate this, in the very prestigious Corvin Cinema complex in Budapest. This included the award ceremony for an art contest for children that the Society had organised, the prizes given out by Árpád Göncz; and a roundtable discussion on Tolkien.[8] The event was so successful that in 2004 the entire Corvin Cinema complex was taken over by the Society for the big day, and several lectures[9] and discussions were held, all on the topic of "Reading Tolkien", and providing various contexts. One discussion focused on reading him as children's literature,[10] another one on reading him as "literature proper",[11] yet another looked at the connections of the text and the films,[12] and a fourth at Tolkien in the context of fantasy/RPG.[13] By this time, the Society had already formed its connections with institutions, publishers, literary figures (some of whom, like Anikó Sohár or Béla Rigó, had been actively writing about Tolkien for decades.[14]) Editor Ervin Tézsla from the Szeged publisher Szukits turned up quite accidentally at the founding meeting in 2002, and from then on worked very closely with the Society, who advised the publisher on what to bring out and offered expertise in looking through translated texts before publication.

But another explicit aim of the Society was to further academic work on Tolkien's writings, and this was a field I took responsibility for. The founding meeting's few papers were a good start, and in February 2003, we organised the first academic conference in Hungary fully devoted to Tolkien's work, "J.R.R. Tolkien between the Disciplines: Parallels, Texts, Uses". The event was supported by two departments of the University of Szeged, and held in the prestigious Szeged headquarters of the Hungarian Academy of Sciences. More than twenty papers were read, and nearly all the biggest Hungarian universities were represented at the conference by graduate students and faculty. Donald E. Morse from Debrecen and Fulbright scholar Jon Roberts (teaching in Szeged that year) made the event international. Next year, the conference "J.R.R. Tolkien: Language,

42   *Gergely Nagy*

Tradition, Interpretation" was held in Pécs in April 2004. The keynote lecture was delivered by Prof. Jane Chance of Rice University, who went on to give two lectures in Budapest. In 2005, the conference returned to Szeged, "J.R.R. Tolkien and the Text: Meaning and Sources" being a smaller, one-day meeting. Even though after the first three years it became clear that a yearly event was not yet tenable in Hungary (there did not seem to be a point for the same people to do this every year), the Society did not give up the idea and returned to organising conferences in the 2010s, in Budapest.

But the Society first and foremost defined itself as a community of people, and there were more "esoteric" activities too. Apart from the yearly long-expected parties (LEPs), the tradition of the Tolkien Society summer camp was established, and there were several creative subgroups who also started meetings, in the spring and autumn of every year, which continue to this day. The officials of the Society, most frequently me and Füzessy, were invited to give lectures and interviews (one year there was a series of programmes at Budapest's Sziget Festival where I talked about Tolkien, and in the National Library of Foreign Literature, I spoke next to Árpád Göncz about Tolkien's poems), and we also took part in the translation and overdubbing of the Jackson films (starting with *The Two Towers*). When national television put on the Hungarian version of *The Big Read* (*A Nagy Könyv*, 2005–2006), a series of programmes where viewers were invited to vote for their favourite book, *The Lord of the Rings* effortlessly made it into the shortlist of twelve books, but finally came in only eighth (the only foreign works to do better were George Orwell's *1984*, *Winnie-the-Pooh*, and Saint-Exupery's *The Little Prince*; *Harry Potter and the Philosopher's Stone* followed directly at the ninth place). Etologist Vilmos Csányi was asked to be the "face" of the book in the shortlist phase, appearing in a short film shown on television to promote the book. The Society was consulted and involved in the programme, and at the gala broadcast in December 2005, Judit Gálvölgyi, the translator of *The Silmarillion*, and I were present at the *Lord of the Rings* table.

The Society also started a magazine entitled *Lassi Laurië* [Golden Leaves], where reports, essays, interviews, and creative writing were published. Among other things, an interview with American Tolkien scholar Mike Drout appeared here, whose discovery of an "unknown" Tolkien manuscript in the Bodleian Library in Oxford (in reality, the versions of Tolkien's *Beowulf* lecture, which Drout published in 2002) which made the news all around the world, was one of the topics he discussed here. Over the years, interviews were published with Tolkien translators Judit Gálvölgyi, Anikó Németh, Gábor Koltai and Svetlana Lihachova; Tolkien scholars Thomas Honegger and Marcel Aubron-Bülles; renowned Tolkien illustrator and artist Ted Nasmith; the illustrator of the first Hungarian

Lord of the Rings edition, Győző Vida; and actors John Rhys-Davies, Craig Parker, Nathaniel Lees, and David Prowse. Other articles were sometimes mildly academic, like my own "Samu" (later expanded and published as "Fictitious"), Iván Uhrman's "Bestiarium", Judit Gálvölgyi's "Egy soha" (which was originally delivered at the 2005 Szeged conference), and later the translation of Dimitra Fimi's award-winning "Was Tolkien Really Racist?" ("Tényleg"), and the publication has interesting pieces and interviews offering an insight into a lot of the Society's activities, including the translation and publication work.[15]

Putting Things Right: Revisions

The most important achievements of the 2000s were the revisions of the two main books, *The Hobbit* and *The Lord of the Rings*, followed by *Unfinished Tales* and *The Book of Lost Tales*, which led on to the appearance of further volumes of the *History of Middle-earth*. First published in 1975, *The Hobbit* was a standalone children's book, and its translator, Tibor Szobotka, did not know anything about Tolkien's other works. He consequently translated names he should not have (like the word "hobbit", for which he made up the new word "babó", and so *The Hobbit* was known as *A babó* until the revision) and did not translate others he should have (like the name "Baggins"). Generally, his text was excellent, but the terminological problems between it and the Hungarian edition of *The Lord of the Rings* (first published in 1981) soon made readers clamour for consistency and a revision of the text, at least to put the names right. *The Lord of the Rings* had its own problems, which mostly derived from the great speed with which Árpád Göncz had to deliver the translation. These included names, oversight, or wrong translation of words (like "north" for "south" several times). The most emblematic blunder was that Göncz's oversight of a pronoun caused Merry to kill the Witch-king instead of Éowyn,[16] and so older Hungarian fans could say to this day that they had read *The Lord of the Rings* when it was still Merry who killed Sauron's emissary. Göncz's text otherwise commanded great respect and critical approval, so even suggesting revision was a thorny question. But it clearly had to be done.

The first step, thus, was the revision of *The Hobbit* and *The Lord of the Rings*, and in both, the Tolkien Society was involved. Tibor Szobotka's *Hobbit* text was first made coherent in its use of names and terms with the received Tolkien terminology of *The Lord of the Rings* in preparation for a Hungarian edition of Douglas A. Anderson's *Annotated Hobbit* (2nd ed.) by Tamás Füzessy and Zsuzsa Ürmössy in 2006, for the publisher Cicero. This was the first edition which restored "Hobbit" into the title and the text, dispensing with Szobotka's "babó". But before Cicero could reprint

44 *Gergely Nagy*

this new text in a standalone edition, their copyright lapsed, and the rights of *The Hobbit* were snatched up by Európa, where an entirely new translation was made by László Gy. Horváth (1950–), a writer, translator, and original editor of the 1991 Hungarian *Silmarillion*. The Society was not consulted in the making of this new text, and so when it appeared in 2006 and they had a chance to look through it, Füzessy sent Európa a list of corrigenda so that the new translation should match the terminology. Füzessy recalled that Európa incorporated a part of this list in their first reprint, some more in further reprints, so that now Gy. Horváth's translation exists in at least three different forms (personal communication). It was after this that the Society started on *The Lord of the Rings*. Apparently, Göncz's text was never really checked,[17] and apart from the kinds of errors mentioned above, there was the question of the spelling of some names that the revision restored. For example, Göncz's text had "Szauron", "Szarumán" ("sz" being the Hungarian grapheme for the [s] sound), but since these are Elvish names, the Society argued for restoring the original "Sauron" and "Saruman" (the same happened with *The Hobbit*'s "Smaug", which Szobotka transcribed phonetically to "Szmóg"). The accent in "Frodó" and "Bilbó" was, however, retained, because Hungarian readers have got so used to these forms. The revised edition of *The Lord of the Rings* came out in 2008, published by Európa. The publisher had already dropped Göncz's original afterword from the reprints in 2002, which meant that Göncz's statement about *The Lord of the Rings* being "the longest fairy tale of all time" no longer influenced readers at the very first point of contact with Tolkien.

The revision work continued with *The Book of Lost Tales*, which Holló és Társa had published in 1996. This was translated by the exceptionally inventive and original poet, Dezső Tandori, and while his text was brilliant and enjoyed high critical acclaim in the 1990s, Tandori had the tendency to "Tandorise" everything he translated.[18] Very original and playful, this sometimes did not quite fit Tolkien's text, and a revision was helped by the Tolkien Society, along with a terminological unification with the rest of the Hungarian revised corpus, when the publisher Cartaphilus acquired the rights and put out a one-volume edition in 2011. This already bore the series title "Középfölde históriája" (which would be the official Hungarian title of *The History of Middle-earth*), and some poetic texts were newly translated for it by Zsuzsanna Ürmössy from the Tolkien Society. When the publishing house Helikon took over the publishing of the *History* series in 2017, the two-volume structure was restored, and the Index of Names (translated by Ágnes Füzessy-Bonácz) was added.

Unfinished Tales, which Szukits had published in 1995, fared somewhat similarly. This was acquired by Európa, and reissued, revised with a title closer to the original (*Befejezetlen regék*) in 2012. In 2019, the rights were purchased by Magvető, and so after they also bought *The Silmarillion* in 2018, all the major Tolkien texts were in one publisher's catalogue. *The Silmarillion* also received a new editing at Európa (who published it between 1996 and 2018). The Index of Names, missing from the original Árkádia editions, was restored from 2015 on (done by Ágnes Bonácz), and from 2018, an excerpt from Tolkien's famous letter to Milton Waldman was affixed at the beginning, as in the English editions (this was translated by Judit Gálvölgyi). By the early 2020s, the most fundamental Tolkien texts have gone through several reeditions and revisions, making sure that the reader gets an authentic Tolkien in Hungarian too.

The Third Wave: New Work by and about Tolkien

Parallel to the revision work, new books by and about Tolkien were also published in the 2000s. First, the cooperation of Szukits and the Society yielded some new Tolkien publications. Szukits had already published Robert Foster's *A Complete Guide to Middle-earth* (translated by veteran fantasy translator Zsolt Szántai as *Tolkien enciklopédia A-tól Z-ig*, 2002), an encyclopaedic aid to reading Tolkien. Now Iván Uhrman was enlisted as a translator for an edition of *The Adventures of Tom Bombadil* (*Bombadil Toma kalandjai*, 2002), and I also worked with Szántai on several books, checking his text and providing notes. Two of these were film-related, but Szukits for some reason insisted on bringing out Lin Carter's *Tolkien: A Look Behind The Lord of the Rings*. Since this first came out in 1969, there did not seem to be much point in translating it, and all I could do was supply copious notes to qualify and correct Carter's outdated points. More important was the plan to publish *The Monsters and the Critics*, which Gábor Koltai had translated for Szukits, but the text needed meticulous checking, and it was in any case missing "On Fairy-Stories", which I translated for this edition. I also wrote an essay to go with the book, on Tolkien's scholarly work, to contextualise the pieces for the Hungarian reader ("J.R.R. Tolkien"). The book finally came out only in 2006, because Tézsla's sudden and tragic death in 2005 put the project on hold. *Monsters and the Critics* was one of the most important new Tolkien releases in the early 2000s, since it made available Tolkien's scholarly essays, among them the *Beowulf* lecture and the paper on *Sir Gawain and the Green Knight*, which were important pieces for students of medieval English literature as well.

Another active member of the Society, Tamás Füzessy, also made contact with publishers. Karen Wynn Fonstad's *Atlas of Middle-earth* was one of the first projects the Society did and which established their connection with the publishing house Cicero. This appeared in 2004 (as *Középfölde atlasza*), translated by Gabriella Büki, Tamás Füzessy, and Balázs Tallián. Füzessy also arranged for Bestline–Cinema to bring out Michael

46 Gergely Nagy

Martinez's *Visualising Middle-earth* (translated by Füzessy, Gabriella Büki, and Zsófia Ábrahám as *Középfölde életre kel,* 2004) and the collection of essays edited by Gregory Bassham and Eric Bronson, The Lord of the Rings *and Philosophy* (translated by Füzessy, Büki, and Gergely Fazekas as *A Gyűrűk Ura és a filozófia,* 2004). Neither of these were very important (or even very good) books within the Tolkien scholarship available at the time, but the goal at this point was to provide the general reader with some insight into what kind of interpretive questions can arise from an informed reading of Tolkien.

The new Tolkien books were mostly shorter works, with the notable exception of Christopher Tolkien's one-volume edition of *The Children of Húrin*, the first of the great tales. *Húrin gyermekei* was translated by Judit Gálvölgyi, who had done *The Silmarillion* in 1991, and published by Európa in 2008 (remarkably soon after its original release in 2007). The poetic parts were done by Zsuzsa N. Kiss (1955–), a very experienced translator. Other smaller books were published by Szukits, who (as we saw) maintained a close relationship with the Society. But Szukits had been active even before then: after bringing out *Unfinished Tales* in 1995, they came out with a volume of Tolkien's shorter tales (*J.R.R. Tolkien meséi,* 2000, illustrated by Tibor Szendrei), which had *Farmer Giles* (in Göncz's translation), "Leaf by Niggle" (in Szántai's new translation), *Smith of Wooton Major* (retranslated by József Békési; these last two had appeared in Anikó Németh's translation in the 1990s), and *The Adventures of Tom Bombadil* (done by István Tótfalusi, who had translated the poems for the original Hungarian *Hobbit* in the 1970s). This book would go through numerous reprints in the 2000s and the 2010s (then by another publisher, Partvonal). Békési's text of *Smith of Wooton Major* also appeared separately in 2002, illustrated by István Kelemen, who also worked on the Hungarian edition of *Roverandom* (*Kóborló és a varázsló,* translated by Szántai) in the same year. Partvonal brought out *Mr. Bliss* in 2008 (*Kürtő úr*, with Tolkien's illustrations, translated by Roland Acsai, a poet and translator who also worked on the Percy Jackson books). Another great addition to the Hungarian corpus was the publication of *The Father Christmas Letters* (in Hungarian, entitled just "Christmas letters", *Karácsonyi levelek*) by Cartaphilus in 2016. With good quality reproductions of Tolkien's art, translated by Csilla M. Szabó and poet Mari Falcsik, this volume gave Hungarian readers an insight into Tolkien's family life as well as the ingenious stories in the letters. In 2019, this too was acquired by Magvető and reprinted by them numerous times. So today, Tolkien's shorter works are practically all available for the Hungarian reader.

The second decade of the new millennium saw other new releases, partly those that Christopher Tolkien was bringing out to follow *The Children of Húrin*; but more importantly, work started on the Hungarian version

Reading Tolkien in Hungary, Part II: The 21st Century   47

of the full *History of Middle-earth* series. Apart from bringing *Unfinished Tales* and (the already existing) *Book of Lost Tales* in line with the Unified Hungarian Tolkien Terminology that was starting to take shape at the Tolkien Society (and would come in extremely handy when work on the *History* volumes started), the new releases brought Tolkien's ideas on *Beowulf* and Kullervo to Hungarian readers – the latter especially important since, as speakers of a Finno-Ugric language, the *Kalevala* is much better known to Hungarians than to readers in the Western world. Relating Tolkien to this important text (which is taught in literature classes in Hungary as early as primary school) makes a connection that brings Tolkien closer to the reader and makes it easier to show the beginnings of his world-creation, as well as educating the reader about Lönnrot and his methods in putting together the book (which itself has instructive parallels for what Tolkien was doing).

The further volumes of Christopher Tolkien's editions of the great tales came out in Hungarian too. After *Húrin gyermekei*, it was again Európa who brought out *Beren and Lúthien* (*Beren és Lúthien*) in 2018, translated by László Gy. Horváth, who did the retranslation of *The Hobbit*. The poems were again done by Zsuzsa N. Kiss. *The Fall of Gondolin* (*Gondolin bukása*) followed, this time published by Magvető, in 2019, translated by Judit Gálvölgyi, with another eminently experienced translator, Mónika Mesterházi (1967–) doing the poetic parts. Magvető acquired the first of the great tales, *Húrin gyermekei* in 2019, and will doubtless strive to add *Beren és Lúthien* to their catalogue too. Európa, however, still has *Beowulf* and *The Story of Kullervo*: the former was published in 2015, translated by Andrea Nagy (who would go on to translate the *History* volumes) and István Tótfalusi, a veteran Tolkien translator (*Kullervo története*, 2016). The *Beowulf* volume was just as important, since *Beowulf* as a poem is not very well-known to Hungarian readers (although a full alliterative translation appeared in 1994, done by György Szegő), and connecting it to Tolkien, what is more, reading Tolkien's meticulous commentary, gives them rather a good idea about the poem. The translator, Andrea Nagy, had already made a full translation of *Beowulf* of her own (with Ágnes Kata Miklós), and so translating Tolkien's text proved a challenge, since she needed to focus on rendering Tolkien's *Beowulf*, and not the Old English text (which she knew very well; Tóth-Palásthy 12).

But the greatest step was taken by the publishing house Helikon, when they took over *The Book of Lost Tales* and undertook to follow it with the publication of the rest of the *History of Middle-earth*. *Lost Tales* was already done, and after the revised text was published in 2017, the Tolkien Society started organising the work to push forward. The third volume, *The Lays of Beleriand* (*Beleriand dalai*), came out in 2018. It was a very difficult book to translate, says Andrea Nagy, who did the

48 Gergely Nagy

alliterative poems and their notes: Hungarian does not lend itself easily to the alliterative meter, and the translators tend to fall back on a more common Hungarian meter which, however, should be avoided, as it is a rhyming form and most readers associate it with compulsory readings they met in primary school (personal communication). The "Lay of Leithian" sections were translated by Zsófia Ábrahám, a talented young poet who practically grew up in the Tolkien Society. Ágnes Bonácz (who had worked on a number of other earlier revisions) rounded off the volume with the remaining prose parts. *The Shaping of Middle-earth* (*Középfölde formálása*) followed in 2020, with a team of translators that included Ágnes Bonácz, Gabriella Büki, Viktória Fehér, and Andrea Nagy, by now all experienced in rendering the minutiae of Tolkien's convoluted worldbuilding. The fifth book, *The Lost Road and Other Writings* (*Az Elveszett Út és más írások*) came out in 2021, now translated by Andrea Nagy alone, as was the sixth, *The Return of the Shadow* (*A homály visszatér*, 2022). Nagy is an associate professor at the Károli Gáspár University of the Reformed Church in Hungary (where two Tolkien Society conferences were held in the 2010s), Department of English Linguistics, and in addition to English historical linguistics, she also teaches Old English literature and translates children's books. She has said in an interview that translating *The Lays of Beleriand* had always been a great dream of hers (Tóth-Palásthy 10). The *History* series has now entered the phase where *The Lord of the Rings* versions are published, and this is both a blessing and a curse: it will doubtless generate more interest, even among readers who are otherwise not too enthusiastic about the minutiae of Tolkien's worldbuilding, but at the same time there is immense difficulty in relating the translation of the "earlier versions" to the finished and published Hungarian text. Even so, there is every hope that in a few years Hungarian will become the second foreign language in which the whole of *The History of Middle-earth* is available (the first being Spanish).

Work on Tolkien, Popular, and Scholarly

We saw how Tolkien was already a given, a "reference point" for some fields of popular culture even in the early 2000s. There was even some scholarly interest (most notably, Tamás Bényei's book), but younger scholars also published articles (Hódosy, Bokody), and also had the opportunity to speak about Tolkien at conferences, like those of the Hungarian Society for the Study of English (HUSSE), at whose biannual conferences I too gave two papers on Tolkien in 2003 and 2005.[19] Doubtless partly because of the Tolkien Society's work, but also due to the great interest that the films generated, new scholarly work was now published. Some of these, like Zoltán Kelemen's or Gertrúd Szamosi's papers, were versions of

Reading Tolkien in Hungary, Part II: The 21st Century 49

what they delivered at the Society's conferences, and continued to exhibit a strong cultural historical (Kelemen) and/or theoretical (Szamosi) focus in the Hungarian scholarly reception. Miklós Stemler's paper in the 2003.1 fantasy-themed issue of *Prae* made use of Todorov's and Christine Brooke-Rose's approaches to argue that a theoretically "very interesting variety of fictionality [is present] in the technique with which the elements of Tolkien's textual universe engage in a dialogue with each other to build up the narrated reality" (5). Stemler also concluded that by the device of the Red Book, Tolkien "invests Bilbo, Frodo, and Sam with the role of the fictional author" (12) – an important point in the early 2000s. Norbert Gyuris's argument in his PhD dissertation, defended in 2006 at the University of Pécs, entitled "A szerző alakváltásai: narratológia, szimulációelmélet és hipertextualitás" [The Shape-shifts of the Author: Narratology, Simulation, and Hypertextuality], is likewise theoretically informed. Here, an entire chapter was devoted to Tolkien, in which Gyuris showed how the different functions assigned to the author in *The Lord of the Rings* blur the distinctions between author, translator, and narrator, and that Tolkien's device of fictitious translation can very profitably be interpreted with the help of Baudrillard's ideas about simulation (*Vénember*, ch. 2.4). Gyuris also presented this in a paper at the 2004 Tolkien conference, in Pécs (not published). Writing about Hungarian fantasy literature, Dániel Végh remarked that Tolkien is especially interesting since "in the last decade, he has started to infiltrate the canon" (1154), and making use of Brooke-Rose's term "megatext" (which he takes from Stemler) and Bokody's ideas about RPG, concludes that the megatext, the various paratextual elements in fantasy, are the key to the reader's enjoyment and aesthetic experience (1557). Wolfgang Iser's and Hans-Robert Jauss's theories are brought in to approach the (readerly) fantasy experience.

While the Society kept up organising popularising events and community activities, and also contributed to the growing Tolkien corpus in Hungarian, they also lent their expertise to the translation of secondary literature. Wayne G. Hammond and Christina Scull's wonderful *The Art of* The Hobbit was translated by Ágnes Bonácz and published by Európa in 2012 (*J.R.R. Tolkien: A hobbit művészete*), and Karen Wynn Fonstad's *Atlas of Middle-earth*, one of the first projects the Society did, also went through some revision and correction to be reprinted again in 2017 and 2021. Colin Duriez's *Tolkien and C.S. Lewis: The Gift of Friendship* appeared in Hungarian in 2016, at the Christian publisher Harmat, translated by Teodóra Király (*Tolkien és C.S. Lewis: egy híres barátság története*), and more recently Corvina, one of the publishers that survived from the old communist days (when it published high quality art albums) came out with a translation of John Garth's *Tolkien's Worlds* (*Tolkien világai*, 2021). This was translated by Anikó Németh, who had worked on Tolkien

50   *Gergely Nagy*

texts in the 1990s. Corvina asked Iván Uhrman to read and check the translated text.[20] Garth's book is a welcome addition to the small library of Tolkien-related books in Hungarian, because his knowledgeable and academically informed, yet very accessible writing is a good introduction to more scholarly readings of Tolkien's work. At the other end of the scale, Norbert Gyuris's PhD dissertation, which I cited above as an example of a very theoretically minded approach, and not very widely accessible, came out in e-book form in 2011.

Another important contribution was the Tolkien course that Füzessy started teaching at the Department of History and Philosophy of Science, at the Faculty of Sciences of Eötvös Loránd University. This initially collected the talks he had written and delivered at various Tolkien events over the years, and was always very popular with students. But it was a general education course, not a "professional" one in the sense that Füzessy was not affiliated with any department of the university, which saw his course as a great way to draw in students. After the Department of History and Philosophy of Science ceased to exist, the course continued on ELTE's Faculty of Humanities, and a seminar was launched too. From 2007, it was continued at Károli, and later transformed into an online series of lectures called the "Tolkien Academy". The course offered a rather comprehensive treatment of Tolkien, touching on mythopoesis and fantasy, Germanic, Norse, and Celtic mythology, the creation of languages, social/political patterns in Tolkien's world, its religious and historical aspects, and looked out towards Christian attitudes and other popular franchises (*Star Wars, Harry Potter*, even *Game of Thrones*). A lot of students went through the course during the years, and many of those found that their interest in Tolkien only grew by learning more about his work.

It is thus no surprise that the 2010s brought new developments in scholarly work too. There was a conference on the fantastic ("Visions of Baseless Fabric") organised at Pázmány Péter Catholic University in 2011. No-one spoke explicitly on Tolkien here, but some people who had done so at other, previous gatherings, read papers (Norbert Gyuris and Anikó Sohár). The Tolkien Society also revived their academic conferences in 2012, when they organised "J.R.R. Tolkien: Fantasy and Morality" in Budapest, at Károli Gáspár University, partly in celebration of the tenth anniversary of the Society's founding. Here, Verlyn Flieger and John Garth gave keynote lectures along with Füzessy and myself. Some scholars who had been there from the first read papers too (Anikó Sohár and Zoltán Kelemen), and two young instructors at Károli, Andrea Nagy (whose work on translation we have already seen) and Dóra Pődör, made their first appearance. The conference was held in downtown Budapest, the Humanities building of Károli, and was a very pleasant and productive meeting. Its proceedings, along with some papers from earlier conferences (like Pál Regős's

Reading Tolkien in Hungary, Part II: The 21st Century   51

and Gertrúd Szamosi's) were published by the Tolkien Society in the same year, in what became the first ever volume of papers entirely focusing on Tolkien to be published in Hungarian. The book, however, shows many of the problems of Tolkien scholarship in Hungary as well as some very good and valuable work. It is certainly a good thing that essays by Verlyn Flieger and John Garth were published here in Hungarian, and that university instructors such as Sohár, Pődör, Szamosi, and Kelemen all gave papers to publish: they each brought to Tolkien something from their own field (Sohár, her research on contemporary fantastic/fantasy literature; Szamosi, the theory; Pődör, historical lexicography; Kelemen, comparative literature and cultural history), but many other papers read like seminar papers from a Tolkien course: sources and parallels chosen rather haphazardly and arbitrarily, with not a very good knowledge of Tolkien scholarship, and thus often making points that had been made decades before. On the whole, the volume is significant more as a milestone and less as scholarship. In the "Foreword" that I wrote for the book, I warned about exactly this: that there cannot be any more excuses for provincial and repetitive work ("Nincs több" 15–16).

The Society organised another conference in 2015, this time at Pázmány Péter Catholic University, and with a more international attendance. Thomas Honegger and Allan Turner (from Friedrich Schiller University in Jena) delivered keynote lectures, and there were several English sessions too, with participants from France, Italy, and Serbia. A much slimmer volume, entitled, as the conference was, *J.R.R. Tolkien: egyén, közösség, társadalom* [*J.R.R. Tolkien: Individual, Community, Society*] resulted from this, again published by the Tolkien Society, and edited by Andrea Nagy, Ágnes Bonácz, and Kincső Kiss. This sadly had all the issues the previous one had had in plenty, and since six of the nine papers in it were translations from English, sometimes this added to the problems.

One of the great achievements in all of this was that Tolkien Studies were established at all Hungarian universities, and this furthered a wider acceptance of Tolkien's work as "serious literature". The press often reported on the various Tolkien conferences (see Cs. Molnár, Thomka), the first volume of essays (Szathmáry, Thomka), and later, the ongoing translation projects (Csepregi), often quoting contributors, translators, and generally producing more and more competent articles with less simplification. The fortieth anniversary of the first Hungarian edition of *The Lord of the Rings* was also publicised (Juhász, see also Orthmayr, "Negyvenéves"), and Tolkien now counted so firmly as one of the basic, "iconic texts" of Generation Y that Mónika Miklya Luzsányi, in an article in *Theologiai Szemle* [Studies in Theology] used his work (along with *Harry Potter, Star Wars*, and *The Matrix*) to outline religious or almost-religious elements in how this generation sees the world (Miklya Luzsányi). It seems that Tolkien has eventually found

52   Gergely Nagy

his place, if not in the Hungarian academic world, then at least in popular culture. But unlike the early 2000s, since the second and the third decades of the millennium, sources are not scarce at all, and Hungarian scholars can access any scholarship that is available to students of Tolkien anywhere in the world. This could even mean that more of them enter the international scene of Tolkien Studies, but so far this has not been the case: to date, there are only a handful of Hungarian scholars who made any impact on international Tolkien criticism. Anikó Sohár's book (*Cultural Transfer*) touched on Tolkien's reception in Hungary in the 1990s. I started publishing abroad on Tolkien in the early 2000s, and was very happy when Mike Drout invited me to be on the editorial board of the then starting *Tolkien Studies* in 2003. I wrote the article on *The Silmarillion* both in *The J.R.R. Tolkien Encyclopaedia* (published in 2006) and in the Wiley-Blackwell *Companion to J.R.R. Tolkien* (ed. by Stuart D. Lee), and it gave me particular pleasure that an old student of mine, Péter Kristóf Makai was also invited to contribute (the *Companion* appeared in 2014, and was recently revised for a second edition, which came out in 2022). Makai had by then already published an important essay on "On Fairy-Stories" and the (virtual) reality of computer games in *Tolkien Studies*. Another contributor of the first Hungarian volume of essays, Tibor Tarcsay (then a PhD student at Pázmány Péter Catholic University), also published an article on archetypes in Tolkien's Earendel in *Mythlore* in 2015.

Conclusion: The Myth of Many Places

It seems that Tolkien has found his place in Hungary, in popular culture and in the academy too, and it is more than one place: from medieval literature through contemporary fantastic literature (and fantasy) to digital formats and virtual reality, he has many contexts that can be examined profitably. Some view him as an outdated classic, but for others his work is very much fresh and alive, and this can be seen from the interest evidenced at the Tolkien Society's events. Supporting Peter Jackson's *Hobbit* movies, the Society organised events in 2012, 2013, and 2014, and also kept up the tradition of "LEPs" on or around 3 January every year (now called "Tolkien Days"). The Society remains a vibrant community whose summer camps are now filled with the children of those who founded the Society in 2002; but also a productive workshop of creative pursuits, and of course the centre of translation and organisation work. Quite of lot of the important steps that Tolkien's reception in Hungary took in the 2000s were due to the Society's work, the greatest being the revision of the older Tolkien translations and arranging the translation of *The History of Middle-earth*. This means that Hungarian readers have good and authoritative Tolkien texts to read, and what they do with them is also more diverse than it has ever been.

Reading Tolkien in Hungary, Part II: The 21st Century   53

Tolkien is now not confined within science fiction, children's literature, nor even fantasy. Hungarian readers have all they need to start engaging with his work in various meaningful ways, only one of which is scholarly research and interpretation. The Hungarian scholarly reception is, as we have seen, varied: it includes some very good work (Uhrman, Stemler on fantasy, Gyuris, Hódosy, and especially Bényei) that could certainly hold their own even in an international context, while also containing outdated or repetitious papers. As sources are now much more freely available and accessible than they used to be, and instruction on Tolkien can even be obtained at universities (if not in courses, then certainly by the supervision of instructors), there is every hope that young Hungarian scholars can enter the international scene if they want to. But non-academic readers and fans can find him and engage with him in more places than ever too.

Notes

In writing and researching this survey, I attempted to talk to as many people who make an appearance in the story as possible. I am grateful to Bálint Barna, Vera Benczik, Ágnes Bonácz, Adrienn Deák, Tamás Füzessy, Norbert Gyuris, József Kazár, Andrea Nagy, Donald E. Morse, Flóra Orthmayr, Szonja Selmeczi, Anikó Sohár, Gertrúd Szamosi, Péter Tick, Iván Uhrman, Illés Varga, and Dániel Varró for taking the time to answer questions or their help. In all quotations from Hungarian texts, the translations are mine.

1 Todorov's own work on the fantastic was published in Hungarian in 2002 (translated by Gábor Gelléri).
2 Hungarian readers had already seen Tolkien connected to the antiutopian tradition of SF in Sam Lundwall's *Holnap történt*: see previous chapter 19. Bényei stresses that *The Lord of the Rings* is simultaneously in the tradition of nostalgia and antiutopia (194).
3 A review of the book by Gábor Tamás Molnár points out how Bényei's treatment highlights the "reflexive tropes at work in Tolkien's worldbuilding process, as the narration posits the emergence of the fictitious world as a sort of philological reconstruction" (G.T. Molnár, 110).
4 As fantasya.hu is no longer online, the original date of Kornya's essay is uncertain, but there certainly was discussion about in on messageboards in 2003. The original is archived at https://web.archive.org/web/20070927192449/ http://www.fantasya.hu/index.php?modul=cikk&mod=mutat&id=204&kez des=0 (accessed: 12 Feb 2023).
5 Another related point is the total lack of sex and sensuality (8), something that critics often brought up in the 1970s: see previous chapter 17.
6 In private, he did not hesitate to admit he did not mean this very seriously (Illés Varga, personal communication).
7 These two were even mentioned in the press: Magyar 13.
8 The participants were literary critic Anikó Sohár, film aesthete András Réz, Tolkien translator Gábor Koltai, psychologist Zsuzsanna Vajda, and literary historian Béla Rigó. I moderated the discussion.

54   Gergely Nagy

9 Pál Regős, Iván Uhrman (of the Aurin circle, see previous chapter 24–25), and Tamás Füzessy, Tamás Ferencz, and Károly Baksai from the Tolkien Society gave lectures.

10 Literary historians Zoltán Kelemen and Béla Rigó, and the translator of the *Harry Potter* books, Tamás Boldizsár Tóth took part in this.

11 Here, the participants were Iván Uhrman, media scholar Benedek Tóth, and me.

12 Literary historian György Endre Szőnyi, fantasy specialist Miklós Stemler, Attila Varró from the periodical *Filmvilág* [Film World], and András Réz participated in this discussion.

13 This discussion had the most participants: fantasy authors/translators Csanád Novák and András Gáspár, all three members of the Aurin circle (Péter Tick, József Kazár, and Illés Varga), Tamás Pollák, ex-editor of the RPG magazine *Dragon*, editor Ervin Tézsla from the publishing house Szukits, and Norbert Tóth from fantasya.hu.

14 Rigó wrote several very competent articles for young readers in *Kincskereső* [Treasure Seeker], which he edited ("Tolkien", "A Két Torony", and "A filmbirodalom"), advising them to "read first if you want to really enjoy the film" ("A filmbirodalom" 13).

15 *Lassi Laurië* is now available online at https://tolkien.hu/mtt/kiadvanyok/lassi-laurie, with a useful, thematically arranged, and comprehensive table of contents at https://tolkien.hu/mtt/item/3334-lassi-laurie-egyesitett-tartalomjegyzek.

16 In his provocative essay, Zsolt Kornya reproaches Tolkien for Merry's "backstabbing" killing of the Witch-king while he is occupied by Éowyn (5), even though he claims to have read the book in English too (which was clearly true, but this detail shows how attentively). Kornya also says he had no problem with the Szobotka translation of *The Hobbit* (1, an unpopular view to express).

17 Although the colophon of the early editions claimed Éva Avarossy was responsible for "checking the translation against the original": see Orthmayr, "Negyvenéves", 32.

18 To the point that Anikó Sohár called his translation of Stephen Donaldson's *Lord Foul's Bane* "often undecipherable, unmeaningful" (*Cultural Transfer* 112), and Kornya also mentioned that Tandori's translations "end up more as works by Tandori, not by the original author" (2).

19 "Sauron and the Sign: from Mythological Sign to Mythological Subject" at HUSSE 6 in 2003 (Debrecen), and "Old Poems: Fictitious Poetic Traditions in Tolkien's Fiction of Culture" at HUSSE 7 in 2005 (Veszprém).

20 See Flóra Orthmayr's interview with Németh: "Tolkien meséi".

Works Cited

Adorján, Sebestyén. "J.R.R. Tolkien: A szilmarilok" [J.R.R. Tolkien: *The Silmarillion*]. *Igen*. 16 August 1991, 60–61.

Bényei, Tamás. *Az ártatlan ország. Az angol regény 1945 után* [*The Innocent Country. The English Novel after 1945*]. Debrecen: Debreceni Egyetemi Kiadó, 2003.

Bokody, Péter. "Szerepjáték és fantasy" [Role-playing Games and Fantasy]. *Holmi* 14.10 (2002): 1299–1307.

Carpenter, Humphrey. *J.R.R. Tolkien: az ember a mű mögött*. Transl. Éva Koncz and István Tótfalusi. Budapest: Cicero, 2001.

Csepregi, Evelyn. "Abszolút jó és abszolút rossz. Tolkien titka" [Absolute Good and Absolute Evil. Tolkien's Secret]. *Népszava*. 26 June 2019, 11.

Reading Tolkien in Hungary, Part II: The 21st Century 55

Fimi, Dimitra. "Tényleg rasszista volt Tolkien?" [Was Tolkien Really Racist?]. Transl. Zsófia Feró. *Lassi Laurië* 19.2 (2022): 14–15.

Fónod, Zoltán. "Utak, lehetőségek, kihívások. A kor világirodalmának fontosabb jelenségei" [Roads, Opportunies, Challenges. The Most Important Phenomena in Contemporary World Literature]. *Irodalmi szemle* 45.7 (2002): 56–76.

Gálvölgyi, Judit. "Egy soha meg nem írt szakdolgozat helyett" [In place of a never-written thesis]. *Lassi Laurië* 4.2 (2005): 6–8.

Gyuris, Norbert. *A vénember lábnyoma: metafikció, szimuláció, hipertextualitás és szerzőség* [*The Old Man's Footprint: Metafiction, Simulation, Hypertextuality, and Authorship*]. Szeged: Americana E-books, 2011. Avalailable: https://ebooks.americanaejournal.hu/hu/konyvek/a-venember-labnyoma/ Accessed 27 April 2022.

———. "Rev. of Jane Chance, The Lord of the Rings: *The Mythology of Power*". *Helikon* 49.1–2 (2003): 141–143.

"Harry Potter kerekasztal" [Harry Potter Roundtable]. *Kincskereső* 28.5 (2001): 8–14.

Hódosy, Annamária. "A fantázia informatikája" [The Informatics of Fantasy]. *Literatura* 3 (2000): 300–316.

Kapitány, Ágnes and Gábor Kapitány. "Modern mitológiák" [Modern Mythologies]. *Kultúra és Közösség* 27.4 (2000): 127–145.

Kelemen, Zoltán. "Így rendezték ők a lovas Hektór temetését" [Thus, then, did they celebrate the funeral of Hektor tamer of horses]. *Új Forrás* 36.4 (2004): 66–74.

Kende B., Hanna. *Harry Potter titka. A gyermek csodavilága* [*The Secret of Harry Potter. The Miraculous World of Children*]. Budapest: Osiris, 2001.

Kornya, Zsolt [Raoul Renier]. "Miért van elegem Tolkienből?" [Why Am I Fed Up with Tolkien?]. *fantasya.hu*, archived at https://web.archive.org/web/20070927192449/http://www.fantasya.hu/index.php?modul=cikk&mod=mutat&id=204&kezdes=0 Accessed 12 February 2023. Also available: https://docplayer.hu/43553-Miert-van-elegem-tolkienbol-avagy-rendhagyo-eszmefuttatas-a-fantasy-irodalom-berkeiben.html Accessed 11 February 2023.

László, Dóra. "Olvasás, nevelés, művészet. Négyszögletű kerekasztal a gyermekirodalomról" [Reading, Education, Art. A Roundtable on Children's Literature]. *Magyar Nemzet*. 25 January 2001, 14.

Lovász, Andrea. "'mi egy képes a képtelenhez képest?' Mesék a jelenkori gyermekirodalomban" [what's a possible compared to the impossible? Tales in Contemporary Children's Literature]. *Tiszatáj* 56.12 (2002): 53–75.

———. "A meseregény kora. Vázlat a meseregény megközelítéséhez." [The Age of the Fairy-tale novel. A Sketch of an Approach to Fairy-tale-novels]. *Korunk* 13.10 (2002): 7–12.

———. "Harry Potter avagy a jelen idejű holnemvolt" [Harry Potter, or the Present "Once Upon a Time']. *Új Forrás* 33.9 (2001): 49–59.

———. "A tizenharmadik tündér. Mese, álom, halál" [The Thirteenth Fairy. Fairy-tale, Dream, Death]. *Art Limes* 12.44 (2000): 9–19.

Maár, Judit. *A fantasztikus irodalom* [*Fantastic Literature*]. Budapest: Osiris, 2001.

Magyar, Katalin. "Frodo, Sam, Gandalf és a többiek" [Frodo, Sam, Gandalf and the others]. *Népszava*. 16 May 2001, 13.

56 Gergely Nagy

Miklya Luzsányi, Mónika. "Ót és újat. Vallási-teológiai elemek a digitális nemzedék világképét meghatározó művekben, különös tekintettel a kereszténységre" [Old and New. Religious-theological Elements in Works Determining the Worldview of the Digital Generation, with Especial Focus on Christianity]. *Theologiai Szemle* 58.4 (2015): 233–241.

Molnár, Csaba. "Tündetudomány. J.R.R. Tolkien helye a világirodalomban és a magyar tudósok képzeletében" [Elvish Scholarship. The Place of J.R.R. Tolkien in World Literature and the Imagination of Hungarian Academics]. *Magyar Nemzet.* 30 June 2012, 30.

Molnár, Gábor Tamás. "Poetológiai és ideológiai határhelyzetek. Bényei Tamás: *Az ártatlan ország*" [Liminal Situations Poetological and Ideological. Tamás Bényei's *The Innocent Country*]. *Alföld* 58.11 (2007): 107–111.

Nagy, Andrea, Ágnes Bonácz, Kincső Kiss, eds. *J.R.R. Tolkien: egyén, közösség, társadalom* [*J.R.R. Tolkien: Individual, Community, Society*]. Budapest: Magyar Tolkien Társaság, 2018.

Nagy, Gergely. "Nincs több mentség. A Tolkien-kutatások Magyarországon" [No More Excuses: Tolkien Studies in Hungary]. *J.R.R. Tolkien: Fantázia és erkölcs.* Ed. Dóra Pődör, Andrea Nagy, and Tamás Füzessy. Budapest: Magyar Tolkien Társaság, 2012. 13–17.

———. "Fictitious Fairy Tales: Writing a Fictitious Character in *The Lord of the Rings*". *Postmodern Reinterpretations of Fairy Tales. How Applying New Methods Generates New Meanings.* Ed. Anna Kérchy. Lewiston, Lampeter: The Edwin Mellen Press, 2011. 367–382.

———. "J.R.R. Tolkien tudományos munkája: az író és a kritikus" [J.R.R. Tolkien's Academic Work: the Writer and the Critic]. J.R.R. Tolkien, *Szörnyek és ítészek.* Transl. Gábor Koltai and Gergely Nagy. Szeged: Szukits, 2006. 351–363.

———. "Samu és a szilmarilok". *Lassi Laurië* 2.2 (2003): 8–10.

———. "That Fantastic Century. Tom Shippey's *J.R.R. Tolkien: Author of the Century*". *The AnaChronist* (2002): 327–338.

Nyilasy, Balázs. "A tündérmese, a műmese, a vágy és a csoda" [Fairy tales, Literary Tales, Desire, and Miracle]. *Korunk* 13.10 (2002): 19–24.

Orthmayr, Flóra. "Negyvenéves a *Gyűrűk Ura* első magyar kiadása" [Forty Years Ago: the First Hungarian Edition of *The Lord of the Rings*]. *Lassi Laurië* 18.2 (2021): 32.

———. "Tolkien meséi és világa" [Tolkien's Tales and World]. *Lassi Laurië* 18.2 (2021): 18–19.

Pődör, Dóra, Andrea Nagy, and Tamás Füzessy, eds. *J.R.R. Tolkien: Fantázia és erkölcs* [*J.R.R. Tolkien: Fantasy and Morality*]. Budapest: Magyar Tolkien Társaság, 2012.

Rigó, Béla. "A filmbirodalom visszavág. Fanyalgások *A király visszatér* megtekintése után" [The Filmic Empire Strikes Back. Grumbling after *The Return of the King*]. *Kincskereső* 31.1–2 (2004): 10–13.

———. "*A két torony*, avagy *A Gyűrűk Ura* második része a filmvásznon" [*The Two Towers*, the Second Part of *The Lord of the Rings* on the Big Screen]. *Kincskereső* 30.1 (2003): 26–28.

———. [Góbé]. "Tolkien, a gyűrűk ura" [Tolkien, Lord of the Rings]. *Kincskereső* 29.1–2 (2002): 36–43.

Reading Tolkien in Hungary, Part II: The 21st Century 57

Schlemmer, Éva. "Nemi szerepek és olvasási szokások" [Gender Roles and Reading Habits]. *Valóság* 45.12 (2002): 17–37.

Shippey, Tom. *J.R.R. Tolkien: Author of the Century*. Boston and New York: Houghton Mifflin, 2001.

Sohár, Anikó. "Importált kulturális javak: a populáris műfajok fordítása. Science fiction és fantasy" [Imported Cultural Goods: the Translation of Popular Genres. Science Fiction and Fantasy]. *Modern Filológiai Közlemények/Papers in English Philology* 2.1 (2000): 5–13.

———. "Thy Speech Betrayeth Thee: Thou Shalt Not Steal The Prestige of Foreign Literatures. Pseudotranslations in Hungary After 1989". *Hungarian Studies* 14.1 (2000): 55–83.

———. *The Cultural Transfer of Science Fiction and Fantasy in Hungary 1989–1995*. Frankfurt am Main: Peter Lang, 1999.

Stemler, Miklós. "A világteremtés poétikája" [The Poetics of World-building]. *Prae* 5.1 (2003): 5–13.

Szamosi, Gertrúd. "Szubjektum és a hatalom diskurzusai a *Gyűrűk Urában*" [The Subject and the Discourses of Power in *The Lord of the Rings*]. *Opus* 7 (2010): 44–58. Also in *J.R.R. Tolkien: Fantázia és erkölcs*. Eds. Dóra Pődör, Andrea Nagy, and Tamás Füzessy. Budapest: Magyar Tolkien Társaság, 2012. 195–208.

Szathmáry, István Pál. "Tolkien örökségéről tudományosan" [On Tolkien's Heritage through Scholarship]. *Magyar Nemzet*. 11 January 2013, 15.

Thomka, Orsolya. "Új mese a halálról és a megváltásról" [A New Tale about Death and Salvation]. *Reformátusok Lapja*. 5 May 2013, 11.

Todorov, Tzvetan. *Bevezetés a fantasztikus irodalomba*. Transl. Gábor Gelléri. Budapest: Napvilág, 2002.

Tóth-Palásthy, Luca. "A *Középfölde Históriája* fordításáról" [On the Translation of *The History of Middle-earth*]. *Lassi Laurië* 16.1 (2019): 10–13.

Uhrman, Iván. "Bestiarium Terrae Mediae, Part II". *Lassi Laurië* 6.1 (2007): 16–19.

———. "Bestiarium Terrae Mediae, Part I". *Lassi Laurië* 5.1 (2006): 8–11.

Valastyán, Tamás. "Valóságos csodavilág" [A Real World of Miracles]. *Hajdúbihari Napló*. 28 October 2000, 9.

Varró, Dániel. *Túl a Maszat-hegyen* [*Beyond Mt. Smudge*]. Budapest: Magvető, 2003.

Part II

Reception and Translations of Tolkien in Czechoslovakia and Its Succeeding Countries

3 Mythologia Non Grata
Tolkien and Socialist Czechoslovakia

Janka Kascakova

Introduction

The First World War in which Tolkien fought and lost so many friends and which so significantly impacted his whole generation also gave rise to a new country, an experiment of sorts, in the very heart of Europe. Czechoslovakia was and remains one of the most interesting historical ventures of modern European history. When it became obvious that the massive Austrian-Hungarian Empire consisting of many different nations would crumble, the representatives of Czechs and Slovaks came up with a rather novel idea of two small countries joining forces rather than attaching themselves to some larger unit, to have a go at being independent with less chance of being swallowed up again soon by some other giant. And while, in the relatively brief joint history of the two nations, the "swallowing" did happen twice anyway – once in the division of the spheres of interest during the Second World War, the second time in the 20 years of Soviet occupation – the experiment proved to be generally successful and yielded very interesting results. Although it eventually ended in separation whose reasons are manifold and outside of the scope of this chapter, the crucial aspect is that it all ended peacefully and in a civilized manner. There was no need to heal the wounds of war as in other similar cases, and, ironically, many areas of tension disappeared while the cooperation in others remained and flourished. Both the geographical and linguistic closeness of the two nations created a particular cultural environment which, in spite of the split, or maybe even because of it, is getting even stronger. Most of the inhabitants of Czechoslovakia were bilingual, if not in their active, then certainly in a passive knowledge of the other language. This was supported on many different levels, not least by the national television broadcasting in both languages. Although there were separate cultural and other newspapers and magazines, they were available in both parts of the country and there were some which were published countrywide and with articles in Czech and Slovak depending on the mother tongue of their author.

DOI: 10.4324/9781003407171-6

62   *Janka Kascakova*

There has always been and will always be an element of (mostly friendly) competition between the two nations, although the ones more prone to compete are usually the Slovaks. It is most obvious in ice hockey yet has existed also in the field of culture, for example in translations. Most of the great works of world literature (those that were approved by the censorship in the socialist era) were translated to both languages, and it was not an exception for learned people to read both translations and contemplate the merits of one over the other.[1] And although some works were available only in Czech as they formed two-thirds of the country's inhabitants and thus a bigger market, there was no language barrier and thus no imbalance in the access to the work in question. Even now, thirty years after, the mutual influence still needs to be taken into consideration. While the bilingualism became more uneven – Slovaks generally remaining better at Czech than Czechs at Slovak – the cultural ties are still very strong.

However, the closeness never meant sameness, although, at the beginning of the common country, some politicians were trying to pass all the inhabitants of the common state as one Czechoslovak nation speaking the Czechoslovak language. The intention was to strengthen the claims of legitimacy but instead, it created many problems and hard feelings. While being aware of the dangers of stereotyping, it still is useful to generalize and explain the differences between the two parts of the country that help understand the difference in the reception and approaches to the cultural stimuli in question and Tolkien in particular.

Due to the differences in the historical development of the two nations, the Czechs were seen as more self-assured, cosmopolitan, and comfortable with their national identity. In the past, for a long time, the Czech kingdom played an important role in the European political arena and even after the infamous 1620 Battle of White Mountain, which ended the last remains of self-rule and independence within the Habsburg monarchy, they still had aristocracy that professed to be Czech. Furthermore, at the beginning of the common state, the Czech part of the country was more industrial and technologically developed than the Slovak part and was more advanced in terms of education.

Unlike the Czechs, the Slovaks never really experienced home rule, and at the beginning of their alliance with the Czechs, the area was mostly agricultural, deeply religious, and less exposed to higher education. In the context of the discussion of the reception of J.R.R. Tolkien, it is of interest to say that most of the inhabitants were Catholics, yet the Protestant minority was very visible and contributed in a major way to the cultural and political uplifting of the nation in the 19th-century national revival movements. From the outset, thus, the two parts were uneven and kept developing unevenly for many years. From this stems the, often one-sided, desire of Slovaks to compete and to get even, to show off to their "older" brothers.

Mythologia Non Grata: Tolkien and Socialist Czechoslovakia   63

From 1948, however, the whole country had to cope with a new, tradition-breaking and destructive regime that distorted the political, social, and cultural development of the country and whose methods were violent and their consequences far-reaching. It is into this environment that J.R.R. Tolkien's work was introduced or, rather, against which it had to struggle to be even allowed to enter. This chapter deals with Tolkien's reception in some of the most difficult times of the two nations' joint history, the twenty plus last years of the socialist country, a country which was seemingly independent, yet in reality, suffering under the yoke of the Soviet influence and occupied by its armies.

The Literary Magazines and Tolkien Translated for the First Time

Speaking of the good-natured competition, the very first mention of Tolkien's work in the Czechoslovak press happened in Slovakia and that relatively late, in 1970. In three successive volumes of the literary magazine *Revue svetovej literatúry* [Review of World Literature], a renowned linguist and translator Viktor Krupa (1936–2021) opened a window to Tolkien's world by first offering a serious long study of Tolkien's life and work and then translations of selected chapters from *The Lord of the Rings*.[2] Apparently, Krupa was hoping to test the waters or whet the appetite of a potential publisher for the whole work. However, the historical context of the publication date gives the whole attempt a more sinister atmosphere. The early 1970s were not good times in general and even less so for a writing of Tolkien's kind. The decade before was full of enthusiasm and hope. The shackles of communist oppression were loosening, artists were suddenly free to express their ideas; not only heretofore forbidden books were being translated, but original production flourished too. People were hoping for a more positive existence and a freedom of expression. As Zuzana Bujačková demonstrates, several literary magazines founded in the 1960s, including *Revue svetovej literatúry,* began publishing text and visual art absolutely inaccessible until then and thus contributed to the translation and literary renaissance of that era (13). It all ended (in)famously in the summer of 1968 when the "friendly" armies of the Warsaw pact entered Czechoslovakia and cut all hopes of the period of democratic processes known as the "Prague Spring".[3] Some would soon leave, but the Soviet army settled in for the very long twenty years. The censorship, weakened and ineffective in the years leading to 1968, was back in full force and since the socialist cadres preferred and enforced the one-dimensional and unequivocal socialist realism, the censors were skilled close readers and proficient at spotting dangerous ambiguities and symbolism that could potentially be interpreted in an anti-establishment way. Many people still recall some of the most hilarious reasons given for

64 Janka Kascakova

compulsory modification or complete banishment of some artistic production. However, it was laughing through tears, as the 1970s began the era of what the leading communists would call "normalization". It meant the loss of jobs for many artists and intellectuals involved in the Prague Spring, a wave of emigration of those who no longer wanted to stay or were forced to leave and a bleak and grey existence in a nightmarish reality for those who had to or chose to remain. 1970 was certainly not the year of hope for a publication of Tolkien.

Since Victor Krupa is no longer alive and there are not many records as to what exactly happened and in what order, the sequence of events related to the publications or attempts at the publication of Tolkien remains unclear. The only fact is that *The Lord of the Rings* was not published in the Slovak translation until the early 2000s.[4] One can only conjecture that, encouraged by the unprecedented explosion of translations of the works of world literatures in the 1960s, Krupa originally contemplated translating his favourite author and possibly even started with several chapters. When the abrupt change came and his suggestion was not favourably received – the director of the publishing house allegedly telling him it was "hogwash for children and a waste of paper" (Rehák n.p)[5] – he at least attempted an ideologically much less sensitive, *The Hobbit,* which he was the first in Czechoslovakia to translate and publish in 1973.[6] As Krupa stated in an interview years later, he became familiar with Tolkien while studying abroad and offered the publisher his translation of *The Hobbit* which was welcome with open arms. However, when he suggested *The Lord of the Rings,* he kept meeting with refusal even after the regime was over (Aľakša 11–12).

It is a great pity and loss for the Slovak translation literature that Krupa's original effort was thwarted. He would have been an ideal translator of *The Lord of the Rings* as he had a lot in common with Tolkien and understood him and his aims much better than many other translators in other countries. For one, Krupa, just like Tolkien, was a deeply knowledgeable and enthusiastic linguist, although his field of expertise lay in a very different linguistic and geographical area. Krupa was an expert on languages, literatures, and cultures of the Pacific Ocean nations (mostly Maori and Polynesian), but he also translated from English and Japanese, among some other languages ("Viktor Krupa" n.p.). Similar to Tolkien, he was deeply interested in folktales and mythologies and translated some during his fruitful career. It is obvious that at the time of the writing of the article and translations for *Revue svetovej literatúry,* he was not only familiar with *The Lord of the Rings* but had a rather extensive knowledge of its author and his opinions and background as well. In the introductory study on Tolkien's work entitled, slightly provocatively "Mýtus večne živý" [The myth forever alive],[7] he quotes from various sources and offers a valuable introduction to

Mythologia Non Grata: Tolkien and Socialist Czechoslovakia 65

Tolkien's world and its background. Krupa calls *The Lord of the Rings* "a masterpiece" (104) and explains its spontaneous and "unexpected success" by "an incredible attention to detail", consistency, deep faith in the victory of good over evil, and Tolkien's storytelling genius (105). According to him, it is an "anti-sociological novel" that displays moral and psychological truthfulness (105). He is fascinated by the presentation of evil, he sees it not as a result of our ignorance (it is not passive), but as an autonomous principle, capable of regeneration: it is "the devil of Manichaeism able to constantly change its tactics" (107). Finally, in opposition to the opinion of many critics, he believes the pessimism makes the work not really fairy-tale-like (107). Krupa could not avoid some of the "compulsory" vocabulary of those times and called the hobbits "robotný roľnícky ľud" [hardworking agricultural/peasant people] (106), yet this would not appeal only to the pro-regime censors but also to common Slovaks who could very easily identify with hobbits in this respect. Unfortunately, it was not enough to warrant the permission to publish as there were other dangerous aspects which greatly prevailed. Those are usually illustrated by a legend that still reappears from time to time in articles about Tolkien and Czechoslovakia. According to it, in 1977, the leading communist daily *Rudé právo* [The Red Right] published a short review of *The Lord of the Rings* in which, in the typical language of the era, the reviewer denounces the work as an obvious imperialist allegory that would have us believe that ugliness and evil are coming from the East, presenting the "good" communists as orcs. In reality, no such article exists, and the origins of the legend go back to a similar review appearing in Poland in 1971 (Rehák n.p.). However, even if not true in reality, it is true in spirit: anybody who experienced the reasoning of censors recognizes immediately the verisimilitude of such incidents. This also remains one of the most frequent reasons given by various scholars and fans as to why *The Lord of the Rings* was so objectionable in the former Soviet Bloc. There are, however, many other potentially sensitive aspects of the book, the most comprehensive appearing at its end, where, as I argued before, the whole scouring of the Shire by Saruman's lackeys is strongly reminiscent of the communist collectivization of land and a "fair" distribution of gains resulting in nobody having anything and being much worse off than before (Kascakova 94).[8] It is, however, highly unlikely that a person at the helm of a publishing house would have such detailed knowledge of a work whose translation did not exist yet. Most probably, the strong aversion was really caused by the basic information that Mordor is situated in the East (works of art were banned for lesser reasons than this in those times), but there was also the fact that Tolkien was not only a living Englishman but also a devout Catholic, which did not help either.[9] Religion was perceived as the most dangerous sort of "blunder" the communists wanted to keep well away from their "robotný roľnícky ľud" who,

66   Janka Kascakova

despite all the efforts to the contrary, still insisted on keeping their faith and certainly needed no further encouragement. These might also be the reasons why an almost identical answer, or rather a poor excuse about the shortage of paper, awaited the Czech translator of *The Lord of the Rings,* Stanislava Pošustová-Menšíková, when she presented her finished manuscript to a Czech publishing house in 1980.

As already mentioned, in Slovakia, Krupa's three extracts from *The Lord of the Rings* in the three successive volumes of *Revue svetovej literatúry* in 1970 remain the only tantalizing insight into what might have been under different circumstances. Krupa thus had to move on and, as mentioned above, only got to publish *The Hobbit* in 1973.[10] The Czech translation of *The Hobbit* came out in 1979.[11] Its translator, František Vrba (1920–1985), was not allowed to publish due to ideological reasons and the translation was thus signed by Lubomír Dorůžka (1924–2013).[12] This was a common practice and a way how to help out friends who fell into the displeasure of the authorities and that not only in this regime. A very similar situation happened during the Nazi occupation of the Czech Republic during the Second World War when a famous Shakespeare translator, Erik A. Saudek (1904–1963), was not allowed to work due to his Jewish origin, so his works were published under the name of another renowned translator, Aloys Skoumal (Blümlová 32). Vrba's knowledge of languages was also very impressive, he translated from English, French, German, and Russian. Unlike Krupa, however, he seemed to have no deeper interest in Tolkien and no reverence for what Krupa knew lay behind the simple tale for children. As Krupa's daughter, Martina Bucková, remembers: "Tolkien was father's favourite, he was quite disappointed by the Czech translation. He felt they hadn't understood that it was mythology" (Rehák n.p.). Vrba's translation is indeed very different. He uses all the unique qualities that the Czech, and other Slavic languages, possess – for example, a wide variety of diminutives, colloquial, and childish words – to make the translation high-spirited, playful, almost comical. This is reinforced by the colourful and grotesque illustrations by one of the best Czech illustrators Jiří Šalamoun. As Blanka Stehlíková pointed out, Šalamoun was not one of those illustrators whose books resemble one another. He entered into the spirit of the text and attempted to adapt his illustration to it (592). The final result is thus rather far not only from Krupa's much more sober translation with black-and-white illustrations by Naďa Rappensbergerová, but also from Tolkien's original.

The Strange Case of the First Adaptation of *The Hobbit*

While this chapter is primarily concerned with literary reception as appearing in contemporary newspapers or magazines, for the sake of completeness, it is necessary to mention a rather curious case of, what seems to

Mythologia Non Grata: Tolkien and Socialist Czechoslovakia 67

be, the first film adaptation of *The Hobbit*. While both the director Gene Deitch (1924–2020) and the producer William L. Snyder (1918–1998) were Americans, their 1966 ultra-short 12-minute animated film was made in Prague animation studios with drawings of another renowned Czech illustrator, Adolf Born (1930–2016) (RembrandtFilms). The story surrounding this film is emblematic of the experimental time it was born in. Snyder owned rights to the film adaptation that were soon to expire unless he at least produced something. So, within a short period of one month, he did and, the story has it, stood in the street in front of a cinema in New York and paid people to come in and watch it. (Koníčková n.p.).

The film itself has very little in common with the original. Obviously, for such a short time, it makes sense that the number of characters had to be reduced. Thus, there are Thorin, Gandalf, the dragon called Slag and Bilbo-the dragon slayer. Gollum is there too, under the name Groans. What makes less sense, however, are additions of the characters of a watch and a princess. The film further deviates from Tolkien in the plot which basically abandons the original at the first opportunity and adds the element of prophecy and a love story. It would seem that apart from being the product of necessity, this is a practical joke or an exercise in absurdity and innovation, so typical for the 1960s. It is interesting to observe that, whether aware of the film or not, Vrba's translation is in a similar vein of playfulness.

Snyder, now in possession of the extended copyright, had more time and could contemplate a more serious and extensive adaptation. Interestingly, he remained in the Czech Republic and addressed Jiří Trnka (1912–1969), one of the founders of Czech animated films, who made some preliminary sketches of characters in 1967. Unfortunately, not long after that, Trnka died, and the remaining sketches offer just a glimpse into what could have possibly been the plan for the final work. Trnka's Gandalf, unlike the original and also Born's, is ominous and almost harlequin-like, with very pronounced bushy eyebrows, ballet posture, and no hat. Gollum is a frog-like creature with webbed fingers and, it seems this was important either to Snyder or to both illustrators, there is an unknown woman yet again – resembling a fairy from Czech folklore, with blond hair, a slim waist, rather bulky calves, balancing on her foot in an obvious dancing position (see "Hobit a Československo").

While these two are not more than fragments and probably bear witness more to the originality and creativity of Czech animators than to some serious reception of Tolkien's *Hobbit*, the presence of the female characters in both predates and anticipates very similar concerns of later critics who saw the lack of any female character as a handicap and, just like Peter Jackson many decades after them, felt the need to give a more important role to a woman and add a more pronounced element of romance.

68 Janka Kascakova

Tolkien and the Czech Underground and Dissident Circles

After the 1970s and the two translations of *The Hobbit* into Slovak and Czech, Tolkien almost disappears from the contemporary magazines or newspapers and re-emerges literally at the very moment of the Velvet Revolution in 1989 (see Dědinová in this volume 78–82). In both parts of the country, there are a few little reappearances of his name throughout the 1980s. In Slovakia, they are especially connected to the name of Daniel Hevier, the bard of Slovak children's literature, then just a rising star. On several occasions, he mentions *The Hobbit* as one of the books he admired. He also wrote a short article on Tolkien in the magazine for children *Ohník* [Little Fire] as an introduction to an extract from Krupa's translation of *The Hobbit*. There is no indication, however, that Hevier knew *The Lord of the Rings* then or had the opportunity to read it and his mentions keep Tolkien firmly where the regime wanted him to be, in the realm of children's literature. It is no accident then, that most of these little mentions appear in the joint Czechoslovak magazine about children's literature *Zlatý máj* [the Golden May]. There is one more short allusion to Tolkien in this magazine in 1987, this time by a Czech literary critic Michal Peprník, reviewing Richard Adams' *Watership Down*, published that year in the Czech translation. He expresses his admiration for Adams' work and compares it to that of Tolkien and *The Hobbit*. What he sees as comparable is the world of "small, underestimated beings" who seem to be "helpless and harmless", but it turns out that in a critical situation they can be heroes, sacrifice their lives for others, and be more compassionate than men (534). He also observes that rather than fairy tales, both works are myths for: "myth goes beyond the fairy tale. It clarifies the notions of good and evil, gives things and all creatures their place in the natural order" (534).

If one judged according to the number and quality of articles on Tolkien in these years, it would seem he was all but forgotten, but it was far from being the case. While much of the evidence emerges in the form of memories of intellectuals from those times and often exists only in oral tradition or tantalizing little pieces of information scattered here and there, some cases are recorded in a greater length too. Notably, it is Tolkien's significant role in the Czech underground and dissident circles of the 1970s and 1980s which came to be known only after the change of the regime. It is well-documented (see Putna; Neubauer and Putna) and forms one of the most interesting chapters of the Czech cultural history. Tolkien is especially strongly connected with the group of intellectuals who called themselves Kampademie (Kampademy – Academy of Kampa),[13] on the example of and as a continuation of Plato's Academy. They were some of the most influential members of the Czech dissent and after the change became leading

Mythologia Non Grata: Tolkien and Socialist Czechoslovakia 69

figures in Czech political, cultural, and academic life. Apart from their academic interests and intellectual debates, their activities included walking tours of the Czech countryside (Putna 871), strongly reminiscent of similar ventures of Tolkien's and Lewis' Inklings. They also chose nicknames from *The Lord of the Rings*: Daniel Kroupa (1949–), currently a philosopher and politician, was Frodo; Tomáš Halík (1948–), currently a Catholic priest and university professor, was Gandalf; Radim Palouš (1924–2015), a philosopher and the first post-socialist rector of the Charles University, was Elrond, as he offered his house in the countryside to serve as a refuge, some sort of Rivendell, etc. (Neubauer and Putna 45–46). Apart from the practical necessity of having code-names to be able to freely speak on the phone with the secret police always listening (Neubauer and Putna 46), the members of the Kampademy had other reasons to appreciate a discussion on Tolkien. While the important element of the Czech underground and dissent was their Christianity, one did not have to be a Catholic or a monarchist to yearn for the return of the King, or rather, for the return of some more natural order of things, a less distorted rule than: "the ocean of dull grey stupidity of Husák's late socialism" (Neubauer and Putna 92).[14] Another member of Kampademy, Zdeněk Neubauer (1942–2016), a biologist and philosopher, one of the most fascinating figures of this period, was also a great admirer of Tolkien and thanks to him the memories of those times and the importance of Tolkien saw the light of the day. His memories are significant also because they include another member of Kampademy, one of those personalities that surpassed the Czech and Czechoslovak context and became known and respected all over the world, the writer and politician Václav Havel (1936–2011).

Neubauer's belief in the importance of *The Lord of the Rings* was so strong that, as he noted, when Václav Havel returned from prison in 1983 and showed Neubauer:

> the pile of samizdats at Hrádeček [his house] which had come out in the mean time [sic], and asked me – as if I was the holder of authority – which of them were worth reading, I didn't want to give away the fact that I hadn't read any of those various Škvoreckýs and Vaculíks, no chance, so I told him not to bother with it and that instead he should read *The Lord of the Rings* (Neubauer and Putna 105).

Neubauer will later explain his fascination with Tolkien and mythology in a book companion to *The Lord of the Rings,* first published in 1990. Rather surprisingly for a primarily natural scientist, especially in the light of the current Central European great divide between humanities and natural sciences, Neubauer believed myths to be essential for the return of the rationalist man to his roots, "to the world of archetypes, proto-tales about

70   Janka Kascakova

the search for his place in the universe and about the journey of spiritual maturing and change" (Putna 884). Neubauer claimed that reading Tolkien "is a road to adulthood that does not cancel childhood" (66) and that his work steeped in mythology has a genuinely pedagogical effect; through it, we can actually "find a new relationship with the so-called facts from biology, chemistry or history" – we can see them as "a part of a tale – one of many tales – such ones in which we can appear, whose part we form and which we can become better aware of" (67). Paradoxically, not directly but through myths people can thus become more skilled in exploring and understanding the world around them, even in the case of natural sciences.

A historical role in this unofficial alternative culture connected to Tolkien belonged to Stanislava Pošustová-Menšíková (1948-) and her 1980 samizdat translation of *The Lord of the Rings*. This translation together with Vrba's 1979 translation of *The Hobbit* introduced Tolkien not only to those who could not read English or had no access to the original but also, surprisingly, to those who did. Neubauer himself having first read *The Fellowship of the Ring* in English was not really impressed. The moment of revelation came when he visited a friend whose children ran around chanting the poems from *The Hobbit* and was offered the samizdat translation of *The Lord of the Rings*. As he recalled:

> Suddenly the Word opened up to me. The Czech vernacular had the effect that what I read before was a mere narrative, now flowered with colour and imagination. However well I understand them, words in a learned language simply can't engage the imagination. (Neubauer and Putna 103).

While not all non-native readers would have the same opinion or experience – there are those for whom the original and its beautiful language does engage the imagination better than any translation – Neubauer was certainly not the only one who felt like that. It is then no wonder that *The Lord of the Rings*' translation was published practically immediately after the Velvet Revolution[15] and became, not only for the Czechs but for Slovaks equally, one of the cultural landmarks of the late 20th century.

Conclusion

This study showed the peculiar character of Tolkien's reception in socialist Czechoslovakia, one that is incidentally in line with the historical period he so admired and was inspired by in his works – the early Middle Ages. Just like then, what was actually written down was just a very small portion of what existed in reality; literature, legends, stories, and myths were transmitted orally, or more than that, they were lived and experienced in real time and most of them did not get recorded. However, that did not

Mythologia Non Grata: Tolkien and Socialist Czechoslovakia   71

make them less real than those that did. Although for different reasons, most of the Czechoslovak reception of Tolkien is equally irreparably lost with those who are no longer alive and whose stories did not get recorded. Yet what remains is still a fascinating story of admiration, inspiration, and encouragement. Tolkien spoke to some of the people of that difficult era from behind the cultural and political divide, literally over the Iron Curtain, which is yet another proof of the unique and universal character of his works.

Notes

1 See Pevčíková a Urbanová's chapter in this volume for frequent discussions and comparisons of Slovak and Czech translations of Tolkien (93–114).

2 *Revue svetovej literatúry* 1970, volumes 4, 5, 6. As a matter of fact, they are not entirely translations as Krupa decided to squeeze the whole of *The Fellowship of the Ring* into some 30 odd pages. For that reason, he alternates between translations and brief summaries of what happened in between. The first instalment is chapter 2, the discussion between Gandalf and Frodo about the Ring and Sam joining in through the window. The second begins in Hobbiton yet ends in Lórien; the third begins with the mirror of Galadriel and ends at Rauros with the funeral of Boromir.

3 This is reflected in the very design and, of course, the content of *Revue svetovej literatúry* from that moment on. The experimental and colourful covers had to give way to white uniformity, certain kinds of art disappeared, and the content was carefully supervised (Bujačková 18).

4 Tolkien, J.R.R. *Pán Prsteňov: Spoločenstvo prsteňa*. Bratislava: Slovart, 2001; *Pán prsteňov: Dve veže*. Bratislava: Slovart, 2001; *Pán prsteňov: Návrat kráľa*. Bratislava: Slovart, 2002.

5 Unless indicated otherwise, all translations of the texts from Czech or Slovak are mine.

6 It was published under a puzzling title *Hobbiti*, which translates as hobbits in the plural. His translation was reprinted twice (in 1994 and 2002, respectively) with the title then corrected to the singular. Tolkien, J.R.R. *Hobbiti*. Bratislava: Mladé letá, 1973.

7 The era of socialism was known for stale slogans and phrases that were repeated ad nauseam on every occasion and taught from an early age. One of them would be a reference to one of the "icons" of communism, V.I. Lenin, as "Lenin večne živý" [Immortal Lenin or Lenin forever alive], which could be understood ambiguously, both a reference to his legacy and to his rather spooky and by science never explained perfect mummy in Moscow. In this context, Krupa's title sounds like one of the thousands of small acts of defiance against the occupation abounding in that period.

8 A similar point was also made by Markova and Hooker (165).

9 While Western production, in general, was frowned upon, there were some notable exceptions; the socialist cadres allowed the translations of many great works of the 19th century English and French realism, probably because, according to them, they criticized all that was bad with capitalism and the Western society. Their authors were also safely dead and thus more easily manageable by propaganda.

10 See Jela Kehoe's discussion of this translation in this volume.

72   Janka Kascakova

11 *Hobit aneb cesta tam a zase zpátky*. Praha: Odeon, 1979.
12 Most of Vrba's 1970s and 1980s translations were published under different names.
13 Kampa is an island on the river Vltava in Prague, where one of the members of the group had an apartment.
14 Gustáv Husák (1913–1991) was the 8th president of Czechoslovakia from 1975 till 1989 when he was replaced by Václav Havel.
15 *The Fellowship of the Ring* in 1990, *The Two Towers* in 1990 and *The Return of the King* in 1992. After that, Pošustová-Menšíková became almost the exclusive Czech translator of Tolkien with most of his works translated and published in the 30 years since.

Works Cited

Aľakša, Ivan. "Z archívu: Krupa bol prvý" [From the archive: Krupa was the first]. *Fantázia* 4 (2001): 11–12.

Blümlová, Dagmar. "Život a názory blahorodého pana Aloyse Skoumala" [The Life and Opinions of the Honourable Aloys Skoumal]. *Aloys Skoumal (1904–1988) v průsečníku cest české kultury 20. století.* Ed. Dagmar Blümlová. České Budějovice: Jihočeská univerzita v Českých Budějovicích, Historický Ústav, ve spolupráci s NTP Pelhřimov, 2004.

Bujačková, Zuzana. "Revue svetovej literatúry v kontexte Pražskej jari" [*Review of World Literature* in the context of the Prague Spring]. *Prekladateľské listy* 9 (2020): 11–20.

"Hobit a Československo? Vždy patřilo k sobě! Proslavit jej mohl také Jiří Trnka" [Hobbit and Czechoslovakia? They always belonged together! It could have been made famous also by Jiří Trnka]. http://hobbit.news/zajimavost/hobit-a-ceskoslovensko-vzdy-patrilo-k-sobe-proslavit-jej-mohl-take-jiri-trnka/. Accessed 24 March 2022.

Kascakova, Janka. "'It snowed Food and Rained Drink' in *The Lord of the Rings*". *Middle-earth and beyond: Essays on the world of J.R.R. Tolkien.* Ed. Kathleen Dubs and Janka Kascakova. Newcastle-upon-Tyne: Cambridge Scholars Publishing, 2010. 91–104.

Koníčková, Olga. "Hobit – neočekávaná cesta aneb Kdy už s ním konečne skončíme?" [Hobbit – an unexpected journey or when are we finally going to end this?] https://kultura21.cz/film/5677-hobit-neocekavana-cesta. Accessed 15 November 2022.

Krupa, Viktor. "Mýtus večne živý. J.R.R. Tolkien a jeho trilógia Pán Prsteňov" [Myth forever alive. J.R.R. Tolkien and his trilogy *The Lord of the Rings*]. *Revue svetovej literatúry* 6.4 (1970): 104–107.

———. transl. "J.R.R. Tolkien: Bratstvo prsteňa" [The Fellowship of the Ring]. *Revue svetovej literatúry* 6.6 (1970): 128–145.

———. "J.R.R. Tolkien: Galadrielino zrkadlo, 1. zväzok, Bratstvo prsteňa, kniha 2, kapitola 7" [The Mirror of Galadriel]. *Revue svetovej literatúry* 6.5 (1970): 75–79.

Markova, Olga and Mark T. Hooker. "When Philology Becomes Ideology: The Russian Perspective of J.R.R. Tolkien". *Tolkien Studies* 1 (2004): 163–170.

Neubauer, Zdeněk. *Do světa na zkušenou čili o cestách tam a zase zpátky. Malá rukověť k trilogii J.R.R. Tolkiena.* [To the world and back: A small handbook to the trilogy of J.R.R. Tolkien]. Praha: Michal Jůza & Eva Jůzová, 1990.

Neubauer, Zdeněk and Martin C. Putna. "'When I write, It's an Expression of the Fact that I've Glimpsed Something ...' A Conversation about a Saint John's Day trip, Kampademy, letters from prison and letters to prison, about *Consolatio philosophiae* and about Hrádeček, and also about Catholicism, magic mushrooms, and Tolkien". *Consolatio Philosophiae Hodierna: k Šestnácti dopisům Václava Havla/ To Sixteen Letters of Václav Havel.* Transl. Václav Paris. Praha: Knihovna Václava Havla, 2010.

Peprník, Michal. "Daleká cesta za domovem" [A long way home]. *Zlatý máj, časopis o dětské literatuře* 31.9 (1987): 532–535.

Putna, Martin C. *Česká katolická literatura v kontextech 1945–1989* [The Czech Catholic literature in contexts 1945–1989]. Praha: Torst, 2017.

Rehák, Oliver. "Čo prekážalo komunistom na Pánovi Prsteňov" [What bothered the communists about *The Lord of the Rings*]. *Sme,* 19 December 2014. https://kultura.sme.sk/c/7554711/co-prekazalo-komunistom-na-panovi-prstenov.html. Accessed 24 March 2022.

RembrandtFilms. "First Animated Hobbit – directed by Gene Deitch, produced by Rembrandt Films". *YouTube,* uploaded by RembrandtFilms 13 August 2013, https://www.youtube.com/watch?v=UBnVL1Y2src.

Stehlíková, Blanka. "Groteskní svět Jiřího Šalamouna" [The Grotesque World of Jiří Šalamoun]. *Zlatý máj, časopis o dětské literatuře* 29.10 (1985): 592–595.

"Viktor Krupa: Životopis autora" [Author's biography]. Slovenské literárne centrum, https://www.litcentrum.sk/autor/viktor-krupa/zivotopis-autora. Accessed 27 November 2022.

4 "Through darkness you have come to your hope"

The Dynamics of J.R.R. Tolkien's Work Reception in the Czech Context

Tereza Dědinová

"It was indeed as if elven light was falling on the child's soul from somewhere through a crack in the fabric of the grey universe" (Kozák n.p.).[1] This is how the Czech religious studies scholar Jan A. Kozák described his first encounter with J.R.R. Tolkien's work as a child when his parents read to him from a samizdat translation of *The Lord of the Rings* during communist totalitarianism. At a time when those in power could not allow the official publication of books beloved in the West because the fight against Mordor could "remind readers of something" (sus 11), readers thus accessed Tolkien's books through friends and secretly read typescripts and repeatedly xeroxed manuscripts circulating in dissident circles. As a result, the books used to be "truly magical" (Kozák n.p.) in their very form, resembling medieval manuscripts, with many mistakes and typos, with passages challenging to read, forcing the reader to decipher the text and guess "whether the given letter is an 'o', 'e' or 'a'" (Kozák n.p.). Where the fascinating world of Middle-earth enchanted the child, the adult readers, trapped in the bleakness of the seemingly eternal communist regime, were keenly aware of the themes of freedom and responsibility, the crucial role of the small hands, the need for foolish determination, and the necessity to fight against evil.

In the early years of freedom in the early 1990s, during which *The Lord of the Rings* was first officially published in Czech, reviews and magazine articles, as well as the personal recollections of contemporaries, attest to the continuing sensitivity to the depth and complexity of Tolkien's world, along with the perceptible overlap of the fictional world and story into the historical and social experiences of readers. How is *The Lord of the Rings* and, more generally, Tolkien's work perceived more than thirty years later by readers born to the free Czechia, digital natives, who overwhelmingly encountered Jackson's adaptations first and read the books after seeing the films, if at all? And how has their reception been influenced by the significant shifts of recent decades in the cultural perception and portrayal of evil, otherness, gender, and environmental issues?[2]

DOI: 10.4324/9781003407171-7

"Through Darkness You Have Come to Your Hope" 75

This chapter aims to capture and analyse possible shifts in Tolkien's work reception over time. To do so, it begins by introducing when and under which circumstances the first Czech translations of Tolkien's novel appeared. After examining contemporary written responses to the first official publications, it will turn to the memories of several representative readers significantly inspired by Tolkien's work. While aware that every personal experience is highly individual and can make no claim to a complete and objective portrayal of the situation, these testimonies offer valuable insights into the unique impact of Tolkien's work at a specific time and fill in the contours drawn by reviews and critical commentary. To trace the dynamics of the reception of Tolkien's work, a significant portion of the chapter then examines contemporary readers and their perception primarily of *The Lord of the Rings* in particular and Tolkien's texts in general. In doing so, it starts from the assumption that the profoundly different political and socio-cultural situation of the second decade of the new millennia, together with specific characteristics of the young generation in general (see Wolf 2018), necessarily affects readers' responses to a certain extent. However, the second premise is that Tolkien's Middle-earth's inner consistency and depth resist the flow of time and – like other classical works of literature – keeps its autonomy and stays relevant for new generations. Arguably more influential than a general development of sensitivity to gendered, racial, or environmental representations in the arts has been exposure to the Peter Jackson-directed film adaptation of *The Lord of the Rings* and *The Hobbit*.[3] One might expect that readers who have read the books after seeing the adaptations would prefer colourful scenes and adventure along with a simplified plot, would have less patience with archaic language and longer expository passages, and their interpretation of the book would tend to be superficial.

To analyse the reception of contemporary young readers, the questionnaire survey results will mainly be used, in which the participants familiar with Tolkien's work first answered questions concerning their relationship to it and the topics they considered vital. They were then led to ponder the portrayal of good and evil, the representation of otherness, racism, and feminist and environmental themes. Due to the nature of memory, it is practically impossible to distinguish overall impressions from the books and their adaptations in the case of respondents familiar with both, however, follow-up questions after preferences provide additional information. Together, the following analyses of readers' responses and survey provide a platform for understanding the reception of Tolkien's works among Czech readers and its dynamics concerning the reflection of issues essential for twenty and twenty-first-century society.

There and Back Again: First Glimpses of the Middle-earth

Unlike other Tolkien works, *The Hobbit, or There and Back Again* was translated and officially published in Czech during communist totalitarianism in 1979. The publication was aided by its apparent focus on children as readers, the possibility to include it in the shelf of fairy tales and, as Kozák ironically glosses, how it could quite easily be interpreted in line with regime values: "a group of impoverished dwarves (i.e. workers, labourers) set out to retrieve a treasure stolen from them by an evil dragon ('capitalist') who merely sits on the treasure and shares his wealth with no one" (n.p.). But even so, the paranoid regime had its effect on the translation's path to readers: first, *The Hobbit* was published in, at the time, a minimalist number of 8,500 copies, and second, the author of the afterword, Lubomír Dorůžka, signed the translation. Not unusually for the time, the author of the translation was someone else, a "politically unreliable" and therefore an officially banned translator of classics from English, French, German, and Russian, František Vrba. Both in the afterword (Dorůžka) and contemporary review (ml) basic information could be found about Tolkien and the massive success of his works, especially *The Lord of the Rings*, in the world. As was necessary under the communist regime, the works of authors from the "enemy camp", if published at all, had to be interpreted in the afterword in accordance with the ideology promoted by the state. Therefore, Dorůžka links *The Hobbit* to folktales and interprets its central topic as a reflection on the dangers of greediness: "The desire for property is the root cause of all evil in Tolkien, perhaps even more so than in the folktales" (378). He attributes the popularity and value of the book in particular to the character of Bilbo, the "little peaceful man" (378) who is the only one who can resist the attraction of gold.[4] The review, signed with the abbreviation ml, only mentions *The Hobbit*, then briefly introduces *The Lord of the Rings* and *The Silmarillion*, and reflects or rather marvels at Tolkien's success even though "his books are far from what is described as appealing to readers" (14). Its author finds the answer in a period-contingent reading: "*The Silmarillion* is an escape from capitalist society, but not from its problems" (14). Topics and values crucial for Tolkien's life and work (e.g. aversion to industrialisation and environmental destruction) are thus interpreted solely as resistance to capitalism. In another – very short – review, science fiction writer and journalist Ondřej Neff identifies the book as a straightforward fairy tale that, however, crossed over to an adult audience, which has found a "childish delight in it" (4). Comparing it to *Alice in Wonderland*, Neff describes *The Hobbit* as a mystery-free novel, but one that moves and enthrals its readers. He also pointed out *The Lord of the Rings*, "a monumental work" discussed on all platforms focused on Anglo-Saxon sci-fi (4).

"Through Darkness You Have Come to Your Hope" 77

Neff's likening of *The Lord of the Rings* to science fiction points to the cluelessness of reviewers encountering a genre that is entirely new to them. *The Hobbit* became the first, and for a long time, the only fantasy book published in Czech until Michael Ende's *The Neverending Story* was translated in 1987 (Bronec 103). Readers who, thanks to their knowledge of English and foreign friends, had encountered fantasy literature referred to it with a feeling of slight helplessness as "feudal science fiction" – that is, science fiction set in the Middle Ages inhabited by dragons and wizards.

An evident success of *The Hobbit* translation did not convince the censors of the time to allow the publication of *The Lord of the Rings*, so it was not officially released until the early 1990s. However, its translation was already there as, in secret and through networks of friends, copies of Stanislava Pošustová-Menšíková's translation circulated and were eagerly devoured by readers of all ages. Pošustová-Menšíková came across the books by chance: the library of the Institute of English and American Studies at Charles University, where she still works, bought them in an antiquarian bookshop. After initial hesitation – "I heard it was a fairy-tale who-knows-what. I thought it must be some kind of rubbish" (Pošustová-Menšíková, Kales n.p.) – she opened the first book during the holidays of 1979 and as she claims, "I haven't put it down since" (Pošustová-Menšíková, Behún n.p.). That same year she began translating the books, initially so that her father could read them. With the help of the translator and editor Jiří Josek, a contract was signed in December 1980 to produce the translation in the publishing house Mladá fronta. Nevertheless, the publication was delayed for the next nine years under the pretext of paper shortage, "but in reality for ideological reasons. In the book, the West was the seat of good, the East the seat of evil" (Pošustová-Menšíková, Mocková n.p.). However much Tolkien resisted an allegorical reading of his work, the mere geographical location of Mordor was suspicious enough for the official apparatus. Truth be told, their worries were right, as with many speculative fiction works, readers yearning for hidden meanings and social critique found them even where there were none. It is safe to assume, then, that Mordor's location to the East was greeted with mischievous glee. It was neither the first nor only direct application of the readers' experience to the political situation. In the revolutionary days, little flyers "Gandalf na Hrad!" (Gandalf to the Castle, meaning Gandalf for president) occasionally appeared among the many leaflets circulating in the streets – a cry for the wise wizard to symbolically oversee the "return to the natural order of being in our country" (Savický "Gandalf na Hrad!" n.p.). Much more important, though, was a sensitive application of *The Lord of the Rings'* essential topics and values on the contemporary situation, an appreciation of the richness and complexity of the fictional world together with the fierce determination and perhaps foolish hope so prominent in the story.

78 Tereza Dědinová

Pošustová-Menšíková asserts that the books' distinct ethos with its clear divide between good and evil and the necessity for each being to make a free moral choice between the two, makes *The Lord of the Rings* valuable for readers of all generations, and elevates it above other fantasy stories. "For it has the power to arouse in the reader a passion for the good, to strengthen his moral sensibility" (Pošustová-Menšíková, Mocková n.p.). None of this could have been to the liking of a regime built on suppressing freedom and yielding to evil.

As evidenced by the first post-revolutionary reviews of the official edition of the trilogy (translated by Pošustová-Menšíková), the authors, while enthusiastic about the autonomous world of Middle-earth, did not hesitate to apply its principles to their past and present. In his review of *The Return of the King*, Nikolaj Savický interprets it not as an allegory of the two world wars but a reflection of their experience. His reading of the book is very relevant to post-revolutionary efforts to create a civil society, which the previous regime – like all totalitarian regimes – severely repressed. "For the ultimate goal of Tolkien's hobbits is not the establishment of some ideal order, but of what we have come to think of as a civil society. A society of the independent, the self-governing, the proud and the free. It is a stark warning against utopias" ("Návrat krále" 16).

Hana Primusová, in her "Reflections on Tolkien's *The Lord of the Rings*" (1991), quotes the author's rejection of allegorical reading and his appreciation of the freedom of the reader of history – whether genuine or pretended – to apply it according to his thinking and experience. She then applies the theme of freedom of decision and action, which resonated strongly in the revolutionary period, to the history of Middle-earth itself. "That is to say, a man's only real gain is what he has arrived at himself, by his own efforts, quite freely – if we will" (334). In doing so, she compares this knowledge with the recent past: "How unusual for us, who for years have been constantly told by someone what to think about and why" (334) and emphasises that Tolkien's freedom is very far from the Marxist "recognition of necessity" that required the renunciation of personal identity in favour of false ideals. It is equally far from freedom as egocentric self-assertion at the expense of morality and the freedom of others. "It is the freedom that is the prerequisite for a fully human life, the only possible path that allows for creating spiritual and material values" (335). The fact that the pernicious power represented by one the ring is not indestructible, that foolhardy efforts succeed despite the odds, and the belief "that the triumph of freedom is not just a dream", Primusová identifies as another major contribution of the work, emphasising how well "we know from years past" the temptations of power and that not everyone has the strength to resist its pull, the desire to take a bite out of it for themselves. She concludes her essay with another actualisation: "one cannot wonder

"Through Darkness You Have Come to Your Hope" 79

our 'former dark lord' found this particular text unsuitable reading for 'happy subjects'" (335).

There are recurring themes to be found in many reviews and reflections on Tolkien's work in the 1990s; the aforementioned topics of freedom (Primusová, Savický "Návrat krále"), moral choice (Savický "Pán prstenů", "Návrat krále"), and individual responsibility (Eisenbruk), the need for hope (Pošustová-Menšíková, Primusová), and perhaps the foolish attempt to stop evil (Eisenbruk). Sympathy for the hobbits is universal; the "little people", endowed with ordinary human frailties, giving their best under pressure (Peprník) "are the kind of people we would probably all like to be" (Savický "Návrat krále" 16).

The reception of Czech readers in the 1990s, nevertheless, was not limited to extolling the values of Tolkien's work and their possible application in the real world. The common element in many of the articles is, of course, a fascination with the beauty of the language and world of Middle-earth, which for many readers became their first encounter with the world of fantasy. However obvious the distance between Middle-earth and the world of the readers, the reviews often point to the perceived reality of the fictional world and do not understand the story as a non-committal fantasy. There is a frequent reminder of the interdependence between Tolkien the philologist, and the writer, a reflection on Tolkien's resistance to allegorical interpretation and his preference for approaching the work as "the real history". Americanist Michael Peprník, in his 1991 article "The Magical Realm of the Word", remarks on this, "Fortunately, his novel is not mere history; it is a coherent magical work – a true unreal" (10). Savický points out that *The Lord of the Rings* cannot be approached in "hurry, impatience, or fleeting reading" but it rewards the patient and attentive reader "royally" (6). He then analyses the opening chapters of *The Fellowship of the Ring* as a work of history, pointing out that "from the very beginning it creates *the illusion not of reality but of the cognitive processing of that reality*, and thus achieves very effective results. Here the fairy-tale story is given an unsuspected dimension: depth, and also an unsuspected perspective" (6, emphasis mine). Primusová compares the ultimate unknowability of the real world and Middle-earth: "We know the fact that none of us will ever fully know the real world: no one is surprised by it, and we don't ask anyone to be" (334). Literary historian and critic Pavel Janáček argues for the success of Tolkien's work against the postmodern distrust of great stories and concludes that "the appeal of Tolkien's myths, born of language, reveals just how strong our desire for there to be something prior to every story is. The desire to see the law behind every tree" (4). Savický quotes Tolkien's lecture "Beowulf: The Monsters and the Critics" (1936), where he famously compared modern critics to those who misunderstood a man building a tower from old stones of a former house. They did not grasp

80   *Tereza Dědinová*

or even consider that "from the top of that tower the man had been able to look out upon the sea" (Tolkien *"Beowulf"* 55). Savický then glosses:

> Readers of Tolkien's work can see that sea in the distance and hear the distant cry of seagulls. The fairy tale has got out of hand. It became the heroic epic of the 20th century. [...] It cannot be so bad for Euro-American civilization if a Tolkienesque narrative has such resonance. (1).

A number of Czech artists who mostly encountered *The Lord of the Rings* before the revolution in the form of samizdat amateur and professional translations, described the literal immersion in Tolkien's work. Čestmír Šuška[5] recalls that he fell into illustrating *The Lord of the Rings* "as if into a dream" (Zvelebil 4) and for about a year was creating Tolkien-inspired drawings, paintings, and sculptures. Strong inspiration from Tolkien's works can also be found in works of his generational colleagues Jaroslav Róna[6] and František Skála[7], and film director Václav Marhoul declared in the 1990s that making a feature adaptation of *The Lord of the Rings* was his greatest dream (Zvelebil 4). In his article, Jan Zvelebil also draws attention to other, not only visual, artists and recalls the semi-legal theatrical adaptation of *The Hobbit* by Ctibor Turba or the musicalisation of songs from *The Lord of the Rings* by Pavel Richter and Jim Čert (4).

The Birth of the Fellowship

After the Velvet Revolution in 1989, the literary market opened widely to English-language production, and Czech readers quickly encountered other works of the fantasy genre, albeit somewhat indiscriminately – alongside *The Lord of the Rings*, Howard's *Conan the Barbarian* appeared and gained popularity. As early as 1990, the Czech version of *Dungeons & Dragons* called *Dragon's Den* was created, and a group of friends in Prague founded *The Fellowship of J.R.R. Tolkien*, the first fandom club devoted to Tolkien's works that published a fanzine called *Imladris* (1998–2010), organised miscellaneous events, and re-enacted famous battles from *The Lord of the Rings*. In spring 1992, another community, called *The Fellowship of Friends of the Work of Mr J.R.R. Tolkien*, established itself in Brno. In addition to the two fanzines – *Palantír* and *Thorin* – they issued many one-off publications, met regularly on the celebrations of Bilbo's birthday and of the destruction of the one ring, in and summers then re-enacted the battle called Bitva Pána prstenů (The Lord of the Rings Battle), which was arguably one of the first live-action role-playing games where wooden swords were used in Czechia (Grunt "Email" n.p.). According to former board member of *The Fellowship* and editor of *Palantír* and *Thorin* Jiří Grunt, one of *The Fellowship's* outstanding actions was a stage game for

"Through Darkness You Have Come to Your Hope"   81

Prague children on the occasion of the production of *The Hobbit* by the theatre Minor. Loosely connected *Poetic fellowship* focused on the writing and performing of the Middle-earth inspired songs. The power of the fictional world and stories brought together a "group of very different people who wanted to share the experience and who had something to say to each other for some time" (Grunt "Email" n.p.). Grunt further emphasises the particularity of the 1990s given by the restoration of freedom and the relative scarcity and inaccessibility of information, both of which contributed to the specific reception of Tolkien's work. On the one hand, the already mentioned application of the sensitively perceived themes of freedom and personal responsibility, on the other hand, the need for initiative and more than little patience in acquiring books. Some of Tolkien's books could be bought in English in Prague, but at a rather high price, especially for students. Therefore, many of them brought the books back from their summer jobs in the UK. The long wait for translations into Czech and the uncertainty as to whether they would be published at all had an air of adventure. During this time, as Grunt recalls, very different people came together on a single topic, united by the powerful experience of "the first and the only truly autonomous fictional world" (n.p.).

It is neither within the intent nor scope of this chapter to capture the richness and diversity of artistic and social responses to the inspiration of Tolkien's work. As exciting and thought-provoking as that work would be, it is necessary to let someone else follow upon existing research.[8]

Before turning attention to selected themes that will be used to analyse today's readers' responses to Tolkien's work, it is necessary to briefly comment on the rather characteristic understanding of fantasy literature (including *The Lord of the Rings*) as a fairy tale for adults in the Czech context. Outside of fandom and interested readers, readership both in and outside the academia tend to evaluate the whole of fantasy literature as an unpretentious genre intended primarily for children and young-adult audiences. Particularly the readers unfamiliar with the genre and its best works assume little or zero significance or value from the fantasy worlds and stories, deeming them as mere escapism. As Tolkien reflected in his 1945 essay "On Fairy Stories", literature that did not copy the real world was accused of cowardly desertion of so-called real life. On the contrary, Tolkien likened literary escape to a prisoner's dream of a world beyond the walls of his cell and emphasised that "The world outside has not become less real because the prisoner cannot see it" ("The Monsters" 148). Sadly, his distinction between "the Escape of the Prisoner with the Flight of the Deserter" is still largely unknown. The foundations of the condescending approach to fantasy can perhaps be seen in some of the early reviews of both *The Hobbit* and *The Lord of the Rings* before and shortly after the Velvet Revolution. While Savický, in his above-quoted reviews, emphasises

82 *Tereza Dědinová*

the depth and perspective of the "fairy-tale story" and comments on the transformation of the fairy tale to the heroic epic, some other reviewers, because of the specific world and characters of Middle-earth, have read and labelled *The Lord of the Rings* as a mere fairy tale. A review signed with the initials "sus" begins as follows: "The magical world of fictional Middle-earth and the story of the fairy-tale hobbit Frodo..." (11). Likewise, Tylšová describes *The Lord of the Rings* as a "Fairy tale for adults". Although she eventually notes that "fairy-tale characters are not actually fairy-tale at all" (43), the overall tone of her short article confirms the fairy-tale reading (for instance "good wizard Gandalf", "the strange power of the rings").

The Story as Knowledge of the World: About the Journey of Experience

The following paragraphs will turn to the selected themes of transformation by reading, approaching Middle-earth in its own terms and understanding evil in Arda, crucial for readers' reception of Tolkien's work as presented in the reflections of selected Czech personalities. Subsequent passages will compare how today's young readers think about these themes.

At the beginning of the 1990s, postmodern philosopher, biologist, and a long-time promoter of Tolkien Zdeněk Neubauer published a longer study called *Out into the world to experience: On journeys there and back again* (1992), the most complex Czech response to Arda to date. As he asserts in the introduction, its contemplation is intended for "the lucky ones. Those who have gone through Tolkien's trilogy (by which he means *The Hobbit, The Lord of the Rings* and *The Silmarillion*) found themselves in its world, and returned transformed" (8). This transformation by reading lies at the core of Neubauer's interpretation. Starting with an understanding of philology as recognition of meaning and stories as vehicles for discovering the world, Neubauer leads his readers into appreciating Tolkien's work as initiation not into the fictional world of Arda but their own world. The afore-mentioned transformation occurs only after a critical turning point: "the moment when [the reader] stops projecting his experience onto the reality of Arda and sees his reality, common to us all, in the light of Arda's experience" (36). Meditating on the mythic and narrative foundation of the reality and in accord with Tolkien himself, Neubauer sees the crucial value of Tolkien's work as a means of opening one's eyes and recognising new connections of the old things: "He will see them as part of a story – one of many stories – ones in which we can find ourselves, of which we are a part, and to which we can awaken" (67). Of course, initiation by its very nature is not easy nor free; the hero of the story and the attentive reader of Tolkien returns to his world different. The result, then, is an intimate

"Through Darkness You Have Come to Your Hope" 83

relationship with reality – when we learn to feel at home in reality, we get a chance to "know and create our own story" (72).

Literary scholar and fantasy writer Luisa Nováková encountered *The Lord of the Rings* in the early 1990s, and her account of the reading experience is at times reminiscent of Neubauer's words about the transformation by reading:

> The texts affected me deeply. In part, in a way that I perceive as uncommunicable. I found stories that made me shiver and resonate, a world in which I felt strangely safe and, in a way, naturally at home, and in Tolkien, the storyteller a guide who is in many ways extremely close to me humanly. One does not have many such fundamental literary experiences in one's life. (n.p.).

Nováková sees *The Lord of the Rings* as "a symbolic statement about the world, about human life, about what it is to be a real human being at all in the best sense of the word, about the necessity of standing up to evil even when it hurts (and maybe hurts a lot)" (n.p.) and further mentions topics of hope and faith in good endings, the temptations of power and pride, humility and the power of small and nameless, willingness to sacrifice oneself for others, and respect for nature and otherness. In her contemplation, she emphasises the need to approach the work in its own terms, not succumb to the temptation of allegory or interpretation through "realist glasses". Equally damaging, according to Nováková, is focusing only on the storyline and removing details and partial motifs from the context of the work. Readers who do not give Tolkien "ear, attention and time" (n.p.) will be easily disappointed. A superficial reading produces incomprehension: "we will end up in the same way as if we were to blame a painting for not giving us an account of the world in the same straightforward way as, say, reportage photographs" (n.p.). And like Neubauer, she relates the experience of reading Tolkien's work to the experience of the real world when concluding that if we accept the symbolism of *The Lord of the Rings*, "we encounter a story that says so much about the world, the real world in which we live today, right now, that it is hard to say more – just as a good picture captures reality more completely than a documentary photo from a cell phone" (n.p.).

For Jiří Grunt, the essential theme is the autonomy of Arda, as evidenced in his critical texts and in the emails in which he reflects on his experience as a reader.

> Stories have – like art in general – their autonomy. Their value is not reducible to entertainment, truth, utility, beauty, simply any other value, or even any complex of other values. Good stories prove themselves

84 *Tereza Dědinová*

dramatically, and there is nothing else beyond that. And because they have autonomy, they don't necessarily start from assumptions that are "right" in terms of some other area, even if it's an area as essential and jealous as ethics. ("Erika Johansenová" 21).

This understanding of Tolkien's world is crucial when considering the representation of evil, which, particularly in *The Lord of the Rings*, could be faulted for its considerable black-and-whiteness and, in terms of the real world, its rather problematic racial conditioning. But as Grunt points out in one of his reviews, there is a difference between interpreting Tolkien's world from the perspective of the readers' reality and in terms of the rules of Middle-earth.

Taken literally, Tolkien's world is based on a flawed theology that necessarily leads to a false ethic. Yet it is a story not only dramatically compelling but also morally unusually deep. Tolkien has managed to change some of the constitutional elements of our world, not only so that his world remains consistent, but even so that it continues to be able to reach out and affect us in our world to an unprecedented degree. [...] Tolkien's method is acceptable because it creates a new category of evil that we do not have in our world. ("Erika Johansenová" 21).

Reading Skim and Deep: *The Lord of the Rings* in the Digital World

The younger generation of readers, digital natives, are encountering Tolkien's work under very different conditions than their parents ten or even twenty years after the Velvet Revolution, in an age in which the problem is not a lack of information but a flood of it. For them, fantasy is no longer a new and curiosity-inducing genre, but one of the most popular branches of literary production, which in the Czech Republic contains a vast number of conventional texts and is often identified as purely entertaining, unpretentious, and unworthy of serious attention. This reputation is reinforced by Hollywood blockbusters, including Jackson's adaptations that flatten and simplify the story of *The Lord of the Rings*. Moreover, according to current research, the current generation of digital natives is defined by fundamental changes affecting deep reading abilities. As Marianne Wolf opens her seminal monograph *Reader, Come Home: The Reading Brain in a Digital World* (2018):

Together we stand at the threshold of galactic changes over the next few generations. These letters are my invitation to consider an improbable set of facts about reading and the reading brain, whose implications will

"Through Darkness You Have Come to Your Hope" 85

lead to significant cognitive changes in you, the next generation, and possibly our species. (Letter One).

The questionnaire, the results of which are interpreted in this subsection with regard to the competencies of deep and skim reading, focused mainly on the survey of the general reader's reception of *The Lord of the Rings* and possibly other works by Tolkien, the relationship of readers to the books and the film adaptations, and on the work's valued and criticised aspects. These broad questions were accompanied by targeted inquiries about issues of the representation of female characters, good and evil, race, and nature.

The survey, distributed online primarily to college and high school students, had 93 respondents; 58.1% were college students, 20.4% were high school students, 4.3% were elementary school students, and the remaining 15.1% identified themselves as other. 72% claimed to be under the age of twenty-five, with the majority (55.9%) being between eighteen and twenty-five. 67.4% of them first encountered Tolkien's work in the first decade of the twenty-first century, and 19.6% only in the last twelve years. There was no one among them who was not familiar with any of Jackson's film adaptations, while 17.2% had never read the books. As could be expected, given the age of most respondents, nearly half had first seen Jackson's films before reading the books, and 34.4% had seen the movies after reading one or more of the books.

When asked whether they return to Tolkien's works or his film adaptations, 91% answered affirmatively. The most common justifications for these returns include an appreciation of the complexity of the fictional world and the appeal of the story, with many emphasising that they notice something new each time they read the book (and, to a lesser extent, watch the adaptations). Repeatedly, respondents recall the emotional connection and nostalgia they feel for Tolkien's work and its adaptations – both the books and films influenced them as children, they grew up with them, the stories contain a community dimension for the respondents (watching the movie with friends and family, friendship ties in the fan community). For many, a fundamental reason for returning to Tolkien's works is an escape from reality and the hope and comfort they derive from them.

When asked whether they prefer book originals or film adaptations, rather surprisingly, nearly three-fifths (58.7%) of respondents who knew both (82.7% of the total) chose the books. The rationale for the responses to this question both captures the primary differences between the original and the adaptation and speaks to what individual respondents expect from the work. Respondents who prefer books typically emphasise the complexity and meaningfulness of the fictional world and story, disappearing from adaptations. They also appreciate details and characters missing

86   Tereza Dědinová

from the films (e.g. Glorfindel and Tom Bombadil), directly mentioning the opportunity to enjoy an idea-rich and linguistically beautiful text and engage their own imaginations. One response sums up what many others notes: "The opportunity to go more in-depth, to create a world of my own, to spend more time there, a deeper and more complex experience". For the film adaptations, then, there is criticism of their black-and-white simplification, the vanishing of many allusions to *The Silmarillion*, and widespread dissatisfaction with the adaptation of *The Hobbit*, which even many of the respondents favourable to *The Lord of the Rings* adaptation describe as inferior to disastrous.

On the other hand, respondents who prefer films mention fewer demands on watching films than reading texts, which some describe as too long, descriptive and their language as difficult (one respondent uses films as a backdrop when cleaning the house). For them, films are better for relaxation, the plot is faster, and the whole is more action-packed and suspenseful. Some also argue that there is not enough time to read; films are not so time-consuming. In one case, the respondent considers films to be more "adult", taking away the "fairy-tale feeling" that the respondent felt from the original books (including *The Lord of the Rings*). As with the question asking for motivations for returning to *The Lord of the Rings* and *The Hobbit*, respondents mention nostalgia, the closeness evoked by repeated viewing of the films, and the soundtrack's influence. It should be noted here that a significant number of respondents who indicated a preference for films over books in the closed question added in a follow-up comment that they found it difficult to choose; they liked both.

In the following questions, attempts to separate the experience of the films and the books were not made if only because for many recipients, adaptations are part of – in some cases, the dominant – reception of Tolkien's work. However, correlations of some responses with preferences for the original or adaptations were analysed. Whether they prefer the books or the films, many readers, in response to what they like best about Tolkien's work, emphasise an elaborate world with its own cosmology, mythology, history, fleshed-out characters, and a strong sense of hope. Respondents favouring books also highlight the melancholy and nostalgia of a passing age, the uniqueness of the story and the beauty of the language, intelligent humour, atmosphere, the depiction of beautiful nature, the use of contrasts, and the diversity of characters and world. One response mentions that Tolkien's books "open a gateway to new possibilities", and another appreciates "a specific type of beauty and a kind of grandeur that (Tolkien) manages to create an almost perfect, believable world". Viewers enjoy the epic scale and visuals – "I'm amazed by the sight of Rivendell every time" – and the "strong emotions" that many of the adaptation's shots evoke, or the drama of the plot: "even after hours, there is no weak spot and no time to get bored".

"Through Darkness You Have Come to Your Hope" 87

When asked what they did not appreciate about Tolkien's work, the two groups' answers again did not differ significantly. While some respondents did not find anything to dislike, the most frequent complaints concerned long descriptive passages, depictions of nature and emotions in particular, and the extensiveness of *The Lord of the Rings*. Some respondents, even those who prefer books to films, cited literally "unnecessary descriptions of scenery" and "lengthy descriptions of surroundings". Occasional objections included impatience with the songs and poems in the text, the complexity and "lesser momentum" of the plot, the intricacy of the language, and too many characters. Several respondents missed the lack of a greater representation of strong female characters in the work (see more below). A respondent who is only familiar with Jackson's adaptations complains about the excessive fighting and violence. One response mentions Tolkien's aversion to technological progress, another a dislike of the character of Tom Bombadil and a sense of the black-and-white nature of the story. The critical voices collected in the questionnaire coincide with the comments on the Databáze knih/Book Database (the Czech equivalent of Goodreads) of those readers who rated some or all of Tolkien's works with two stars or less out of five. On this database, Tolkien's works have a very high overall rating (the three *Lord of the Rings* books received overall ratings of 93, 94, and 95%. *The Fellowship of the Ring* was rated by 7,547 readers, and the following two books by about 1,000 fewer). An analysis of the critical comments (dated between 2012 and the present, with a preponderance of entries from the past few years) shows that readers most often struggle with the language and style of the work, with complaints about "wordy descriptions", "lengthiness", "boring descriptions of landscapes", and "little plot flow" recurring in the questionnaire as well. Overall, they correspond to the general observation that the current generation does not abound with patience for longer and more complicated texts; moreover, when they are written in a specific and archaic style. Readers often compare books to films, considered significantly better than the original in the case of low book ratings, and mention disappointed expectations. The books did not give them what they expected based on the films.

In response to the question of which themes they consider most important in Tolkien's work, respondents emphasise similar themes to those found in written responses from the 1990s. Thus, they most often mention the value of friendship, loyalty, self-sacrifice, hope and courage, and the determination to resist evil even at the cost of personal danger and suffering. More respondents also write about the love of nature and home and the power of the little ones: "Even a little hobbit can save the world". After all, hobbits, especially Samwise Gamgee, often appear among readers' favourite characters.

88   *Tereza Dědinová*

The following paragraphs will briefly present the results of the questions concerning the portrayal of female characters, good and evil, nature, and racism in *The Lord of the Rings*. 87.1% of readers believe that there are strong female characters in *The Lord of the Rings*, most often naming Éowyn for her warrior spirit, courage, and determination to control her life, and Galadriel, the Lady of the Forest, who protects her people and holds one of the three powerful rings. Arwen is frequently named in third place, mainly because she defies expectations and chooses a mortal life for love. 80.6% of readers then do not perceive the representation of female characters as problematic. However, the remaining nearly one-fifth of readers point to the underrepresentation of strong female characters, and many sense female characters as more passive, complementary to male characters rather than independent personalities. Some respondents perceive the female characters as stiff, which they attribute to the lesser space they have in *The Lord of the Rings* story. One response points to the "constant emphasis on beauty" of the female protagonists, while another calls to attention that while Arwen, for example, changes and gives up her immortality for her love of Aragorn, Aragorn does not undergo a similar transformation. However, this is indirectly contradicted by some of the answers to the following question of whether female characters are essential in *The Lord of the Rings*. More respondents here highlight the influence of Arwen and her love on Aragorn. As one respondent writes: "Aragorn fights for Arwen so that they can live their lives in peace. Because of Arwen, he becomes who he is meant to be". Overall, 40.9% of respondents consider the role of female characters to be essential, another 33.3% tend to agree with this statement, and 19.4% tend to disagree. 6.5% chose the answer "I don't know"; no one said that female characters do not play any essential role in *The Lord of the Rings*.

In a shorter series of questions targeting perceptions of the distribution of good and evil in *The Lord of the Rings*, most respondents (80.6%) did not believe that all characters in *The Lord of the Rings* were either good or bad. However, when asked if they would "describe *The Lord of the Rings* as a story with a clear to black and white distribution of good and evil", respondents were less clear in their answers. 42% responded in agreement, 54.8% in disagreement, and the remainder chose to answer that they do not know. Almost three-quarters of respondents realise that the defeat of Sauron in *The Lord of the Rings* does not result in a definitive victory of good over evil and that Middle-earth may be threatened by evil again.

85% of respondents consider nature very important in *The Lord of the Rings*, and 74.2% believe that *The Lord of the Rings* highlights the need to protect nature. Positive characters have a strong relationship with nature, according to 82.8% of respondents, and 56% find inspiration in *The Lord of the Rings* for thinking about how humans treat nature.

"Through Darkness You Have Come to Your Hope" 89

87.1% of respondents do not find the representation of races in *The Lord of the Rings* problematic. The remaining 12.9% referred in their responses to the perceived black-and-white nature of the portrayal of Orcs in particular. 54.9% of respondents had never sympathised with an Orc while reading *The Lord of the Rings*, 15.1% did not know, and the remaining 30%, with varying degrees of certainty, responded that they did feel some sympathy for Orcs – in some cases due to the knowledge of the orcs' origin, which evokes compassion.

Collectively, responses covering the themes of representations of women, good and evil, nature, and race indicate overall satisfaction with their portrayal within the fictional world. Some respondents add that while they are sensitive to issues of race or gender in the actual world, Tolkien's fictional world has different rules, and they do not feel the need to compare too much. Answering to what extent this result ensues purely from the acceptance of the rules of the fictional world and to what extent it corresponds to the respondents' views on this issue, in general, would require further research.

Conclusion: Canary and Frodo Baggins in the Mines

When introducing the theme of her book *Reader, Come Home: The Reading Brain in a Digital World*, Marianne Wolf refers to Kurt Vonnegut's famous comparison of the artist's role in society to that of the canary in the mines: to warn of danger. But to do that, readers need the competency of deep reading – attentive, contemplative, engaging critical thinking, empathy, fantasy, and self-reflection (Letter One). Wolf equates the Aristotelian three lives of a good society to those of the good reader; he or she should manage reading on three levels: of extracting information, entertainment, and contemplation. While people learn the first level and are inundated with the second one, the third deep level of life (and reading) "is daily threatened in our culture" (Letter One). Analysis of the changes in Tolkien's reception from the early 1990s to the present necessarily touches on these three reading levels. The samizdat translation of *The Lord of the Rings* had been circulating in worn-out copies among readers eager to escape the bleak reality communism and catch at least a glimpse of the fuller world on the other side of the iron curtain. And the beauty and complexity of Tolkien's writing were felt to be a part of this forbidden world where people were free to think, speak, and act, accepting responsibility for their own choices. The first official edition, which spread among a multitude of readers, came at a unique time in the early 1990s, in the wake of the Velvet Revolution ending the dictatorship, when the experience of freedom was something new and exhilarating, with people learning to find their position in the new world. Young enthusiasts gathered to share

90   *Tereza Dědinová*

the still somewhat scant information, talked long and deeply about their reading, and fell in love with Middle-earth, just as other people around the world had decades earlier. The themes of personal responsibility, freedom, hope, defiance, and the necessity to face evil resonated deeply. Perhaps this situation supported the deep reading that allowed what Neubauer calls "the transformation by reading". Not for all readers, of course: many did read Tolkien as a mere adventure.

The question is whether the influence of Jackson's adaptations and the digital world – affecting the very structure of the brain – on the one hand, and the deepening sensitivity to the portrayals of races and women characters, on the other, notably changed the reader's perception of Tolkien's work. As the results of the survey show, a significant number of young readers perceive *The Lord of the Rings* primarily as entertainment; many of them prefer the adaptations over the books, appreciating the suspense of the story and complaining about the demanding text and lengthy descriptions. Keeping Wolf's characterisation of the three lives of the reader in mind, the question is whether the transformation by reading happens to impatient readers. The most likely answer is no, they will not leave this world to return altered by the experience of Arda, and Tolkien's work will remain largely hidden from them, since they only scratch the very surface level of it.

However, the survey confirmed the initial assumption, namely that the complexity of Tolkien's work is such that his texts retain their autonomy over time and remain relevant to today's young readers. Many find inspiration, beauty, and depth in them, appreciate the magic of storytelling and willingly undertake the long and tiring journey with the hobbit travellers, admiring their courage, friendship, and hope. I believe that lot of these readers, after putting down their books, view their world in the light of Arda's experience (Neubauer 36).

And finally, a crucial function of Tolkien's work emphasised by many respondents, regardless of the level at which they read his texts, should not be overlooked: for them, the Middle-earth experience is an escape from everyday reality and a returning to something familiar and beloved. It is a place where they feel at home. I write this conclusion in the seventh week of the war in Ukraine, and many of the current events evoke reminiscences of the pre-1989 era. In the atmosphere of uncertainty and threat in which the dark lord once again resides in the East, the need for hope, belonging, and defiance against evil that *The Lord of the Rings* tells of is essential to everyone's life.

Notes

1 All excerpts from the Czech Press and personal emails were translated by Tereza Dědinová.
2 Critical analyses of these themes can be found in many studies; for example, see Fimi and Young ("Diversity and Difference", "Race and Popular Fantasy Literature") or the comprehensive compendia edited by Drout and Lee.

3 For a detailed survey of the reception of both adaptations, see Barker and Mathijs and *The World Hobbit Project*. An excellent analysis of the flattening and simplification of *The Hobbit* in the film adaptation is provided by Marek Oziewicz.

4 Even though the afterword was significantly conforming to the communist regime, it was retained in the post-revolutionary publication of the book in 1991.

5 See www.suska.cz/en

6 See www.jaroslav-rona.cz

7 See www.frantisekskala.com/en/index.html

8 In the case of exploring fandom, see a study by Antonín K. K. Kudláč, which analyses both of the above-mentioned societies.

Works Cited

Barker, Martin and Ernest Mathijs. *Watching The Lord of the Rings: Tolkien's World Audiences*. New York: Peter Lang, 2007.

———. *The World Hobbit Project*. www.globalhobbitca.wordpress.com/home-a/. Accessed 4 March 2022.

Bronec, Michael. "Poznámka k vydání a překladu". *Rejstřík k hobitovi*. Ed. Daniela Binderová. Praha: Straky na vrbě, 2002. 103–106.

Eisenbruk, Vladimír. "Frodo stále žije". *Tvar* 3.22 (1992): 11.

Fimi, Dimitra. *Tolkien, Race and Cultural History: From Fairies to Hobbits*. Basingstoke: Palgrave Macmillan, 2008.

Grunt, Jiří. "Proměny recepce Tolkienova díla ve střední Evropě_prosba". Received by Tereza Dědinová, 4 March 2022.

———. "Erika Johansenová: Osud Tearlingu (dokončení)". *Interkom* 8–9 (2019): 18–23. www.interkom.vecnost.cz/pdf/ik201908-09cl.pdf. Accessed 5 March 2022.

Janáček, Pavel. "Čarovný kotlík pána příběhů". *Lidové noviny*. 27 January1994, III.

Kozák, Jan A. "Tolkienův mýtus". *itvar*, 2020 www.itvar.cz/tolkienuv-mytus. Accessed 25 February 2022.

Kudláč, Antonín K. K. *Anatomie pocitu úžasu*. Brno: Host, 2016.

Lee, Stuart D., ed. *A Companion to J.R.R. Tolkien. Blackwell Companions to Literature and Culture*. Hoboken: Wiley-Blackwell, 2014.

Menšíková, Stanislava. "Tolkien". *Labyrint* 3.4 (1993): 34.

Michael D.C. Drout, ed. *J.R.R. Tolkien Encyclopedia: Scholarship and Critical Assessment*. New York: Routledge, 2007.

ml. "Fascinace mýtem". *Tvorba* 22 (1979): 14.

Mocková, Zuzana. "Pána prstenů šířila Charta 77, Východ byl totiž sídlem zla". *Aktuálně.cz*, September 9, 2014. www.magazin.aktualne.cz/prekladatelka-posustova-pana-prstenu-sirila-charta-77/r~ce788efe37fe11e494d7002590604 f2e/. Accessed 25 February 2022.

Neff, Ondřej. "Skřítek pana profesora". *Mladá fronta*. 7 September 1979, 4.

Nováková, Luisa. "Re: Par dotazu k inspiraci dilem J.R.R. Tolkiena". Received byTereza Dědinová, 4 March 2022.

Nováková, Luisa. "Fantasy jako cesta ad fontes". *Ladění* 10.2 (2005): 2–4.

———. "Fantasy jako prostor duchovního hledání a proměny". *Bohemica litteraria* 16.1 (2013): 103–111.

Oziewicz, Marek. "Peter Jackson's The Hobbit: A Beautiful Disaster". *Journal of the Fantastic in the Arts* 27.2 (2016): 248–269.

92 Tereza Dědinová

Peprník, Michael. "Magická říše slova". *Literární noviny* 44 (1991): 10.

Pošustová-Menšíková, Stanislava and Josef Kales. "Rozhovor s paní Pošustovou, překladatelkou Tolkienových děl do češtiny". *Tolkien.cz*, February 6, 2002. www.fantasy-scifi.net/jrr_tolkien/vite_ze/vite_ze.php?cl=285. Accessed 25 February 2022.

Pošustová-Menšíková, Stanislava and Pavel Janáček. "Tolkien nám dává naději. Rozhovor s překladatelkou jeho děl". *Lidové noviny*. 11 May 1994, 9.

Pošustová-Menšíková, Stanislava and Petr Behún. "Interview s legendární českou překladatelkou – 1. Díl". *Proofreading.cz*, December 31, 2014. www.proofreading.cz/interview-s-legendarni-ceskou-prekladatelkou/. Accessed 25 February 2022.

Primusová, Hana. "Poznaná nutnost opravdu není svoboda: Zamyšlení nad Tolkienovým Pánem prstenů". *Zlatý máj* 35.6 (1991): 334.

Savický, Nikolaj, jr. "Gandalf na Hrad! aneb O kořenech tolkienománie". *Mladá Fronta Dnes, Magazín Dnes*. 4 December 1993, 5.

———. "Textologie jako šlágr. O nedokončených příbězích J.R.R. Tolkiena". *Respekt*. 14 and 20 November 1994, 15.

———. "Pán prstenů". *Svobodný zítřek* 1.37 (1990): 6.

———. "Návrat krále". *Nové knihy* 18–19 (1992): 16.

sus: "Tvůrce pohádkového světa". *Lidové noviny*. 4 September 1998, 11.

Tolkien, J.R.R. *The Monsters and the Critics and Other Essays*. London: HarperCollins, 1997.

———. *Beowulf: The Monsters and the Critics*. Sir Israel Gollancz Lecture 1936.

Tylšová, Lída. "Tolkienovi hobiti". *Mladý svět*. 10 July 1992, 43.

Wolf, Marianne. *Reader, Come Home: The Reading Brain in a Digital World*. London: HarperCollins, 2018.

Young, Helen. "Diversity and Difference: Cosmopolitanism and *The Lord of the Rings*". *Journal of the Fantastic in the Arts* 21.3 (2010): 351–365.

———. *Race and Popular Fantasy Literature: Habits of Whiteness*. New York: Routledge, 2016.

Zvelebil, Jan. "Causa J.R.R.Tolkien". *Reflex*. 23 August 1993, 50–52.

5 J.R.R. Tolkien in the Slovak Press

Situation After 1990

Jozefa Pevčíková, Eva Urbanová
translated by Jela Kehoe

Introduction

The goal of our research was to analyse J.R.R. Tolkien's reception in Slovak periodicals after 1990 and the situation relating to Slovak translations of his works. We focused mainly on scholarly literary magazines and fandom magazines, the so-called fanzines. An additional dimension was provided by the daily press and internet magazine portals operating at a random periodicity and periodicals focusing on translation studies. The starting point was the issue of delayed translations of Tolkien's works into Slovak and how this delay impacted the number and type of the examined reactions. Only then could we analyse the reception and responses obtained from the scholarly press and compare them to those found in fandom magazines and the daily press of the given period.

(Un)Wanted Tolkien: On the History of Slovak Editions of Tolkien's Works

The analysis of Slovak translations of Tolkien's works focused on the chronology and selection of translated texts, as well as criticism of these translations, yielding results from which the following hypotheses can be drawn:

1 On the one hand, Tolkien's texts translated into Slovak represent a relatively rigid cross-section of his fiction – the selection includes the most famous texts associated with Middle-earth: *The Hobbit, The Lord of the Rings, The Silmarillion, Unfinished Tales, The Children of Húrin,* and one text from his work for children (*Roverandom*). On the other, publishers seemed uninterested as far as Tolkien's other works of fiction, his linguistic texts and essays, or his correspondence and other separate stories from the world of Middle-earth are concerned.

DOI: 10.4324/9781003407171-8

94   *Jozefa Pevčíková, Eva Urbanová*

2 Chronologically, the Slovak editions can be divided into four phases:

   a the early phase (1973–1994)[1]
   b the first wave coinciding with the creation of *The Lord of the Rings* film trilogy (2001–2003)
   c the second wave caused by further editions of already published works and the latest translations of new texts (2006–2008)
   d and finally, the third wave, brought about by the appearance of *The Hobb*it film trilogy (2012–2013).

3 Critiques of Slovak translations in the examined period were more often generated by the fan base of Tolkien's work, or by mass media, rather than by professionals and scholars.

While the first point is supported by the comparison of searches of Slovak and original English editions, the second point goes beyond the boundaries of literature as a medium and points to the changing social order (socio-historical context) as well as to the firmer anchoring of Tolkien's myth in transmedia mainstream popular culture.

The first Slovak translation of Tolkien's work was published in 1973, coincidentally in the year of Tolkien's death. It was *The Hobbit*, which was translated by Viktor Krupa and published under the title *Hobbiti* [The Hobbits]. As Krupa mentioned in an interview, he became familiar with Tolkien's work during his study abroad and subsequently he offered his translation to a Slovak publisher on his own initiative: "[since] I was enthusiastic about The Hobbit, I translated it and offered it to the Mladé letá publishing house. They then, as it goes, 'jumped at the chance' to publish the translation and immediately released it" (Aľakša, "Z archívu" 11). Despite this historical regional lead, it was afterwards possible to observe a relatively long period during which no other Slovak translation of any text by Tolkien was published until the re-release of *The Hobbit* in 1994. It was Krupa's revised translation under a revised title at the publishing house Slovenský spisovateľ.

An interesting, although unrealised, undertaking was an attempt by the publishing house Mladé letá in 1990. They were hoping to release the second edition of Krupa's original translation with illustrations by Peter Kľúčik, a renowned artist and illustrator. However, due to some issues with the release, the project was not successful. The collection of 37 original colour illustrations did not appear in any other edition and was presented to the public at an exhibition in Šariš gallery in Prešov in 2002 (frk.). In connection with a later rerun of the exhibition, the press reported on its preparation, quoting Kľúčik and reflecting on the situation surrounding the unrealised edition (Opoldusová; TASR). In addition to the demise of several publishing houses in the early 1990s, both articles also point to a

J.R.R. Tolkien in the Slovak Press: Situation After 1990   95

fact that is symptomatic of translated fantasy literature in Slovakia to this day: the existence of Czech translations. An illustrated Czech version of *The Hobbit* was published around the same time. Klúčik emphasised the potential of the Slovak edition: "The Czech edition is more moderately and rather 'intellectually' illustrated, while the Slovak edition would be more visually captivating for a child reader. [Daniel] Hevier wanted to publish the book then, but the Slovenský spisovateľ publishing house, which did not want all the illustrations but only one for the cover, had the rights. I refused that" (Aľakša, "Rozhovor" 39).[2]

The early phase of interest in Slovak editions of Tolkien's works is thus officially concluded by the revised second edition of Krupa's translation of *The Hobbit* from 1994. No other Tolkien's texts were published in Slovak language until 2001. In an interview, Krupa mentions the lack of interest of Slovak publishers despite his initiative: "As early as in the seventies, I published excerpts from *The Lord of the Rings* in magazines, but nothing budged. I made the last attempt last year [in 2000], however, it was not successful either" (Aľakša, "Z archívu" 12). Krupa thus indirectly confirms the importance of *The Lord of the Rings* movie trilogy in the increase of interest in Tolkien's work in Slovakia. This pop culture event can therefore be seen as triggering the beginning of the first wave of a deeper interest in translating Tolkien's work into Slovak. Peter Karpinský came to the same conclusion: "The filming and subsequent release of the first part of *The Lord of the Rings* trilogy [...] kicked off an unprecedented interest in the work of J.R.R. Tolkien in Slovakia (and not only in Slovakia)" (64). Already in 2001, during the release of Peter Jackson's first film, the first two parts of the book trilogy *The Fellowship of the Ring* and *The Two Towers* were published by Slovart publishing house for the first time in a Slovak translation by Otakar Kořínek.

If the first wave of the "Tolkien craze" in Slovakia was the most fruitful in the history of publishing Tolkien's works in Slovak language, then 2002 can be considered the most prolific year of Slovak Tolkien publications ever. Simultaneously with the release of *The Two Towers* film, the third part of the book trilogy, *The Return of the King*, again translated by Kořínek, was published in Slovak language together with the third edition of *The Hobbit* translated by Krupa,[3] as well as the first edition of *The Hobbit* translated by Kořínek with illustrations by Alan Lee, and also the complete second edition of *The Lord of the Rings* trilogy (with Lee's illustrations, too), all published by Slovart. Above all, the release of the illustrated versions can be seen as a reaction to the popularity of the film series, as Alan Lee was one of the three concept artists collaborating on Jackson's films and was also the author of the illustrations for the English editions of *The Hobbit* and *The Lord of the Rings* from the late 90s. The year 2002 also saw the publication of Krupa's latest new contribution (this time in collaboration

96 Jozefa Pevčíková, Eva Urbanová

with his daughter, Martina Bucková) to add to the Slovak translations of Tolkien's texts; it was the first and only edition of the children's book *Roverandom* in the publishing house SPN – Mladé letá.

The year 2003 symbolically marked the end of the first wave of interest in Tolkien in Slovakia. At the same time as the third film, *The Return of the King*, the Slovak translation of the mythology of Middle-earth *The Silmarillion* (Slovart, translated by Branislav Varsik and Katarína Varsiková) was published as the last, up until then untranslated, essential component of the stories about Middle-earth.

Finally, an outstanding achievement of this period was also the adaptation of *The Lord of the Rings* in the form of an eighteen-part radio play co-produced by Radio Twist and Slovak Radio, translated by Viliam Klimáček and directed by Jaroslav Rihák. This achievement was commented on by Aľakša: "[i]t is actually the world premiere of a radio play based on the motifs of *The Lord of the Rings* – Slovakia was the first in the world to receive the copyright for a radio dramatization of this saga" ("Svetové prvenstvo" 12).[4]

As part of the second wave of Slovak language translations (2006–2008), the latest Slovak versions of Tolkien's works were published. They were the *Unfinished Tales* (2006, Slovart) and a separate edition of the story *The Children of Húrin* (2007, Slovart) with illustrations by Alan Lee. *The Children of Húrin* is particularly specific within the researched topic; this is the only Tolkien's book that was published in a Slovak translation at almost the same time as the original. Matúš "Loki" Hyžný even states in the fanzine *Athelas*: "So we were second in the world to get *The Children of Húrin*, regardless of the quality of the translation" ("O Húrinových deťoch" 7). During this period – until 2008 – *The Hobbit, The Lord of the Rings* and *The Silmarillion* were also re-released.

The third wave of Slovak translations can then be seen as a summarising one, and one that was significantly influenced by the release of *The Hobbit* film trilogy. In the period of 2012–2013, two different editions of *The Hobbit* and *The Lord of the Rings* appeared. In response to the popularity of the films, they were published as paperbacks with film illustrations on the cover, but at the same time they were also released in hard cover with the same cover design as the first, non-illustrated edition of *The Lord of the Rings* from 2001–2003. This is the first visually uniform non-illustrated edition of the texts about Middle-earth; *The Hobbit* was the only such publication that did not correspond visually to a single edition of other books before.

In summary, it can be said that the publication of Slovak translations of Tolkien's texts was closely connected with the increasing or decreasing popularity of Tolkien's myth within the global popular culture. A significant difference in the reception and processing of Tolkien's works can be

J.R.R. Tolkien in the Slovak Press: Situation After 1990   97

observed primarily between the early phase and the later waves of Slovak language editions. While in the early phase, before the emergence of films as visual references, Slovak publishers tended to supplement the editions of *The Hobbit* with original illustrations by Slovak artists, after 2001, the influence of global pop culture and films led to the creation of editions whose appearance more closely followed world trends. The analysis of the research material has also shown the differences in the reception of the Tolkien myth. As shown in the following part, there is a significant difference between the texts from the fandom environment (in the sense of the subculture of fans of popular culture), the mainstream press texts, and the texts of an academic nature.

Critique of Translations in the Slovak Academic and Popular Environment

While the curve of critical interest in Slovak translations of Tolkien's texts tends to follow the sinusoid of the popularity of the Tolkien myth and the various waves of the Slovak language editions' releases, there are however certain differences, which we will discuss in a more detailed way.

In general, the reception of Slovak translations typically has two forms: interviews with translators of Tolkien's texts and texts focusing on criticism of selected translations. A specific set of responses are articles published in fan periodicals and genre periodicals specialising in commentaries on popular culture, including fantasy, across all media. This type of reception is characterised by its comparative nature – the articles compare Slovak translations with Czech ones, as well as Slovak translations with one another. This is a result of the fact that the authors of these analyses are typically readers/fans who have in-depth knowledge of Tolkien's work, of Czech translations as well as original texts, and openly declare this fact.

The first mention of Slovak post-1990 editions of Tolkien's texts can be found in the magazine *Fantázia* (the most popular genre magazine in Slovakia published between 1997 and 2011), which in 1999 featured Aľakša's interview with Peter Kľúčik ("Rozhovor" 39) supplemented with a sample of his unused illustrations for *The Hobbit*. The first reaction to the Slovak translation is Miloš Drastich's review of *The Fellowship of the Ring*. Apart from a short approving comment, the review confirms the tendency to compare the Czech and Slovak translations: "[t]he translation itself was not particularly demanding, but we mustn't forget the fairly widespread opinion among Slovak readers that the Czech translations are better than the Slovak ones" (Drastich, "Kontinuita" 10).

The topic is given more comprehensive coverage by *Fantázia* magazine again, which, on the occasion of the release of *The Fellowship of the Ring* film in 2001, dedicated an entire issue to Tolkien and his work. In addition

98   Jozefa Pevčíková, Eva Urbanová

to the extensive biographical information about the author, which places his life and his works into a wider cultural context, it also provides behind-the-scenes film production information, an overview of other adaptations (comics, animated film, music), a review of the Slovak edition of *The Fellowship of the Ring*, a humorous report on the "Slovak Hobbiton" near the village of Liptovská Teplička in the north of Slovakia, thematic short stories by Slovak authors, information about a radio play being developed, and interviews with all three translators of Tolkien's works into Slovak language – Viktor Krupa (about the translation of *The Hobbit*), Otakar Kořínek (*The Lord of the Rings*), and Viliam Klimáček (*The Lord of the Rings* radio play). In these interviews, those aspects of the translations that are subject to criticism in the later period are also mentioned: comparison with the Czech translation, translation of proper nouns and geographical names, specifically the translation of the terms "orc" and "goblin" and the etymology of these translations, as well as Kořínek's utilisation of the richness of the Slovak language.

Some of these points reoccur in Miloš Ferko's review of the book edition of *The Fellowship of the Ring* in the same publication. At the very beginning of the section dedicated to Kořínek's translation, Ferko claims: "Perhaps the Czech translation is so deeply etched in my mind, perhaps [...] In any case, I have my reservations about the use of the word 'ohyzda' (or 'ohyzd') instead of 'orc' or 'goblin'" ("Na cestu" 26). He also mentions the translation of proper nouns (for example, the case of Merry being called "Chicholm"), geographical names (Shire as "Kraj"), and even the case of "the wrong (specifically masculine) gender attributed to Galadriel in the final paragraph of the Prologue" (26). In spite of these reservations, Ferko's review is one of the few that, as a whole, evaluate Kořínek's translation positively: "Despite these minor flaws, we should not forget the remarkable dimensions of the text, Kořínek's command of rich vocabulary and poetic language – and above all – the fact that it is the historically first translation of this masterpiece of fantasy into Slovak language" (26).

Alena Gottweisová's text published online around the same time is more critical. She also focuses on translations of proper nouns and place names. She compares Czech and Slovak translations (*The Hobbit* and *The Lord of the Rings* books, and *The Lord of the Rings* radio adaptation) and points out some factual errors (the masculine gender used for Galadriel; the name Gil-Galad appearing as a toponym instead of a proper noun), shifts in meaning in the etymology of the translation (Frodo Baggins vs. "Frodo Lazník"), as well as the inconsistency of the Slovak translations compared to the Czech: While Glum [Czech translation of Gollum] remains the same throughout, in Slovak translation "the name fares differently: in the Slovak translation of *The Hobbit*, Gollum was made into 'Glgúň'. The same character is called 'Gloch' in *The Lord of the Rings.* To add to the confusion, in the radio dramatization, we face 'Glum' again" (n.p.).

Daniel Suchý presents a similar opinion in his review of the film *The Lord of the Rings: The Fellowship of the Ring*: "In addition to the popular Czech translation of the book, a Slovak translation is finally available, though it struggles to set itself apart in any way. There is also a radio adaptation in the works, hovering somewhere in between" (8). In the same issue of the magazine *Kultúrny život*, in a review of the book translation of *The Fellowship of the Ring*, Jaroslav Kušnír in turn acknowledges Tolkien's writing qualities "together with the quality of the translation by Otakar Kořínek" (8).

The split in the evaluation of the Slovak translations of Tolkien's works – especially Kořínek's translations – is also evident in other texts from the time of the first wave of interest. In this period, however, a tendency that is noticeable later, too, emerges – a great amount of time and space dedicated to the translators' methods and strategies, especially in fan texts and periodicals.

In addition to the aforementioned "triple interview" with all the translators in a special issue of *Fantázia*, an interview with Kořínek was published in 2003 in the fanzine *Athelas*. Apart from an explanation of the origin of the translation of the terms "orc" or "Baggins", the interview is also interesting due to the translator's self-reflective statement, to which a certain share of the unfavourable reception of the Slovak translation by fans can be attributed: "I probably angered many Tolkienists when I said that it [*The Lord of the Rings*] is just a beautifully, marvellously written fairy tale, nothing more. I do not consider this work to be exceptional" (J. Katka "Crankia", "Interview" 7). In addition, right after this interview, another criticism of Kořínek's translation skills follows, written by Tomáš "Frey" Mašek: "I have read several books translated by O. Kořínek and not all of them were of such dubious quality as his *The Lord of the Rings*" (7).

Martina Bucková and Viktor Krupa's translation of the fairy tale *Roverandom* was also published during this wave. However, the media reports about it primarily focused on the plot of the story and the circumstances of the creation of the work, while the quality of translation was only mentioned in passing (Karpinský; Jurdáková; Ferko, "Psí zázrak").

In the period between the first and second wave of interest in Tolkien, we can also find probably the only overview of Slovak translations of Tolkien's texts, penned by Matúš "Loki" Hyžný in the fanzine *Athelas* no. 8. It lists all translations and editions published up to 2005.

A similar polarity of opinions can also be observed in the reception piece of the Slovak translation of *The Children of Húrin*, which was published during the second wave (2006–2008). Literary-oriented periodicals leaned towards approving rhetoric. Bohuš Bodacz, writing for journal *Slovenské pohľady*, mentions "Otakar Kořínek's excellent translation" (119) and Lucia Winklerová discusses Kořínek's work on Tolkien's texts in a more comprehensive way in the journal *Romboid*, only marginally mentioning the already known criticism, relegating it to the realm of fandom: "Otakar Kořínek's prompt but still cultured translations of J.R.R. Tolkien were awarded a prize by the UNESCO's International Board on Books for Young People in 2004. Certain inaccuracies in the translation are being discussed on the Internet" (Winklerová, "Ďalší rozvoj fenoménu" 82).

An arguably more convincing and objective discussion of Kořínek's translations of Tolkien's texts can be found in the fanzine *Athelas* no. 14. On the occasion of the Slovak edition of *The Children Húrin*, Hyžný notes that Tolkien fans are willing to wait for the Czech edition rather than read the Slovak one. He cites Kořínek as the reason: "On the one hand, he is a renowned translator active in the literary field for many years. On the other hand, he is known for his infamous translation of *The Lord of the Rings*" ("O Húrinových deťoch" 6). The article yet again brings a comparison to the Czech translation, but this time with a significantly positive result: "Those who read *The Lord of the Rings* in Slovak language are aware that Mr. Kořínek really knows how to translate. Some passages sound even more beautiful than the legendary Czech translation by Stanislava Pošustová". He further states that Kořínek's translation is in many ways "very clever and inventive. I dare say that Mr. Kořínek coming up with the term *ohyzd* is absolutely fantastic, because from an etymological point of view, it describes the essence of the concept of *orc* more than the Czech word" (6). Hyžný thus offers a new perspective on the problematic aspects of Kořínek's translations, and aptly identifies the partial reservations of fans which, as we state below, are supported by later translation studies: "The most conspicuous issue one notices when reading the Slovak *The Lord of the Rings* is the absolute failure in the matter of in-depth awareness of Middle-earth realia" (6).

Another short essay by Hyžný, published in another issue of *Athelas*, focuses on the etymology of the words "orc" and "goblin", tracing their origins to Germanic and Scandinavian languages and cultures, and points to the transformations these words underwent in Tolkien's works themselves. It also briefly evaluates the cultural-historical anchoring, quality, and use of these words in the Slovak translations by Krupa and Kořínek, and the Czech versions by Vrba and Pošustová-Menšíková, as well as the Polish translation by Maria Skibniewská ("Jazykové pozadie" 10–11).

However, within the second wave, most of the attention was devoted to *The Children of Húrin*. The only brief mention of another translation of Tolkien's text into Slovak can be found in Miloš Ferko's summary in the magazine *Fantázia*: "The publishing house Slovart completes the first

J.R.R. Tolkien in the Slovak Press: Situation After 1990   101

Slovak edition of J.R.R. Tolkien's texts about Middle-earth by publishing *Unfinished Tales*" ("Uhorky" 52).

The third wave of Tolkien's popularity (2012–2013) and also the later period (2014-up to the present), are marked by the change in the nature of the reception of Tolkien's translations. Their quantity is significantly reduced, and the change in their character and the intended reader is apparent. While in the case of fan periodicals and internet sources we can see the redistribution of interest in Tolkien into new media and genres (comics, video games, wargaming, music, pastiches, parodies, etc.), the literary periodicals do not pay any attention to this topic. This is probably connected to the fact that in the third wave of Slovak language translations we can only find unmodified re-releases.

Translations are also discussed in the most current source – Adrián Berecz's 2021 online interview with Slovak Tolkienists for the daily *Denník N*. The interview contemplates Tolkien's life and works in a wider cultural-literary context (biographical data, Christianity, Tolkien's presence in Oxford, etc.), and at the same time comments on the constant presence of Tolkien's myth in popular culture. Kořínek's translation, however, again receives a predominantly negative reaction and a comparison with the Czech translation. Michal Gendiar in this interview said: "there are various factual errors in the Slovak translation, which persist there despite the fact that more than 20 years and several editions have passed since the first edition. As Tolkienists, we are disappointed and dissatisfied with this. The very reactions of Mr. Kořínek also contributed to the dissatisfaction" (n.p.).

Analysing the discourse in the mentioned media, our attention was finally drawn to an article by Martina Juričková published on the Christian platform Slovo+. Juričková uses Tolkien's letters to support her arguments in her criticism of the current state of the Catholic Church: "Even J.R.R. Tolkien, a British writer, otherwise a deeply religious man, had to deal with a period of certain spiritual waning" (n.p.). The author's loose translation of the letters no. 250 and 43 is apparently the only Slovak translation of Tolkien's correspondence apart from the letters cited in books about Middle-earth.

While the references to Tolkien and Slovak translations were rare in mainstream and literature-popularising media from the mentioned period, the situation was different in translation studies academic journals, where criticisms of Slovak translations and analyses of Tolkien's manner of creation of new terms and proper nouns were published mainly during the years 2012–2016.

A comparative criticism of the Slovak translation of functional names in *The Lord of the Rings* was written by Daniela Klučariková for the journal *Prekladateľské listy*. She pays particular attention to place names and surnames, and in the conclusion, she also mentions the problematic translation

102 Jozefa Pevčíková, Eva Urbanová

of the term "Gladden Fields". After an etymological analysis of the original English names, she offers more suitable Slovak equivalents (29–34).

The problem of translation of the terms "orc" and "goblin" is dealt with in another study in the later issue of the same journal, this time by Igor Tyšš (2013). Although the text is not primarily focused on the analysis of the translation of Tolkien's text, Tyšš takes into account all three translation solutions (Krupa – Kořínek – Klimáček) as well as the justifications for their use. It is worth mentioning that he refers to the information published in the "Tolkien" issue of *Fantázia* magazine, which we have mentioned several times (119–120).

The most complex – and probably also the most ambitious – contribution to the translational discourse concerning Tolkien is the study by Zuzana Kraviarová and Michal Gendiar in the 2013 volume of the journal *Kritika prekladu*. It is dedicated exclusively to a critical analysis of the Slovak translations of *The Hobbit* with an emphasis on the latest translation by Kořínek. The authors place them in a broad context – the study contains biographical information about Tolkien, their own critical analysis, Kořínek's reactions, which the authors obtained from a new interview with the translator, as well as an extensive section devoted to the reception of the Slovak translation in the fan community, or readers in general. The study recalls the fact that Tolkien created a translation guide for his works, explaining the origin of various names and suggesting possible translation strategies. "However, the situation of Otakar Kořínek was quite complicated, because he did not have the guide at his disposal and, to make everything even more difficult, the Czech translations were already established and very popular in Slovakia at the time of the creation of the latest Slovak translation" (66). In the end, the authors evaluate Kořínek's translation extremely positively: "The translator's utilisation of the Slovak language (except for a few minor instances) is excellent and must be admired. He managed to realise the 'fairy-tale' character of the work perfectly, it even sounds beautiful when read aloud" (82). Still, they also remind the reader of several shortcomings and inappropriate translations: "[t]he translator may really have acted with the best intentions for creating new and original Slovak equivalents, we are not sure if it was the best strategy when translating a work that has a strong reader base of hard-core fans" (83). In the end, this is also the only study that takes into account the fact that Kořínek did not take into consideration "explicit instructions of the author, who took the trouble to prepare an extensive material of instructions and explanations for the translators" (83). Considering the complex investigation of the issue, we must say that it is a pity that the authors' promise about a series of studies dedicated to the translation of Tolkien into Slovak language was not fulfilled and no further critical analysis was published in the mentioned periodical.

J.R.R. Tolkien in the Slovak Press: Situation After 1990   103

The last traceable study is the analysis by Ivo Poláček in *Prekladateľské listy* in 2016, which is, however, concerned more with etymology rather than with translation procedure. By analysing and comparing the symbolism used in Tolkien's texts, Nordic and Slavic mythology and biblical stories, he tries to find a suitable interpretative approach applicable in the Slovak translation.

In conclusion to this part, we can state that the analysis of the critical reception of Slovak translations of Tolkien's texts indicates the following: in-depth and more critical reception texts dealing with these translations appeared more often in the period of the first and the second wave of Tolkien's popularity, primarily in fan and genre periodicals and in contributions on the internet. Positive, but briefer and more superficial feedback came from literary periodicals during the entire examined period. It was only in the later period (the third wave to the present day) that we received more precise and objective criticism, or analysis published in academic periodicals focusing on translation studies.

How to Critique Tolkien: The Question of the Genre of J.R.R. Tolkien's Works in Slovak Reception Texts

From the issue of the reception of the translations, we come to the actual criticism of J.R.R. Tolkien's works in the Slovak literary environment. We found that the evaluation of the artistic side of the available Tolkien's books is related to the broader problem of acceptance of fantasy as a sub-genre of speculative fiction.

We particularly focused on academic literary criticism journals. We assumed that those journals would dedicate the most space to the works of such a world renown author, or at least as much space as the fandom magazines. This hypothesis was not confirmed. The reception pieces found in academic journals that went beyond mention or brief information were the following: *Knižná revue, Kultúrny život, Rak, Romboid, Literárny týždenník, Slovenské pohľady, Slovenský jazyk a literatúra v škole, Knižnica, Litikon, A&P, Bibiana,* and *Impulz.* Of these, only five of the named periodicals devoted space to Tolkien's works more than once. The situation was quite different in fanzines, which regularly published pieces on J.R.R. Tolkien's works from 1990 onwards. In addition to the popular genre magazine *Fantázia* (1997–2011), the fanzine *Athelas*[5] was also formed, which was published by the civic association Spoločenstvo Tolkiena [Fellowship of Tolkien] in Bratislava. *Fantázia* magazine devoted space to Tolkien regularly, with a completely thematic issue from 2001.

Online periodicals have also regularly discussed Tolkien and his works, life, translations, film adaptations, etc., especially since 2001,[6] when there was a significant increase in the number of articles on the internet devoted

104 *Jozefa Pevčíková, Eva Urbanová*

to Tolkien. Widespread interest can also be seen in magazines with a confessional profile (*Postoj, Katolícke noviny, Impuls,* and others), which is probably caused by the frequent interpretation of Tolkien's works from the point of view of the Catholic faith.

The assumption that defining the genre would naturally be done by the scholars writing for the academic literary criticism journals did not turn out to be true. The vast majority of texts not only avoided the direct inclusion of Tolkien's works in fantasy literature but also the contextualisation of Tolkien in English literature in general. That is also why we have chosen the ability (and need) of reviewers to determine the genre background of J.R.R. Tolkien's works as one of the relevant approaches for classifying the researched reception piece (whether on an academic or on a fandom basis).

At the beginning of the 1990s, fantasy was discussed rarely in the Slovak literary circles. The studies, essays, and monographs of Ondrej Herec or Miloš Ferko can be considered exceptions. To this day, discourse about speculative fiction and its subgenres (fantasy, science fiction, horror, or others) stands outside the main interest of literary scholarship. The competition for the best Slovak prose of the past year, "Anasoft litera", is a prime example of this marginal position, as only sporadically, and only in the last few years, have the works described as "genre" reading managed to "infiltrate" the competition. The fans of popular literature (and specifically speculative fiction) have responded by narrowing the profile of several literary competitions. Two of the most important in this respect are Cena Gustáva Reussa [The Gustáv Reuss Award] (1991–2002), named after the author of the first Slovak science fiction novel, and the Martinus Cena Fantázie [Martinus Fantázia Award].[7]

The reception of speculative fiction as a genre in Slovak academic periodicals during the period under review is characterised by two tendencies. On the one hand, there is the overlooking of and disinterest in fantastic literature – as Viktor Krupa stated in an interview in 1995, referring to his efforts to translate Tolkien's other works "there was even an opinion of a respected person at the Faculty of Arts and Letters of the Comenius University that this work had no literary value" ("Z archívu" 12). On the other hand (and this approach extends to the present), one can identify the need to prove or defend the artistic quality of works identified as speculative fiction.

Overall, from the corpus of scholarly literary reception texts we have worked with, we have discerned three approaches to the issue of J.R.R. Tolkien's works genre:

1 Genre was not defined, or the fantastic nature of the works in question was only mentioned in passing, without commenting on it further
2 The tendency to look for "substitute" terms for the term fantasy, which can also be seen as an incorrect and/or inaccurate genre classification

J.R.R. Tolkien in the Slovak Press: Situation After 1990   105

3 Correct classification of the analysed works within fantasy or speculative fiction, and readiness to work with the fact.

Genre (non)classification has also influenced the value judgement that the authors have made about the works. In general, the genre non-anchoring and rejection of fantasy, or the search for a substitute term, was associated with a negative reception of Tolkien's works, and conversely, the "acknowledgement" of fantasy with an awareness of its diversity in turn led to a positive acceptance of the discussed works as valuable fiction, which was again the stance primarily found in fandom magazines and websites.

The year 2001 can again be considered a turning point (in the section devoted to translation, we called the period 2001–2003 the first wave), which is related both to the release of the film adaptation and to Kořínek's translations. Around this time, several film reviews appeared in academic periodicals which also dealt, at least briefly, with the literary text that the film was based on. However, while in the case of a book the genre can be strategically bypassed, this practice is rare in the case of a film. This is probably why the reviewer of *The Lord of the Rings: The Fellowship of the Ring*, Daniel Suchý, does not doubt the genre background and uses the term "fantasy" quite explicitly, though he does not define it any further, because, as he says, the fantasy genre "is not something that interests" him (8), which also leads him to make a rather vague statement: "Fantasy is simply a specific genre" and in rather derogatory undertones: "Tolkien fanatics", according to him, "are better in Elvish than in the grammar of their native tongue" (8).

In the same issue of the journal *Kultúrny život,* there also appeared the already mentioned review of the book *The Lord of the Rings: The Fellowship of the Ring* by Jaroslav Kušnír. It is interesting that he does not mention the fantasy genre at all and the elements he names (adventure plot, supernatural characters, elements of suspense) he first attributes to the "fairy-tale character" of this book and when this framework is no longer sufficient for his needs (the motif of wandering, complicated composition and nomenclature, allegory, imagination, mystery, adaptation of mythology and history, etc.), he relies on other auxiliary terms such as "saga" and "heroic epic", until finally he defines the work with his own hybrid genre name: "fairy-tale heroic epic" (8). Although such evasive definitions could be considered insufficient or even retrograde at the beginning of the third millennium – especially in the context of the rapidly growing global popularity of the fantasy genre – in the Slovak academic environment they illustrate the state of scholarly discourse on the subject at the time. This is evidenced by the fact that the first history of Slovak speculative fiction by Ondrej Herec and Miloš Ferko, *Slovenská fantastika do roku 2000*

106 *Jozefa Pevčíková, Eva Urbanová*

[Slovak speculative fiction up to year 2000, which also attempts to define the genre, was published as late as in 2001].

On the other hand, the review by literary scholar Miloš Ferko, who commented on fantasy and the work of J.R.R. Tolkien systematically and regularly (especially on the pages of *Fantázia* magazine), has a completely different character. In the same year as the abovementioned reviews, Ferko briefly assessed the freshly translated *The Lord of the Rings: The Fellowship of the Ring* (in the "My Recommendation" section of the *Knižná revue* journal), and unequivocally stated in the very first sentence: "*The Hobbit* and *The Lord of the Rings* made Tolkien one of the founders of a new literary genre, the so-called *fantasy*" ("The Fellowship of the Ring" 1). In a relatively small space, Ferko was able to explain the essential features of fantasy, especially the relationship of fantasy to the mythological heritage, but also to the fairy tale, which is also based on the conflict between good and evil. A positive assessment of the works of J.R.R. Tolkien results in his acceptance into the paradigm of fiction for both adult and child recipients.

In 2002, Ferko continues his commentary on Tolkien's works, this time of *Roverandom*. As in the previous review, he points out the intersections with Celtic, Germanic, and Oriental mythology ("Psí zázrak" 2). Ferko's thoughts on Tolkien can also be traced in the space of fandom, as already mentioned, especially in the magazine *Fantázia*, where he also evaluates in greater detail Tolkien's legacy from the point of view of a reader. He describes his own personal journey in search of Tolkien's works, which, in his opinion, could not be published in our cultural milieu for ideological reasons: "The Forces of Evil cannot reside in the East. The censors had forgotten that, from the point of view of an Englishman during the Second World War, the East was as much fascist Germany as Stalinist Russia. The system clearly did not have a clear conscience. It feared the power of good literature. [...] As we can read in the preface to the second edition, [Tolkien] vehemently refutes an allegorical understanding of his text. *The Lord of the Rings*, according to the author, is not an indirect depiction of the events of the Second World War, but a pure story from the stores of Lady Fantasy" ("On the Road" 26).

In the same year, *Bibiana*, an academic journal devoted to literature for children and adolescents, published a review by Peter Karpinský discussing Tolkien's *Roverandom*. Among other things, he deliberates on the issue of the child and adult reader of Tolkien's works. While he considers the so-called trilogy as a work less suitable for a child recipient (at this point he also implicitly draws attention to the fact that the fantasy genre encourages one to consider the work suitable for children, which is a simplistic idea of the genre in general), he welcomes *Roverandom* as a suitable text for the child reader (66).

J.R.R. Tolkien in the Slovak Press: Situation After 1990   107

Schools and teachers also express their interest in Tolkien, which was shown, for example, by an article in the journal *Slovenský jazyk a literatúra v škole* [Slovak Language and Literature in School], where Andrea Lobová reported on her research on the issue of "film versus book", choosing as her research material not only the three volumes of *The Lord of the Rings* but also the *Harry Potter* series, both of which were popular at the time, especially thanks to their film adaptations. However, Lobová's research does not focus on the suitability of the books in question, but deals directly with the issue of reading. Genre-wise, she places *The Lord of the Rings* squarely in the category of fantasy, even distinguishing subgenres of fantasy literature by referring to an unnamed source who sees Tolkien as the founder of the genre of "modern heroic fantasy literature" (99). She goes on to slightly correct this claim – it is not heroic but epic fantasy – and in the end she concludes that "[h]is epic work is monolithic, made up of wonderful stories that hold the attention of the recipient, presenting a whole, compelling world" (99). The striking detail about this research is that even though both Karpinský (in 2002) and Lobová (in 2005) attest to the immense popularity of these books and films among schoolchildren, this fact has not had any significant impact on increasing the academic interest in Tolkien's works, as shown in the academic literary periodicals of the time.

The abandoning of the genre classification of Tolkien's works, as well as a bias against speculative fiction in general, have often resulted in loose interpretations of the writer's works, misinterpreting Tolkien's legacy by means of weak argumentation. Miloš Drastich, in his brief review in a weekly *Literárny týždenník* (2001), does speak of the emergence of a new complex world and the related emergence of a new genre, but he does not name the genre directly. Instead, he raises a number of questions – allegorical solutions to the reading of *The Lord of the Rings* – which refer not only to the Second World War, but also to "anthrax", the "aviation apocalypse", or political struggles: "Have not the fires of local military political economic power interests been roaring in different places on the planet all the time during the whole peace-time since the end of the Second World War?"; or a little further: "Also, as regards the world of hobbits, elves, ogres, dwarves, people from the ancient times of mankind, and the diversity of their mindsets and languages: is this not strikingly similar to our nowadays widespread coexistence with dogs, cats, exotic birds, and reptiles as well?" ("Kontinuita" 10)

A year later, Drastich ventures even deeper into the realms of overinterpretation in his review of *The Lord of the Rings: The Return of the King*, when he talks at some length and in some detail (one third of the review) about the genetic research on human aggression: "Scientists have found that men with a gene limiting MAO-A production are prone to antisocial

108 Jozefa Pevčíková, Eva Urbanová

behaviour [...] Therefore – the more of us there are, the more evil people, and therefore evil, there will be in the world. And the more readers of *The Lord of the Rings* and similar books there will be" (Drastich, "Svet" 10).

Jozef Bobok's review, boldly titled "Literatúra, mýty a gýče" [Literature, Myths, and Kitsch], in which he "condemns" two films – *Harry Potter* and *The Lord of the Rings* – is also extremely subjective. The problem turns out to be mainly the popularity of the novels the films are based on in America, as well as the genre itself. Here, however, the author oscillates inaccurately between science fiction and fantasy fiction. He considers the novels as means of escape from reality, from real problems, and thus deemed kitsch.

A less traditional interpretation is Igor Zmeták's 2006 article "Pán prsteňov' – etika a mýtus v postmodernej dobe" [The Lord of the Rings – Ethics and Myth in the Postmodern Era]. Although the author does not use the term fantasy genre, he resolutely refuses to classify the novel as a fairy tale. He focuses on references to mythology, connecting them to the problem of contemporary, postmodern times. Indeed, he finds the meaning of Tolkien's works in "the revival of mythology as a model of positive environmental behaviour" (60). He supports this unusual interpretation with thorough arguments, backing it up with concrete examples of how the characters in the text behave towards nature and all living things in general.

Reception texts, especially in academic but also in genre-oriented magazines and fanzines, often included biographical context. This may be due to Tolkien's interesting life story, such as the circumstances of the creation of *The Hobbit,* his family and university relationships, wartime events, and also his commitment to the Catholic faith. Another recurring fact is the emphasis on Tolkien's academic qualifications (university background, philological talent, study of mythological heritage, etc.), which can be interpreted as a kind of apologia, or an attempt to increase the "solemnity" of his works. As if it were necessary to stress that it is not just a "fairy tale", or that the popular fantasy genre as such is not just a "fairy tale". Much more than the works itself, therefore, the circumstances of the creation of Middle-earth stories are discussed.

As an example, Peter Sýkora also explicates several such details concerning Tolkien's creative method. He also draws attention to the issue of allegory, which is the focal point of many interpretations, especially in terms of its similarity to totalitarian regimes. Paraphrasing Tolkien, he names the main idea of his works as "the existential problem of death and life" (43), which is inherent to all mythologies.

Special attention has been paid to Tolkien's life not only in exclusively literary and art periodicals. A detailed biography, for example, appeared in the popular science bimonthly journal *History*. Its author is Eva Juríčková

J.R.R. Tolkien in the Slovak Press: Situation After 1990   109

who writes about facts from the authors' life which are less known in the Slovak environment. Again, it focuses mainly on the circumstances of the creation of the works, but also on Tolkien's family, his heirs, and the impact of his fame. The popularity of his works, however, is in no way linked to the fantasy genre; rather, the article focuses on the Tolkien myth that has developed around the author, not on a deeper penetration into the structure of his works. Such well-conceived, substantial information pieces based on (often archival) research have helped to raise awareness of Tolkien who was increasingly discussed in the media space mostly in the context of successful film adaptations, despite the fact that year 2006 saw not just *The Hobbit* published, but also translations of the trilogy (and their re-releases) and *Roverandom*.

We have identified the beginning of the second wave of popularity of Tolkien's works as the turning point, with a significant change occurring after 2006. Quantitatively, we can observe an increase in reviews around 2007, when *The Children of Húrin* was introduced to the Slovak market. The analysed texts do not define the fantasy genre in depth, and it is still possible to find such that bypass the term altogether or give a dubious genre classification. The situation is not made any easier by Tolkien's own interpretation of his intentions, which is quoted, for example, by Christopher Tolkien in the introduction to the Slovak edition of *The Children of Húrin*; the story of Beren and Lúthien is characterised as a "heroic-tale romance" in one of the quoted letters (8). Lucia Winklerová, in her reviews, incorrectly attributes this genre to *The Children of Húrin* as a whole ("Alegória" 37; "Ďalší rozvoj fenoménu" 81). However, references to mythological inspirations became commonplace (as stated by Winklerová, too), as did comparisons to the *Harry Potter* book series, which indirectly suggests an acknowledgement, albeit unconscious, of the genre matrix. The allegorical dimension of the works, which has been pointed out by some previous reviewers (Sýkora; Ferko; Juríčková), also made a comeback.

The most prevalent group, as far as academic periodicals are concerned, turned out to be journals with a religious focus. Tolkien offers a wide range of interpretations with references to Christian discourse. The most space devoted to his works appeared in the magazine *Impulz – revue pre modernú katolícku kultúru* [Impulse – a Review Magazine for Modern Catholic Culture] – and in the conservative journal *Postoj*. These periodicals enhanced the quality of such reception texts with articles focusing on translations. Among the critical texts is a study by Michael D. O'Brien, who based his analysis on analogies with Holy Scripture. The association with *Harry Potter* (again) is noteworthy, as this time it is literally a confrontation, as the title – "Harry Potter versus Bilbo Baggins" – suggests. It is Harry Potter that comes out worse in the evaluation. The reasons for criticism are

110 *Jozefa Pevčíková, Eva Urbanová*

the disruption of stereotypes of "traditional" heroes and values as well as "eclectic symbolism", "moral decay", the presentation of magic as a "good" or positive element. The igniting of the imagination in a "right" and "wrong" way is also mentioned (77–86). While Tolkien emerges as the victor from this polarised picture, there is a considerable force applied in the usage of theological concepts in the way his legacy is interpreted: "Even so, if we understand the trilogy as the author intended it, especially in the light of his seminal work *The Silmarillion*, the situation is obvious enough. Within a certain tolerance necessary for the imaginative resolution of his themes, Tolkien presents us with a 'theological' foundation for Middle-earth that is essentially identical with the book of Genesis" (85).

It is also possible to find studies that do not recognise fantasy as a genre which creates new worlds, especially in a philosophical or semiotic sense because it goes against the will of God: As Anthony Esolen recently claimed "[w]e call it 'fantasy' for lack of a better word for it, but it is misleading. We cannot create. [...] We can *sub-create*: create as it were in the light of what has already been created, and so our works can express truths that were hidden since the foundation of the world" (n.p.).

A unique and engaging commentary is also provided by Peter Frišo in his review of *Beowulf: The Monsters and the Critics*, translated by Jan Čermák and published by Argo; this is a unique venture, since the subject of the review is the Czech edition of Tolkien's non-fiction text. Frišo focuses especially on analysing Tolkien's enthusiasm for *Beowulf*. He does not, however, use the prism of Christian morality, but accentuates Tolkien's view of *Beowulf* as a poem, and thus the point of view of poetics and imagination (155).

Fandom as a Quiet Recourse

Despite the obvious artistic qualities that have made Tolkien's work part of the canon of English literature, the fact remains that the majority of his readers are pop culture fans. The popularity of Middle-earth stories in fandom is closely related to the historical origins of fandom in the 1920s and to the fact that fantasy, as one of the main subgenres of speculative fiction, has from the very beginning been one of the main points of interest for fans – that is, members of the fandom.

The interest of fandom in Tolkien's work (and person) is evident in the period under review. This is confirmed not only by the number of texts dedicated to the translation, analysis, or criticism of the literary works themselves, but also by the extensive interest in the content, structure, and quality of other adaptations, or new cultural texts that have a different media form, but openly subscribe to Tolkien's legacy. It was the fandom that gave us what we repeatedly refer to in the text as the "Tolkien myth".

J.R.R. Tolkien in the Slovak Press: Situation After 1990   111

This is a specific phenomenon of popular culture, which Juraj Malíček calls pop culture myths: "Their basis is a pop culture artefact, i.e. a pop culture product and its own reception code. Their development lies in all other reactions to the artefact, which together express something fundamental about the artefact itself and at the same time they place in wider pop-cultural contexts" (36).

While the mainstream media and academic periodicals within the official Tolkien discourse respond primarily to Tolkien's texts as independent, "completed" literary works, or respond to film adaptations, fandom expands the discourse to various other, often marginal, areas. These are, for example, discussions linked to individual parts of the plot or history of the fictional world (for example, the question of the similarity of Hobbits and men; Hyžný "Krajový kalendár" 7). We can also find analyses of different aspects of Tolkien's work, current information about further expansions of Tolkien myth: forthcoming video games, wargaming campaigns, etc. – or supplementing the discourse with curious, or particularly specific, marginal information (such as screening of Soviet or Scandinavian adaptations of *The Lord of the Rings* and *The Hobbit* at cons, and analysis of comic book adaptations).

A specific defining creative feature of the fan discourse is fan labor. It can be found in two main forms: as a direct artistic activity expressed through literary works (fan fiction), visual works (fan art), and video montages (fan vid) or music production. It is the musical production associated with Tolkien's works that represents, on the one hand, a very marginal component of the fans' reception of the Tolkien myth, while on the other hand, especially in various issues of magazines *Fantázia* or *Athelas*, we find a significant number of articles representing the music scene abroad and in Slovakia, interviews with band members, complete transcripts of lyrics and their analyses and reviews of individual songs and entire albums.

For example, Dušan "Duke" Fabian provided a brief response to this phenomenon: "[s]peculative fiction influenced the creation of a number of foreign rock and metal groups. Naturally, we can ask whether this phenomenon has also spread here, at home [...] The answer is – it has" (40). Fabian mentions three Slovak groups that mainly composed metal music and openly worked with Tolkien's works, which they referenced even with their names: Orkrist, Galadriel, and Dark Mordor. Orkrist is then given the most space – a short introduction of this Bratislava group, creating within the subgenre "gothic black doom heavy metal" (40) is supplemented by a laudatory review of their debut album *Reginae Mysterium*.

Similarly, Hyžný contemplates the music production associated with Tolkien and introduces the band Galadriel: "Heavy metal bands drawing on the works of Professor Tolkien can be divided into two groups. Those

112 *Jozefa Pevčíková, Eva Urbanová*

who, while borrowing the name of the band from his mythology (such as Gorgoroth, Amon amarth, Burzum), do not particularly focus on Tolkien's works. Then we have the bands for whom the fantasy, and Tolkien in particular, is life (such as Blind Guardian, Orkrist, Summoning). And a dark-doom metal band from Bratislava called Galadriel is one of the latter ones" ("Galadriel" 10).

The interest in Tolkien has also developed a specific type of DIY culture in the form of LARPs (Live Action Role-Play), groups of historical fencing and children's summer camps.[8] The fans did not just create costumes, weapons, props, scripts or puzzles, etc., but also communities which organised gatherings (e.g. "STretká" named after the Slovak Tolkien association, public readings from Tolkien's works as part of Tolkien Reading Day, film marathons and quizzes) or published their own non-professional periodicals (fanzines *Athelas* and *Imladris*).

The civic association Spoločenstvo Tolkiena, združenie fantastiky [The Fellowship of Tolkien, the Speculative Fiction Association] is the most prominent and practically "official" representative of Slovak fans of J.R.R. Tolkien and his works. It can be considered the first significant point of contact between mainstream and fan discourse about Tolkien and his legacy, making it the first significant point of contact between the two forms of the "Tolkien myth". As can be seen from the information on the association's official website (Tolkien.sk), The Fellowship of Tolkien intends to popularise Tolkien, his works, and his legacy by organising gatherings, public events, lectures at cons or events for children and adolescents, either independently or in cooperation with various companies (for example with the Martinus bookstore chain in the organisation of Tolkien Reading Day). At the same time, the Fellowship of Tolkien is in contact with other foreign associations dedicated to the same purpose.

Criticisms of accompanying encyclopaedic publications, which are meant to make it easier for readers to navigate Tolkien's texts (especially those about Middle-earth) or bring more information about Tolkien's inspirations, can be seen as another point of contact between mainstream and fan discourse. For example, Martina Juričková's review of David Day's *The Heroes of Tolkien* from 2019 draws attention to a number of incorrect data and interpretations of Tolkien's symbolism. She claims that the publication "fails in all respects as an academic publication" and she openly does not recommend it "as a relevant source for analysing the symbolism of Tolkien's works". She, however, sees it as "a good starting point for aspiring 'Tolkienists' for whom it might provide a number of interesting claims, the truth and relevance of which they can further investigate, verify and ultimately confirm or refute in a more thorough and above all academic manner" (Juričková, "Ďalší zaujímavý

J.R.R. Tolkien in the Slovak Press: Situation After 1990   113

knižný kúsok" 233). Two facts are worth noting in connection with this review. First, we can already find similar feedback on Day's books in the repeatedly mentioned thematic issue of magazine *Fantázia* from 2001. There, Martina "Llewelyn" Volná, in her overview of publications dedicated to Tolkien, states the following: "only rather inaccurate and unreliable books by David Day were published in the Czech language" (6). Juričková's review can therefore be seen as an expansion of the Slovak academic discourse, and also as a confirmation of the correctness of the original fan – albeit brief – criticism.

Second, and this can be gauged from the introduction of Juričková's review, as well as from the assertions or published texts of other authors (Gendiar; Ferko), the presence of the so-called "aca-fan" phenomenon is confirmed in the Slovak environment as well. The authorship of this term is attributed to a theorist Henry Jenkins who studies fandom.[9] "Aca-fan" refers to a scientific researcher (an academic) who is also a fan of popular culture and openly declares it. The research and publications of "aca-fans" are typically marked by a particular personal motivation for scientific research which, however, does not reduce the quality of the achieved results – on the contrary, personal interest can mean a better starting point, for example, in the sense of knowledge of the wider context of the investigated issue.

In conclusion, we can state that fandom really fulfils both characteristics that we attributed to it in the title of the subchapter – it is parallel to the "mainstream" perception of Tolkien and his works, because we perceive a void between the traditional and fan response to this phenomenon. This void might either be caused by bias against popular culture and speculative fiction, including fantasy, or by a community-building character of fandom, for which is characteristic originality and its own approach to this phenomenon, independent of the surrounding world.

At the same time, however, we can still detect a certain degree of mainstream in this case as well. This fact manifests itself primarily in the context of the transformation of pop culture reception, or rather the reception of Tolkien by the fan base. A curiosity, a fairy tale, a fable, a myth – a marginal type of text – have become part of the canon, both in the case of fantasy literature and in the case of pop culture in general. For fans, knowing Tolkien has become a commitment and at the same time something that they are constantly reminded of through media texts, references, or marketing strategies, and to which they themselves voluntarily and in various ways constantly return. All in all, the activities of the fandom and the constant circulation, transformation, and enhancement of the "Tolkien myth" are one of the essential proofs that the interest in Tolkien in the Slovak environment is continuous and still relevant.

114 *Jozefa Pevčíková, Eva Urbanová*

Notes

1 The period before 1990 is dealt with in a more detailed way by Janka Kascakova in this volume.
2 It is interesting to note that it was the other way around in 1970s; see Kascakova in this volume 66.
3 It is worth noticing the third change in the translation of the book's title: *Hobbiti (1974) – Hobbit (1994) – Hobit (2002)*.
4 We need to correct Aľakša's claim; while the radio adaptation certainly was an important achievement, Slovakia was not the first to stage the "world premiere" of the radio adaptation of *The Lord of the Rings*. Both the UK and the USA radio listeners were able to enjoy this book in radio adaptations before that. However, Slovak radio adaptation was definitely the first in the context of continental Europe.
5 It is a non-professional magazine without ISSN published by the fans.
6 This chronological milestone is primarily related to the availability of technologies and the development of the Web 2.0 internet culture.
7 The Fantázia Award is currently the largest literary competition in Slovakia with a focus on fantastic literature. It was established under the auspices of *Fantázia* magazine in 2003 (originally under the name Raketa). Since 2005, it has been called Cena Fantázie [The Fantázia Award], and since 2013, the Martinus bookstore chain has been its main partner, which is also indicated by its current name: Martinus Cena Fantázie. "The Multiverzum Award for Authors Under 15 Years of Age" is a specific category, which has been part of the competition since 2020. It was created in response to the fact that there is no literary competition for children and teenagers with a fantasy focus in Slovakia – literary competitions organised within the Slovak education system do not recognise speculative fiction as a separate genre.
8 As seen in an advertisement from *Fantázia* 2 (2004): 55.
9 see also: http://henryjenkins.org/blog/2011/06/acafandom_and_beyond_week_two.html

Works Cited

Aľakša, Ivan. "Z archívu: Krupa bol prvý" [From the archive: Krupa was the first]. *Fantázia* 4 (2001): 11–12.
———. "Svetové prvenstvo na Slovensku!" [The World's First in Slovakia] *Fantázia* 4 (2001): 12–13.
———. "Rozhovor: Mal som pred knihou rešpekt a to je znamenie, že je to veľmi dobrá kniha" [Interview: I had respect for the book and that is a sign that it is a very good book]. *Fantázia* 9 (1999): 39.
Berecz, Adrián. "Slovenskí tolkienisti: Preklad Pána prsteňov je aj po rokoch sklamaním, zostali tam zásadné chyby" [Slovak Tolkienists: *The Lord of the Rings* translation is even after years a disappointment, fundamental errors still remain]. *Denník N*, 12 october 2021. https://dennikn.sk/2566998/slovenski-tolkienisti-preklad-pana-prstenov-je-aj-po-rokoch-sklamanim-zostali-tam-zasadne-chyby/. Accessed 14 August 2022.
Bobok, Jozef. "Literatúra, mýty a gýče: najnovšie nekultúrne vlnobitie" [Literature, myths and kitsch]. *Literárny týždenník* 24 (2002): 3.
Bodacz, Bohuš. "Temný príbeh" [A Dark Story]. *Slovenské pohľady* 10 (2007): 118–119.

J.R.R. Tolkien in the Slovak Press: Situation After 1990   115

Drastich, Miloš. "Kontinuita panstva temnôt" [The Realm of Darkness Continuity]. *Literárny týždenník* 44 (2001): 10.

———. "Svet vernosti myšlienkam, ideálom" [The World of Fidelity to Ideas and Ideals]. *Literárny týždenník* 36 (2002): 9–10.

Esolen, Anthony. "Tolkienov útek do reality" [Tolkien's escape to reality]. *Postoj*, 8 February 2020. https://www.postoj.sk/51422/tolkienov-utek-do-reality. Accessed 23 July 2022.

Fabian, "Duke" Dušan. "Keď zuní oceľ alebo Heavy Metal – stála bašta SF & Fantasy" [When the steel sounds or Heavy Metal – the permanent bastion of SF and Fantasy]. *Fantázia* 25 (2003): 40–41.

Ferko, Miloš. "Na cestu" [For the Road]. *Fantázia* 4 (2001): 26.

———. "Pán Prsteňov 1. Spoločenstvo Prsteňa" [The Lord of the Rings: Fellowship of the Ring]. *Knižná revue* 23 (2001): 1.

———. "Psí zázrak" [Doggie miracle]. *Knižná revue* 11 (2002): 5.

———. "Uhorky a knihy: tak nás prikvačilo leto" [Cucumbers and Books: The Summer struggle]. *Fantázia* 36 (2006): 52.

Frišo, Peter. "O netvoroch a o jazyku" [On monsters and language]. *Impulz* 1 (2007): 154–160.

(frk.) "Pripravujú originálnu výstavu Hobbitov Petra Kľúčika" [They are preparing an original exhibition of Peter Kľúčik's hobbits]. 22 April 2002. https://korzar. sme.sk/c/4660206/pripravuju-originalnu-vystavu-hobbitov-petra-klucika.html. Accessed 23 July 2022.

Gottweisová, Alena. "Pán prsteňov – krása a smútok z prekladu" [The Lord of the Rings – Translation's Beauty and Sorrow]. *HN Online*, 6 December 2001. https://hnonline.sk/style/kultura/69992-pan-prstenov-krasa-a-smutok-z-prekladu. Accessed 27 July 2022.

Hyžný, "Loki" Matúš. "Galadriel". *Athelas* 9 (2005): 10.

———. "Jazykové pozadie slova 'ork'" [The linguistic background of the word 'orc']. *Athelas* 15 (2008): 10–11.

———. "Krajový kalendár alebo Ako zaznamenávali čas hobiti" [The Shire calendar of how the hobbits recorded time]. *Athelas* 7 (2005): 7.

———. "O Húrinových deťoch trochu inak" [On The Children of Húrin a little differently]. *Athelas* 14 (2007): 7.

———. "Professor Tolkien a 'Kraj' slovenský" [Professor Tolkien and the Slovak 'Shire']. *Athelas* 8 (2005): 9.

J., "Crankia" Katka. "Interview: Otakar Kořínek". *Athelas* 2 (2003): 6–7.

Jurdáková, "Crankia" Katarína. "J.R.R. Tolkien: Tulák Rover" [Roverandom]. *Athelas* 11 (2006): 3.

Juričková, Martina. "Ďalší zaujímavý knižný kúsok do fanúšikovskej zbierky?" [Another interesting book item for the fan collection?]. *Art, Communicaton & Popculture* 1–2 (2019): 229–233.

———. "O sklamaní cirkvou, pokušení neveriť a jedinom lieku" [On disappointment with the Church, the temptation not to believe, and the only medicine]. *Slovo+*, 22. October 2011. https://www.slovoplus.sk/o-sklamani-cirkvou-pokuseni-neverit-a-jedinom-lieku. Accessed 29 July 2022.

Juríčková, Eva. "John Ronald Tolkien". *História* 4 (2006): 35–37.

Karpinský, Peter. "Roverandom". *Bibiana* 4 (2002): 64–66.

116   Jozefa Pevčíková, Eva Urbanová

Klučariková, Daniela. "Problematika prekladu funkčných mien v diele J.R.R. Tolkiena *Pán prsteňov*" [On some problems in translation of functional names in The Lord of the Rings by J.R.R. Tolkien]. *Prekladateľské listy* 1 (2012): 29–34.

Kraviarová, Zuzana – Gendiar, Michal. "Slovenský *Hobit* – cesta tam alebo späť?" [Slovak Hobbit – The Way There or Back?]. *Kritika prekladu* 1 (2013): 61–83.

Kušnír, Jaroslav. "Legenda" [Legend]. *Kultúrny život* 8 (2002): 8.

Lobová, Andrea. "Fenomén Harry Potter a Pán prsteňov v čítaní pre deti a mládež" [Phenomenon of Harry Potter and The Lord of the Rings in the reading for children and young adults]. *Slovenský jazyk a literatúra v škole* 3–4 (2005–2006): 97–103.

Malíček, Juraj. *Popkultúra: návod na použitie* [Popculture: An instruction manual]. Nitra: Filozofická fakulta UKF v Nitre, 2012.

Mašek, "Frey" Tomáš. "Mini dodatok ohľadom SK prekladu" [Mini addition concerning the Slovak translation]. *Athelas* 2 (2003): 7.

O´Brien, D. Michael. "Harry Potter verzus Bilbo Baggins" [Harry Potter vs. Bilbo Baggins]. *Impulz* 1 (2006): 77–86.

Opoldusová, Jana. "Hobit zaujal Petra Kľúčika severskou bizarnosťou" [Peter Kľúčik was attracted to Hobbit's Nordic bizarreness]. *Pravda,* 4 December 2017. https://kultura.pravda.sk/galeria/clanok/450152-hobit-zaujal-petra-klucika-severskou-bizarnostou/. Accessed 12 February 2022.

Poláček, Ivo. "O niektorých aspektoch používania symbolov v dielach J.R.R. Tolkiena a hľadaní adekvátnych ekvivalentov v slovenskom preklade" [On some aspects of the use of symbols in the works of J.R.R. Tolkien and the search for adequate equivalents in the Slovak translation]. *Prekladateľské listy* 5 (2016): 105–111.

Suchý, Daniel. "Prsteň filmárov zviazal" [The Ring bound the film makers]. *Kultúrny život* 8 (2002): 8.

Sýkora, Peter. "Tolkien – pán svojej mytológie" [Tolkien – the Lord of his mythology]. *Rak – revue aktuálnej kultúry* 2 (2002): 42–44.

TASR. "Iný pohľad na kultového Hobita ponúka nová výstava" [New Exhibition offers a different view of Tolkien]. *Pravda*, 27 August 2018. https://kultura.pravda.sk/galeria/clanok/481843-novy-pohlad-na-kultoveho-hobita-ponuka-galeria-jozefa-kollara/. Accessed 12 April 2022.

Tolkien, J.R.R. *Húrinove deti*. Bratislava: Slovart, 2006.

Tyšš, Igor. "Preklad záhrobnej fantasy. Analýza prekladu žánrových motívov fantasy v knihe *The Graveyard Book*" [Translation of the underworld fantasy. Analysis of the translation of fantasy genre motifs in the Graveyard Book]. *Prekladateľské listy* 2 (2013): 114–124.

Volná, "Llewelyn" Martina. "Tolkien u nás" [Tolkien in our country]. *Fantázia* 4 (2001): 5–6.

Winklerová, Lucia. "Alegória, aktuálnosť, axiológia, a napriek tomu fantasy" [Allegory, relevance, axiology, and yet fantasy]. *Rak – revue aktuálnej kultúry* 8 (2007): 37–38.

———. "Ďalší rozvoj fenoménu J.R.R. Tolkien" [Further Development of the J.R.R. Tolkien Phenomenon]. *Romboid* 9 (2007): 81–82.

Zmeták, Igor. "Pán prsteňov – etika a mýtus v postmodernej kultúre" [The Lord of the Rings – ethics and myth in postmodern culture]. *Knižnica* 5 (2006): 60–61.

6 Unknotting the Translation Knots in *The Hobbit*

A Diachronic Analysis of Slovak Translations from 1973 and 2002

Jela Kehoe

The impact of J.R.R. Tolkien's literary contribution is undeniably present within the context of Central European readership, including the Slovak one. While there are many Slovak readers who read Tolkien in English nowadays, Slovak publishing houses have, every so often, been releasing Slovak translations of different Tolkien's works for over 50 years, in addition to a number of titles being available within the Slovak book market in the Czech language.[1]

This chapter aims to compare two Slovak versions of *The Hobbit*, the first one from 1973, which was translated by Viktor Krupa (1936–2021), and the other from 2002 by Otakar Kořínek (1946-). Both translators experienced the decades of socialism, and both became well-known translators, recognised for their high-quality translations. Their professional backgrounds differ, however. While Viktor Krupa was an academic (researching and publishing in linguistics and Oriental studies, working at Slovak Academy of Sciences), Otakar Kořínek was a lawyer, journalist and, before focusing full-time on translating, also worked in the diplomatic service. The publication of the 1973 version was initiated by Krupa himself. Subsequently, he was keen on translating *The Lord of the Rings* but was not successful in his lobbying of the publishing houses (see Pevčíková and Urbanová's chapter in this volume 95). Because Peter Jackson's *The Lord of the Rings* movies, and later *The Hobbit* movies, brought about a renewed interest in Tolkien, and presumably because he was the author of a Slovak translation of *The Lord of the Rings*, Otakar Kořínek was tasked with creating a new translation of *The Hobbit*.

It is also important to mention the Czech version of *The Hobbit* (*Hobit aneb Cesta tam a zase zpátky,* translated by František Vrba and published in 1979, six years after the Slovak translation) and the Czech version of *The Lord of the Rings* trilogy (translated by Stanislava Pošustová-Menšíková and published between 1990 and 1992, a good decade before the Slovak translation of this work). These translations undeniably impacted more than one generation of Slovak readers, particularly when considering the

DOI: 10.4324/9781003407171-9

118 *Jela Kehoe*

translation of nomenclature in Tolkien's works. Many members of the Slovak Tolkien's fandom have been quite vocal about disliking the Slovak equivalents of Middle-earth proper names, especially those devised by Otakar Kořínek. Others complained about having to deal with new nomenclature every time a new translator handled the source texts. The existence of a number of versions of Tolkien's texts in the two languages (Czech and Slovak), equally accessible to Slovak readers, is the reason why the Czech version of Middle-earth nomenclature will be occasionally discussed in the process of comparative analysis at hand. With almost three decades dividing the two Slovak versions of *The Hobbit* in Slovak language, this chapter focuses mainly on how the translators dealt with the nomenclature referring to people and places of Middle-earth, how they translated some of the culture-specific notions (rooted in the primary world of England) and how the instances of non-standard language used in the source text to distinguish and build the characters made it into the target language.

Translation is a relatively linear process of transposing a text, produced in the context of a source culture, and utilising a source language, into a target language in order for this text to inhabit a certain space within a target culture. Translation of literary texts in particular is seen not only as an act of communication between distinct literary traditions, but also between distinct cultures (see, for example, Bassnett; Lefevere; Toury) with the understanding that the reality in which the author functions and the intentions the author has as a primary creator of the text are as equally relevant as the reality in which the recipients reside and the expectations they have.

In the process of translation, translators must deal with expressions or notions which force them to pause and consider their options, so as to "unknot" the issue in the best possible manner, carrying through not just the core meaning, but also any stylistic features originally encoded within the expression. These knots are typically caused by an asymmetry or lack of equivalence that exists between the source language and culture and the target language and culture. Dealing with translation knots should always be a deliberate, conscious act informed by a thorough knowledge of both the source and target languages and their norms, as well as a deep understanding of the cultures involved. The task of a translator is ultimately to find the best possible solutions for untangling the knots and produce a text which will be as fluid, as informative and (in the case of literary translation) as rich in stylistic features as the original. When coming across a "knot" a translator typically deals with the tension caused by the dilemma of balancing between the approach of domestication and foreignisation when shifting the text from the source language and culture into a target language and culture. As translation strategies, domestication and foreignisation are two ends of a spectrum, allowing a translator

Unknotting the Translation Knots in The Hobbit   119

to make choices which either shape the resultant text to accommodate it to the target audience and to conform to the target culture or retain the cultural aspects of the source text to point to and to honour an "outside" origin of the text, hopefully widening the readers' horizons and enriching the target literature and culture in the process. Translators (particularly those more likely to produce foreignising translations) then function as cultural mediators.

The choice of either domesticating or foreignising a translation is often decided by the age of the target audience; the younger the audience, the greater the likelihood of the domestication. Extreme domestication, where anything outside the experiential horizon of the recipient (for example foreign proper nouns or culturally marked items) is replaced by items readily understood by the recipient (e.g. tapioca pudding as *krupicová kaša* [semolina pudding]), can only be justified when a very young audience (pre-school) is targeted. After all, nowadays, in our globalised world, most children are aware of the existence of other cultures from an early age. Literature written for children, such as fairy tales and fantasy literature, often present yet another layer of potential issues for translators. The stories told in fairy tales and fantasy literature rely on the environment they function in – their world – to contribute to the richness and other-worldness of the text. Therefore, translators need to keep in mind these secondary worlds and other realities.

Fantasy is a genre which creates secondary worlds (with villages, towns, cities surrounded by rivers, mountains, and plains) inhabited by people, creatures, animals, and supernatural beings. Most of these places and beings have names. This means that fantasy inherently contains a plethora of proper nouns which need to be transferred from the source text into the target text during the process of translation. Translation of proper nouns (or nomenclature) which are used in *The Hobbit* into the Slovak language has been discussed a few times both by scholars in academic journals and laymen, usually fans, within the fandom media. Because proper nouns may imply the social status of characters, their circumstances, and their personal qualities, they demand the translator's attention when rendered into a target language. Ferenčík (56) summarised the three translation strategies used and deemed as appropriate within Slovak translation tradition; either proper nouns can be transferred (which means taken unchanged from the source text to the target language) without any change to how they are spelled, or proper nouns can be modified (changing the proper nouns in some way to conform to the phonological and/or graphic conventions of the target language) or, lastly, "functional" proper nouns (those that carry additional information relevant to the character or place and therefore to the story) can be translated using appropriate semantic equivalents with the aim of enabling readers to appreciate the semantic content

120 *Jela Kehoe*

of the proper noun. Within the strategy of translating proper nouns is a strategy called cultural transplantation, a procedure in which the "SL [source language] names are replaced by indigenous TL [target language] names that are not their literal equivalents, but have similar cultural connotations" (Hervey and Higgins 29).

When translating *The Hobbit*, neither Krupa nor Kořínek had access to the abundance of information that Tolkien disclosed about Middle-earth and its people, history, and languages. *The Hobbit* is a story told in English, though as Tolkien himself said – according to Hammond and Scull – "English cannot have been the language of any people at that time. What I have, in fact, done is to equate the Westron or wide-spread Common Speech of the Third Age with English; and translate every-thing, including names such as *The Shire*, that was in the Westron into English terms" (Hammond and Scull 739). English therefore functions as a "default" language, a language denoting the familiar, setting apart the names from other languages (such as elvish or dwarfish) and other cultures, making them non-Hobbit or somewhat foreign.

Nevertheless, both Krupa and Kořínek intuitively handled these "foreign" names by means of transferring them into the target language in their original form (only occasionally modifying some – Dwalin becomes Dvalin in the 2002 version); so the names of the dwarfs, the wizards and the elves, as well as the name of the dragon retain their form: Dwalin, Balin, Kili, Fili, Dori, Nori, Ori, Oin, Gloin, Bifur, Bofur, Bombur, Thror, Thrain, Durin, Gandalf, Elrond, Smaug.

Translating functional proper nouns in *The Hobbit* (and also in *The Lord of the Rings*) has been problematic for many languages and Tolkien himself was famously upset over some of the Dutch and Swedish editions. He verbalised his frustration in respect to the Dutch version: "*In principle* I object as strongly as is possible to the 'translation' of the *nomenclature* at all (even by a competent person). I wonder why a translator should think himself called on or entitled to do any such thing" (Hammond and Scull 750).

This analysis shall focus on the 'knots', the items which in one or both versions required the translators to look for creative solutions and/or those which in one or both versions turned out problematic (suffering from stylistic and/or semantic obscuring or weakening, or even loss) or, quite the opposite, were instances of inspiration and creativity.

The first group of functional proper nouns to be considered will be the names of persons and beings. Tolkien offered an insight into his naming process in Appendix F of *The Lord of the Rings*: "Most of these [Hobbit] surnames had obvious meanings (in the current language being derived from jesting nicknames, or from place-names", the first-names usually "had no meaning at all in their daily language [...]. Of this kind are Bilbo, Bungo, [...] Tanta, Nina, and so on" (1135). This means that translating such names is

Unknotting the Translation Knots in The Hobbit   121

a process of looking for their semantic or cultural equivalents in the target language. The first (and the most important) name to consider is Bilbo Baggins of Bag-End. The first noticeable feature of this name is alliteration. Viktor Krupa's translation *Bilbo Lazník z Lazov* [an occupant of a remote hamlet] partially follows this lead with the repetition of the letter 'l', but, however, semantically fails to connect with the notion of 'a bag'. Otakar Kořínek's solution *Bilbo Bublík z Vreckán* uses alliteration to the same extent as Krupa's. The word *Vreckany* is etymologically connected to the word *vrecko* [pocket], which is a departure from the notion of a bag. Also, *Vreckany* is plural and thus evokes a group of dwellings, a village, which does not line up with Bag End as a reference to one separate home/house. František Vrba in his 1979 Czech translation uses *Pytlík* [little bag] as an equivalent to Baggins. Even though it avoids the alliteration of the original, the pattern of using a suffix *-ík* (creating a diminutive) emulates the playful -ins suffix of the original. Next, let us consider the names Belladonna Took and Bullroarer Took. Krupa used the name *Belladonna Berková* and *Rapkáč Berko*. *Berko/Berková* are good equivalents of the name Took. The solution for Bullroarer is quite interesting. Krupa (possibly being aware of bullroarers being Australian aboriginal artefacts, sort of ritual musical instruments which are swung in circles to produce a sound) used the equivalent *Rapkáč* [cog rattle]. Kořínek used the names *Ručivec Bral* and *Beladona Bralová* to translate these names. Kořínek's solution for Belladonna employs the modification *Beladona*, possibly because Slovak readers are likely to be familiar with a plant of the same name. The surname *Bral/Bralová* [he took *Bral* combined with a feminine surname suffix] would probably be better for the Czech language, as Czech commonly uses past simple verb forms for surnames (e.g. Musil, Donutil). The solution *Ručivec* [the one who roars] for Bullroarer could be seen as a better option than reference to the aboriginal instrument, considering that the hobbits were inspired by rural farming folk where roaring bulls are much more common than a ritual musical instrument from Australia. The last surname item in this hobbit group is the name of the auctioneers handling the sale of (presumed dead) Bilbo's effects; Messrs Grubb, Grubb, and Burrowes. The original name hints at the meaning "grub" (a worm like stage of insects found for example in manure, soil or rotting wood) and Burrowes can be interpreted as "digs". It is possible to claim that Krupa's solution *páni Červeňovci a Králikovci* [červeň can refer to the red colour of playing cards, *králik* means rabbit] does not have quite the same, potentially unpleasant associations for the readers as the source text surnames. Kořínek's solution *kancelária Chmat, Chmat a Hrab* explicates Messrs as *kancelária* [office, firm] and partially follows the semantic hints of the original surnames "Grubb, Grubb, and Burrowes" with *Chmat, Chmat a Hrab* ['a grab, a grab and dig!', Slovak *hrab* can also be connected to an adjective *hrabivý* – greedy], which overall makes for a better solution to this knot.

122 *Jela Kehoe*

Next, we will look at Slovak translations of Thorin Oakenshield, Gollum, and Beorn. Krupa weakened the character by defining Oakenshield with his *Thorin z Dubnej* [*z Dubnej* means from Dubná, denoting a settlement], which can be classed as semantic obscuring. With his *Thorin Dubbin*, Kořínek decided to imply the 'oak' association (*dub* means oak in Slovak). The characterising power of the nickname Oakenshield remains weakened within this solution too. A solution *Zdubaštít* [shield of oak], which semantically and phonologically emulates the original, could, hypothetically be an option. The name Gollum is approached semantically by Krupa – *Glgúň* [derived from *glgať, hltať* which mean to swallow] and phonetically by Kořínek who created the name *Gloch*. Both solutions have their merit, though Kořínek's solution, in our opinion, better mimics the coughing noise that Gollum makes and that his name is based upon. *Glum* is the Czech equivalent devised by František Vrba. It is also the translation of the proper noun Gollum which Slovak fandom seems to favour. Beorn's name reflects that he is a shape-shifter who can change into a large bear. Krupa chose to carry the name into the Slovak translation without any change. Kořínek decided to explicate with his *Grizlo* using a slight adjustment of the spelling [Slovak *grizly* is a loan of English word "grizzly"]. Interesting, as well as creative, is the Czech version of Beorn – *Medděd* – which is a blend of *medvěd* [bear] and *děd* [old man, grandpa], successfully pointing to the fact that Beorn is a bear as well as a man.

Inanimate objects are often assigned names in fantasy literature. Our translators of *The Hobbit* probably paused to come up with creative and expressive names for the descriptive elements of the Elven swords Orcrist, the Goblin-cleaver, and Glamdring, Foe-hammer. While Krupa chose whole clauses to denote the attributes of the two swords in literal translation: *Orcrist, Sekáč na škriatkov* and *Glamdring, Kladivo na nepriateľov*, Kořínek decided to use compounding which resembles the source language strategy and packs in the meaning denoted by the original names; *Orcrist, Škratosek* and *Glamdring, Vrahomlat*. This naming strategy is often found in Slovak fairy tales (for example *Valibuk* [the one who knocks over beech trees] or *Zemetras* [the one who shakes the ground]) and therefore may contribute to Slovak readers' perception of *The Hobbit* being fairy-tale like.

The Arkenstone is a jewel which plays a very important part in the story and the two translators brought their own original solutions, using the same strategy of applying a suffix which denotes stone. Viktor Krupa used the suffix -*it* to create the name *arkenit*. He also applied the grammatical norm of the Slovak language where the names of precious or semi-precious stones are not treated as proper nouns and therefore not capitalised. Otakar Kořínek's solution to this knot is *Archakam*, where the suffix -*kam* points to the noun *drahokam* [a blend of *drahocenný*, meaning precious and *kameň*, meaning stone]. Kořínek kept the capital letter for the name of

Unknotting the Translation Knots in The Hobbit   123

this stone, which could be interpreted as reference to the Arkenstone being the only one in existence, whereas Krupa's solution denotes a type of stone.

The last pieces of nomenclature this chapter will focus on are the "knotty" place names. Three items stand out: Mirkwood, Rivendell, and Withered Heath. Tolkien advised translators to "[T]translate by sense, if possible using elements of poetic or antique tone" (Hammond and Scull 774). Neither translator seems to have been aware of this advice, but both chose to imply "dark wood". The word "mirk" is an old-fashioned spelling of *"murk"* (darkness or thick mist that makes it difficult to see) and Viktor Krupa's Čierny les [black wood] is a straightforward translation without any extra stylistic layer. Otakar Kořínek's solution *Temnohvozd* does introduce that extra stylistic layer, since the word *hvozd* [large thick wood] is no longer in everyday use, rather it is felt to belong to literary, bookish lexicon. Because of this, Kořínek's *Temnohvozd* is technically a more appropriate solution, though the fans of Middle-earth find this name "somewhat distracting" (Kraviarová and Gendiar 69). Not having Tolkien's advice, the Slovak translators were left to their devices when dealing with the place name Rivendell. Krupa's solution *Rivendellská dolina* uses explication by means of adding *dolina* [valley] and using the noun Rivendell as an adjectival element in Slovak translation. Kořínek (making the same interpretative mistake as the Swedish translator) translated the item as *Vododol* [the element *vodo* definitely denotes water, the element *dol* can be interpreted as a valley, but also a pit or a mine], which is inaccurate. František Vrba's *Roklinka* [split/cloven valley] in the 1979 Czech translation can be considered the best of the three as it most successfully follows Tolkien's intention. Translation of the proper noun Withered Heath is the last item within the topic of nomenclature that this chapter will comment on. Krupa translated this place name as *Mŕtvy vres* [dead heather], which is more likely to bring up in readers' minds an image of a dead plant rather than a place or area "where the great dragons bred" (Tolkien, *The Hobbit* 29). Kořínek's *Povädnuté vresovisko* is halfway to a better solution. While the word *vresovisko* [area where heather grows] is narrower in meaning than the word heath, it denotes a place or area. Having said that, the adjective *povädnuté* is closer to the English word wilted than to withered, which weakens the expressive potential of Kořínek's solution. One might suggest the combination of the two solutions (*Mŕtve vresovisko* [dead heath]) could carry the desired meaning and mood.

Translation of nomenclature can be a point of contention between the fanbase and translators. The stories told in books are no longer limited to those books, and now, more than ever before, our existence and our world can be viewed as being interconnected. Because the secondary worlds nowadays often stretch beyond the pages they were written on into new modes and media, the readers are often consumers of non-literary products

124   *Jela Kehoe*

based on these secondary worlds. For example, the Wizarding World or the Marvel Cinematic Universe produce a massive range of merchandise (music scores, clothing, toys, different types of collectables, everyday use objects, such as mugs, pens, calendars, etc.) on top of adaptations of actual texts which can have the form of movies, television series, theatre productions or even computer games. All this might in some way create additional value for the readers, making the secondary world's presence felt in their everyday lives through tangible objects or experiences. A consistent, true-to-the-original target language nomenclature would allow for these worlds to be transplanted to target culture. When the secondary world lives so many lives outside the pages of the book, may be translating the nomenclature should be a team effort, a process of choosing the best versions from different translations (older book translations, newer book translations, radio adaptation translations, subtitling and dubbing, etc.) in order to compile this consistent nomenclature that the audience could enjoy within every reincarnation of the story.

Culture-specific concepts have a potential to complicate the translator's life in two ways. Firstly, when a translator is not fully or at all familiar with the concept in question or has an incorrect understanding of it and secondly, when the concept does not exist in the target language and culture. To find a solution, an appropriate translation typically lies within the scope of either cultural equivalent, functional equivalent, or descriptive equivalent (Newmark 82). Tolkien's *The Hobbit* contains some food related concepts that needed attention to be solved effectively. The following discussion will pertain to culture-specific concepts which Viktor Krupa and Otakar Kořínek left somewhat knotted. We shall start with "buttered scones". Both translators chose the functional equivalent *maslové šišky* (fluffy sweet pastry deep fried and filled with jam) which does not match the idea of scones (drier, more dense, baked pastry). Perhaps, a descriptive equivalent, e.g. *sladké žemličky s maslom* [buttered sweet buns] might be a more suitable solution. Another sweet treat mentioned in *The Hobbit*, "mince-pies", tripped up both Krupa (who used the functional equivalent *pirohy* [boiled, deep fried or baked sweet pastry]) and Kořínek (who explicated the same functional equivalent and used *ovocné pirohy* [boiled, deep fried or baked sweet pastry with fruit]), as *pirohy* do not resemble "mince-pies" neither in shape or texture, nor in flavour. The most problematic out of the culture-specific food stuff is "pork-pies". Savoury/meaty pies with a crust made of pastry are not at all common in Slovak cuisine. Krupa used the quite appropriate functional equivalent *pagáčiky*. *Pagáčik* is a round savoury pastry with bits of cheese, bacon or ground scratchings worked into the pastry, rather than used as filling, as is the case with the pork-pie. Kořínek decided to use the word *tlačenka* which is not the best choice, as there is no dough or pastry used in this dish.

Unknotting the Translation Knots in The Hobbit   125

For the most part, Tolkien wrote *The Hobbit* in standard English. There are, though two unmissable interactions where Tolkien employed a departure from standard English; the first one is when Bilbo met the trolls (whose speech contained dialectal features) and the second one is when Bilbo spoke to Gollum (who used his own idiolect). In comparison to other nations and their languages, Slovak literary tradition is relatively young and so is the Slovak translation canon. The strategies determining when and how to translate non-standard language varied over the years, resulting in some devastatingly weakened target texts (Huckleberry Finn speaking very polite standard Slovak), but also in some experimental English regional to Slovak regional transpositions. Anton Popovič, one the most influential translations studies scholars in Slovakia, suggests that "the standardised version, enriched with colloquial elements and emphasizing unique characteristics, is an equivalent stylistic solution to the original" (175)[2] which uses regional or social dialects. Let us now observe how Viktor Krupa and Otakar Kořínek unknotted the non-standard speech of the trolls and of Gollum. Tolkien used the dialectal speech of the trolls to set them apart from Bilbo, whose speech is proper, educated, sometimes even formal. The trolls' utterances also provide little bit of comic relief, realised through the use of dialect itself, but also other features, for example the fact that the trolls have regular names – William, Bert, and Tom – or the fact that when they prepare their food (apart from animals also unfortunate dwarfs, hobbits, or people), they might use different (on occasion quite sophisticated) ways of cooking them. "'Mutton yesterday, mutton today, and blimey, if it don't look like mutton again tomorer', said one of the trolls. 'Never a blinking bit of manflesh have we had for long enough', said a second. 'What the 'ell William was a -thinkin' of to bring us into these parts at all, beats me'" (43). This excerpt contains non-standard features at the level of lexis (blimey, blinking), grammar (it don't look like, was a -thinkin') and pronunciation (tomorer, 'ell, thinkin'). Krupa's solution "'*Baranina včera, baranina dnes a nech ma čert zoberie, ak si aj zajtra nebudem zasa pochutnávať na baranine,' zavrčal ktorýsi troll. 'Ako dávno sme si nepochutili na ľudskom mäse,' ohlásil sa druhý. 'Sto hrmených, nejde mi do kotrby, načo nás William ťahal do tohto zapadákova'*" (39) has no non-standard grammar, lexis is standard, rather than dialectal and there is no non-standard pronunciation. He uses colloquial expressions (e.g. *nech ma čert zoberie* [let devil take me] instead of "blimey") and strengthened expressiveness (e.g. *zavrčal* [growled] instead of "said" to create equivalent colour and mood. Kořínek uses the same strategy, with slightly different wording: "'*Včera baranina, dnes baranina, a nech ma rozdrapí, ak to nebudeme žrať aj zajtra,' zahuhňal jeden z nich. 'O ľudské maso sme nezavadili, ani sa nepamätám,' prízvukoval druhý. 'Fuj! Načo nás sem Bill zavliekol, to mi teda nejdo do makovice'*" (37). While Krupa

126 Jela Kehoe

added *pochutnávať* [enjoy] mutton, Kořínek also added a verb denoting eating *žrať* [gobble, stuff faces with] his wording is rougher, more what we would expect from a troll. Similar strategies and results can be seen when the following utterance was translated: "Lumme, if I knows! What are yer?" (44). 'Lumme' is an exclamation used to express surprise, interest, or approval. "if I knows" is grammatically non-standard and "yer" is a non-standard pronunciation of "you". Neither Krupa "*Nech sa prepadnem, ak viem! Čo si?*" (40), nor Kořínek "*Nech ma porantá, ak viem! Čo si zač?*" (38) carried through non-standard grammar or pronunciation. The exclamation is translated using cultural equivalents that mean "let me be damned". The sequence "look what I've copped!" (44) contains a non-standard word "copped". Krupa's solution "*pozri, čo som chytil!*"(40) [look what I caught] could be considered a stylistic loss, while Kořínek's version "*pozri, čo som lapil!*" (38) manages to express the non-standard feature by using a colloquial word *lapil*.

Gollum's idiolect is rooted neither in any regional nor social dialect of the English language. It is "Gollum specific"; marked by particular pronunciation with extra sibilants (preciousss, iss, handses), non-standard grammar (ye sits here and chats, we eats it) and by referring to himself in the plural (bless us and splash us … it must have a competition with us). The sibilant marked utterance, so typical for Gollum: "What iss he, my preciouss?" (78), is weakened in Krupa's Slovak translation to the point of stylistic loss: "*Čo je to, môj poklad?*" (70) as it uses standard language with no idiolectal pronunciation. The more contemporary (Kořínek's) translation fares much better because the translator in his version "*Šo je ono zaš, môj milušký?*" (63) successfully carries forth the specific pronunciation (šo, zaš, and *milušký* instead of the standard čo, zač, and *milučký*). Also, *milušký* (as diminutive of "dear") with its sibilant š/č much better emulates the sibilants of the source word than *poklad* [treasure] with no sibilants at all. The idiolectal nature of "What's he got in his handses?" (78), where Gollum addresses Bilbo in the third person singular 'he', 'his' instead of 'you', 'your' is completely lost in Krupa's very much standard "*Čo to máš v rukách?*" (70). Kořínek unknotted this problem with "*Šo to má v rušiškách?*" (63), carrying forth the third person singular and also finding an appropriate equivalent for the idiolectal "handses" (*rušišky* instead of standard *ručičky*). The following excerpt contains a number of interesting knots that the translators had to deal with: "Praps ye sits here and chats with it a bitsy, my precious. It like riddles, praps it does, does it?" (78), for example colloquial pronunciation of "praps" instead of the standard "perhaps", old-fashioned or Irish English inspired "ye", non-standard grammar of "ye/you sits and chats" and idiolectal "a bitsy" instead of the standard "a bit". Viktor Krupa partially maintained Gollum's idiolect with "*Azda ssi tu possedíš a pohovoríšš ss ním trošku,*

Unknotting the Translation Knots in The Hobbit   127

poklad môj. Má rado hádanky, azzda má rado, vššak?" (70), employing only extra sibilants in Gollum's utterance (standard pronunciation would be denoted as *Azda si tu posedíš a pohovoríš s ním trošku, poklad môj. Má rado hádanky, azda má rado, však?* Otakar Kořínek chose a similar strategy: *"Šo keby sme si sadli a trošiška si pobesedovali, môj milušký? Má rád hádanky, hádanšišky? Má?"* (63), though rather than just doubling the existing sibilants like Krupa, Kořínek replaces one sibilant with another to strengthen the idiolectal effect (čo becomes šo, *trošička* becomes *trošiška*, *milučký* becomes *milušký* and *hádanky* [riddles] becomes *hádanšišky* with additional diminutive quality).

The main idiolectal feature of the last excerpt, "If precious asks and it doesn't answer, we eats it, my preciouss, If it asks us, and we doesn't answer, then we does what it wants, eh? We shows it the way out, yes!" (79), is its non-standard grammar ("we eats it", "we doesn't answer", "we shows it"). Viktor Krupa's solution weakens the stylistic, character defining language of the source text with the usage of standard grammar: *"Keď sa poklad opýta, a ono neodpovie, zjeme ho, poklad môj. Keď sa ono opýta nás, a my neodpovieme, potom urobíme to, čo ono chce, hm? Ukážeme mu cestu von, áno!"* (71). Kořínek with his solution *"Keď sa milušký opýta a ono neuhádne, tak zjeme, môj milušký. Keď sa spýta nás a my neuhádneme, potom urobíme, šo ono chce, áno? Ukážme cestu von, tak!"* (64) made use of somewhat non-standard grammar by leaving out objects in two clauses: *tak [ho/to/ťa] zjeme, ukážme [mu/ti] cestu von.*

It is important to acknowledge that any departure from standard language is utilised by the author with a concrete aim in mind and creates opportunity for readers to not only "recognise a speaker's group- or class-membership, but [also] his linguistic idiosyncrasies [which] contribute to the reader's recognition of the protagonist's individualised character. If these typical speech elements are not reproduced in translation, then part of what makes each protagonist unique is lost" (Bayona 69).

The time, the different socio-political context and the differences in motivation and professional experience of the two translators separate the two Slovak versions of *The Hobbit*. Nevertheless, both versions are of very high quality and both translators demonstrated a great deal of creativity and a thorough knowledge of both the source language and the target language when rendering this well-known fantasy into Slovak language.

Notes

1 Even though the ability to read Czech seems to be somewhat in decline amongst the Slovak readers, for decades, while belonging to the same country (Czechoslovakia), the two nations shared the mass media (TV, radio and press). As a result, many Slovak readers are as comfortable reading in Czech as in Slovak.

128 *Jela Kehoe*

2 Author's translation in the text. Original version: [...] spisovná verzia, obohatená o hovorové prvky a zvýrazňujúca kolorit, je ekvivalentným štylistickým riešením originálu.

Works Cited

Bassnett, Susan and André Lefevere, eds. *Constructing Cultures. Essays on Literary Translations.* Clevedon: Multilingual Matters, 1998.

Bayona, Sandra. "Begging your pardon, Con el perdón de usted: Some Socio-Linguistic Features in *The Lord of the Rings* in English and Spanish". *Tolkien in Translation.* Ed. Thomas Honegger. Zurich: Walking Tree Publishers, 2011. 69–90.

Ferenčík, Ján. *Kontexty prekladu* [Contexts of Translation]. Bratislava: Slovenský spisovateľ, 1982.

Hammond, Wayne G. and Christina Scull. *The Lord of The Rings: A Reader's Companion.* London: HarperCollins, 2005.

Hervey, Sándor and Ian Higgins. *Thinking Translation.* London: Routledge, 1992.

Kraviarová, Zuzana and Michal Gendiar. "Slovenský *Hobit* – cesta tam alebo späť?" [Slovak Hobbit – there or back again?] *Kritika prekladu* 1 (2013): 61–83.

Lefevere, André, ed. *Translation/History/Culture.* London: Routledge, 1992.

Newmark, Peter. *A Textbook of Translation.* Hoboken: Prentice Hall, 1988.

Popovič, Anton. *Teória umeleckého prekladu* [Theory of Artistic Translation]. Bratislava: Tatran, 1975.

Toury, Gideon. *Descriptive Translation Studies – And Beyond.* Philadelphia: John Benjamins, 1995.

Tolkien, J.R.R. *Hobbiti.* Bratislava: Mladé letá, 1973.

———. *Hobit aneb Cesta tam a zase zpátky.* Praha: Odeon, 1979.

———. *The Hobbit.* London: HarperCollins, 1993.

———. *Hobit alebo cesta tam a späť.* Bratislava: Slovart, 2002.

———. *The Lord of the Rings.* London: HarperCollins, 2005.

Part III

Studying Fantasy after Tolkien

Legacies and Contemporary Perspectives

7 Growing Up in Fantasy

Inspecting the Convergences of Young Adult Literature and Fantastic Fiction

Martina Vránová

Introduction

Young adult literature (YAL) has firmly established itself as a successful product of book marketing. According to Michael Cart, author and editor of young adult books, in the late 1980s a good year for YAL saw the publication of about 250 titles in the USA; after 2010, it was more than 5,000 titles ("The Present and the Prospective" 14). Cart also states that in 2017 there were at least 27 US publishers' imprints specialising in YAL ("A New Golden Age" 41). Any online search nowadays yields a much higher number. Even though such easily available data comes primarily from the USA, the situation in Europe is very much the same. Since 2000, YAL has been one of the most dominant genres visible not only on bookshelves but also on TV, film, and computer screens. For example, "German literature for children and young adults is wide-ranging and diverse: almost 8,000 first-run titles were released last year (2019)" (Breitmoser and Beccaria n. p.). The problem with YAL, which only got more pronounced and particularly entangled with its booming success, is in its definition by age, which implies a transgression of clear-cut genre boundaries. Short et al. in *Essentials of Young Adult Literature* (2015) list eight main genres of YAL, each of them having several genre variations, including fantasy. The truth is that "fantasy renaissance led by *Harry Potter* and *His Dark Materials* brought a huge financial windfall to the field [of YAL], making publishers realise just how lucrative the market could be if it grew beyond its problem novel origins" (Hunt 142). Even though the slide toward fantasy has manifested itself in many literary genres, I will argue that it is particularly fitting for YAL. This fortunate union of YAL and fantasy is caused by the peculiarities of YA fiction worldbuilding in which the specifics of the audience play a key role. Aided by the use of Jungian psychology informed approaches and cognitive narratology, I inspect the audience's search for identity which is particularly facilitated by their journey into the possible worlds and the sense of otherness, of being a misfit, which is common to both genres. To

DOI: 10.4324/9781003407171-11

132   *Martina Vránová*

portray how YA fantasy intensifies the above-mentioned features, I trace them first in realist YAL, John Green's *Looking for Alaska*, then in fantasy of a traditional type, Andrzej Sapkowski's *The Witcher* series, and finally in YA fantasy, Ransom Rigg's *Miss Peregrine* series.

My initial motivation for working with these three titles was to choose ones that can be as clear examples of their genres as possible (even though, as will be discussed further on, this is very unstable ground to tread on). My criterion was first whether any legacy can be traced to the writings of J.R.R. Tolkien as the founding father of the fantasy genre as we know it now. John Green, chosen as an author of realistic YA fiction, "has been praised for 'saving young adult fiction' by sheer virtue of not writing fantasy like other authors for teenagers" ("The Problem of Fantasy Fiction" n.p.). Ransom Riggs, on the other hand, acknowledges J.R.R. Tolkien and C.S. Lewis as early influences on his imagination ("Ransom Riggs" n.p.), and Sapkowski, himself called the Polish Tolkien, claims reading Tolkien in the 1960s "was a revelation" to him (Gravemaster n.p.). Distinguishing adult fantasy from YA fantasy was more problematic. In an interview, Ransom Riggs acknowledges the role of marketing: "'Miss Peregrine' was not conceived or composed with a young-adult audience in mind, but its central premise – about people who are 'peculiar' in various ways and must struggle not only to survive, but also to save the clueless rest of humanity from violent evildoers – is certainly adolescent-friendly" ("A Book that Started with Its Pictures" n.p.). Similarly, Tolkien faced publication problems with his *The Lord of the Rings*, now considered an essential part of the canon for YAL, which was "not the children's book [like *The Hobbit*] his publishers requested" but "did not fit current fashions of adult fiction either" (Yates 827). However, sometimes marketing may be a bit too greedy to sell. Sapkowski's *The Witcher*, especially after the release of PC and video games, can be found marketed as YAL. Nevertheless, we also find a content warning: "Readers sensitive to mature content should approach the literary Witcher series with caution equitable to how one would approach the video games. Whereas *The Chronicles of Narnia* is written with children in mind, the target audience for the Witcher series is adults" (Pogue n.p.). The truth is that scenes drawing on Slavic folklore which may be "darker than the uncensored Grimm and Perault" and Geralt's endless "cynical stance" (Sims n.p.) and coming to terms with the role of a teacher and surrogate father point towards adult fiction rather than YAL.

Defining YAL

YAL has been notoriously difficult to define. Jonathan Stephens, for example, notes: "As America's readership continues to shrink, marketing departments scramble for new strategies for getting books into readers' hands" (34).

Growing Up in Fantasy 133

The result of this confused marketing, according to Stephens, is that the category of YAL gets packed with anything remotely connected to the lives of adolescents, very often having poor aesthetic value. Scot Smith (2007) also ponders upon the transgression of clear-cut genre boundaries and a frequent merge of realism and fantasy in contemporary YAL and comes to the conclusion that the root of the problematic classification of YAL as a genre is its definition by audience. Indeed, young adulthood or adolescence is the most difficult stage in human life. Teenagers and adolescents are considered problematic as they rebel, stand up to authority, slip through their parents' and educators' fingers. It is then, ironically, only fitting that literature for such an ungraspable crowd should also defy pre-set boundaries. The difficulty of definition is, however, not only caused by the target audience but also by those who want to define the genre. "The genres of children's and young adult literature are themselves fuzzy sets, culturally and structurally protean [...] and resistant to a satisfying poetics [...] This resistance is a result of the competing textual, subtextual, and contextual approaches and agendas of critics, parents, librarians, and teachers" (Cadden 303). The ideas of those in authority over adolescents of what is desirable to be labelled YAL are at odds.

To avoid the sole determination by audience, Stephens identifies five features, the combination of which comprise the genre of YAL. Unconsciously though, he reinforces the definition by audience because his first four features are essential characteristics of the psyche of young adults: "As I see it, the label 'Young Adult' refers to a story that tackles the difficult, and oftentimes adult, issues that arise during an adolescent's journey toward identity, a journey told through a distinctly teen voice that holds the same potential for a literary value as its 'Grownup' peers" (40–41). He goes on in order to present his own criteria: YAL is written about teens, in a distinctly teen voice, portrays a journey towards identity, focuses on tackling adult issues, and has the same potential for literary value as grownup novels (Stephens 41). If we disregard the last didactic criterion, as any literary genre is composed of outstanding pieces as well as works of dubious quality, we can immediately see that Stephens's criteria are particularly character driven. They focus on the hero's character-forming journey complicated but also facilitated by life-threatening obstacles. Moreover, there is an implied informative value for the readers. The readers form a bond with the hero in order to get immersed into a literary world which in the end has an impact on their own lives, cognition, experience formation. The strong, indeed heroic, characters undergoing an ordeal in a fantastic world in order to emerge as changed individuals make up the most common themes of fantasy. This is the reason why I believe these two genres are destined for each other.

Understanding that adolescence means looking for one's place in the world and answering the question "Who am I?" should be acknowledged to

134 *Martina Vránová*

Erik Erikson whose developmental psychology, particularly when it comes to identity formation, has not been surpassed yet. Erikson takes a psychosocial twist on psychoanalysis and claims that each stage of life is characterised by a crisis which is to be resolved so that a human being can develop healthily. As Erikson puts it, "the stage of adolescing becomes an even more marked and conscious period" than all other stages in the human lifecycle (128). This crisis is accompanied by attempts to establish a final definition of oneself, disregarding the fact that growing up is a process never to be finished: "[Y]oung people, beset with the physiological revolution of their genital maturation and the uncertainty of the adult roles ahead, seem much concerned with faddish attempts at establishing an adolescent subculture with what looks like a final rather than transitory [...] identity formation" (128). Such attempts necessarily lead to multiple redefinitions, which is productive in the sense of finding one's way through life but also very confusing and potentially frustrating. These redefinitions, resulting in identity confusion, encompass all aspects of young people's lives:

> [I]t is the inability to settle on an occupational identity which most disturbs young people. To keep themselves together they temporarily overidentify with the heroes of cliques and crowds to the point of an apparently complete loss of individuality. Yet in this stage not even 'falling in love' is entirely, or even primarily, a sexual matter. To a considerable extent adolescent love is an attempt to arrive at a definition of one's identity by projecting one's diffused self-image on another and by seeing it thus reflected and gradually clarified (132).

One of the roles of YAL is then to serve as such mirror image. Not only does a young person, through the experience of reading, compare one's situation to that of the hero's but, through the projection into the hero's fictional quest, he or she encounters many more incentives against which he or she can identify oneself.

Such a setting with endless paths to follow presents a fertile ground for literary production, resulting in the quest motif which is "at the center of virtually all works of fantasy fiction" (Melanson 2). The main protagonist's individual growth from an insignificant, often underprivileged, person to a hero defining not only his or her own destiny but also the future path of his or her fantastic world can be found in most books of fantasy, as the stress on an individual is inherent to it. Melanson formulates the appeal of fantasy, through the lens of Erikson's Jungian psychoanalysis, in the following way: "we relate to a hero's encounter with powerful forces and dangerous obstacles and difficult choices not because they replicate by mimesis our daily struggles, but because they resonate on a grand and imaginative scale with the challenges that life poses to each individual" (5). Even though the referential value of literature to readers' everyday lives cannot be so easily dismissed, the grounding of fantasy in myths and legends indeed makes it possible to view it as an artistic recreation of Jungian archetypes springing from the collective unconscious. It is probably not a coincidence that the two founding fathers of contemporary fantasy and writers for children and young adults, J.R.R. Tolkien and C.S. Lewis, were medievalists. Fantasy may be viewed as a modern rebirth of the medieval romance in which a psychologically incomplete hero sets out on a quest to achieve a tangible goal, ridding a country of a monster or just jousting with other knights, and along the way he also achieves mental, psychological, or moral development. We only have to look back to Timothy R. O'Neill's *The Individuated Hobbit: Jung, Tolkien, and the Archetypes of Middle-earth* in which he focuses on "obvious relevance of Jung's psychology of Self-realization" to Tolkien's works (xi). The purpose of his thorough Jungian analysis is to "demonstrate that the framework of Tolkien's world is truly in harmony with 'real' myth and fairy tale, that they are woven of the same strand of human psyche" (3). Human psychological wiring revealed in archetypes is responsible for both Tolkien's work as well as the mythology he drew on. His followers in the fantasy and YAL genres may be influenced by his work, yet it is the human psyche that is primarily expressed in their works. Tolkien did not consciously write an allegory of Jung's ideas and his followers do not copy him. Nevertheless, the tremendous and ongoing success of his works has played a role in promoting and popularising these genres together with the Jungian archetypes underlying them.

Joseph Campbell's monomyth in its multiple variations has been recognised to be still retold in contemporary literary and cinematic production, particularly in the genre of fantasy. Campbell originally discusses classical myths and legends suggesting that there is an underlying archetypal structure incorporated in them which is modelled on the rite of passage. "The standard path of the mythological adventure of the hero is a magnification of the formula represented in the rites of passage: *separation – initiation – return*: which might be named the nuclear unit of the monomyth" (23). Resolving each of Erikson's life crisis is a reenactment of the archetype of the self as a hero on a quest, which is particularly pronounced in the adolescence.

The Loner on a Quest

A brief survey of realistic YAL, fantasy, and YA fantasy will illuminate this shared feature of a hero on the quest for identity. First, let us start with realistic YAL – John Green's *Looking for Alaska*. Miles is a nerdy boy who has no real friends in his Florida hometown. He himself comes up with the plan to leave and go to his father's boarding school in order to

136   *Martina Vránová*

cultivate his intellect and seek the "Great Perhaps", as François Rabelais said in his last words (Green 5). His parents organise a farewell party for him but in the end, Miles says: "I sat with my parents and stared at the blank TV and wanted to turn it on but knew I shouldn't. I could feel them both looking at me, waiting for me to burst into tears [...] I could feel their pity as they scooped artichoke dip with chips intended for imaginary friends, but they needed the pity more than I did" (4). Green sets up Miles as a misfit in his ordinary life who feels the pressing need to escape. At boarding school Miles engages in self-defining fights with authorities, such as the dean and the religion teacher, as well as with fellow students, the Weekly Warriors. The process of identity formation is, however, always social as one cannot identify oneself without identifying with a group of people; one needs to prove oneself to be loyal to a group and thus learn to trust in oneself. In YAL, as well as in fantasy, it is the misfit of the main character who eventually finds a company of other misfits. Miles thus forms a "band of brothers" with his roommate Chip "The Colonel" Martin, who comes from a poor background and is a strategic mastermind in prank playing, Takumi Hikoto, a Japanese MC and hip-hop enthusiast, Lara Buterskaya, a Romanian immigrant, and Alaska Young, an emotionally unstable girl who is guilt ridden for causing the death of her mother. Only as such a group of misfits are they able to survive in the competitive environment of the boarding school. Miles, now nicknamed Pudge, falls in love with Alaska only to realise when she dies how much this relationship shaped him as a person:

[S]he had embodied the Great Perhaps – she had proved to me that it was worth it to leave behind my minor life for grander maybes, and now she was gone and with her my faith in perhaps [...] You can't just make yourself matter and then die, Alaska, because now I am irretrievably different, and I'm sorry I let you go, yes, but you made the choice. You left me Perhapsless, stuck in your goddamned labyrinth (172).

Even though Miles may sound desperate in this passage, he also knows that through Alaska's mirror he realised some of his potential. His quest for the Great Perhaps is indeed labyrinthine and he needs to set another Perhaps as a goal in order to live. In Campbell's terms, Miles has undergone separation and initiation and is about to return to his original community.

Andrzej Sapkowski's *The Witcher* series is also a contemporary example of the enactment of the monomyth and the rite of passage. The immense success of the books inspiring computer games, comic books, and TV series only proves Melanson's point of the human need to relive Jungian archetypes through the medium of the fantasy genre. Especially in the first two books of short stories, on the surface we can see a

Growing Up in Fantasy 137

uniform structure shared with many legends, myths, and fairy tales. The hero comes into a community with a problem, sets out on a journey to solve this problem, and finally comes back with a boon. Thus, Geralt[1] is hired by a community tormented by a monster which he slays. Yet on a more intimate level, Geralt undergoes the whole psychological cycle of Campbell's hero. Geralt is called to an adventure by a blunder "which reveals an unsuspected world, and the individual is drawn into a relationship with forces that are not rightly understood. [...] The blunder may amount to the opening of a destiny" (Campbell 42). This is the situation when after saving Duny, Geralt foolishly calls in the law of surprise. Even though he knows that he was abandoned as a child by his mother, he falls back on the popular legend that witchers replenish their numbers by demanding that which their debtors are ignorant of owning: "Duny! You will give me that which you already have but do not know. I'll return to Cintra in six years to see if destiny has been kind to me" (*The Last Wish* 178–179). Thus, Geralt is called to the adventure to find his destiny. Campbell's next step in the first stage of departure is the refusal of the call, which happens in "The Sword of Destiny". Six years later Geralt finds Ciri, his child of surprise, in the Brokilon forest. Here he is reminded by the ruler of the forest that the "Sword of Destiny has two blades [...] You are one of them" (*The Sword of Destiny* 295). Even though Ciri begs Geralt not to leave her, he insists that the "only thing everyone is destined for is death. Death is the other blade of the two-edged sword" (313). Campbell's hero then crosses the threshold from his own world into the word of adventure via the help of a magic guardian and an act of self-annihilation and rebirth.

When Geralt calls in the law of surprise again for saving a farmer, he gets seriously injured. He is miraculously saved by an herbalist, who happens to be his mother, an ideal guardian, only to find out that his child of surprise is once again Ciri who was hiding in the farmer's house after the siege of Cintra. Thus, Geralt's initiation starts. It is evident that Geralt's character development is closely tied to those he is destined for, which is not only Ciri but also Yennefer whose love he gets by a wish granted by a genie. Yet, there are also other misfits that Geralt identifies with on his quest. First, there is the witchers' order and their keep in Kaer Morhen where witchers gather for winter and where Ciri starts her education in *Blood of the Elves*. Second, there is the school at the Temple of Melitele where Geralt, Yennefer, and Ciri find asylum at various points of the story. The third, probably the most significant, group of misfits Geralt is part of forms in *Baptism of Fire*. On the quest to find Ciri whom he got separated from, in the midst of a raging war, Geralt joins forces with Dandelion, Milva, a lone hunter who originally ran away from an abusing stepfather, a group of dwarves on their way home from having criminally acquired and buried a treasure, a party of refugee women and children, Cahir, the Black

138 *Martina Vránová*

Knight who saved Ciri from Cintra but recently deserted the Nilfgaardian army, and Regis, a high vampire posing as a barber-surgeon. In Geralt's words: "What a company I ended up with [...] Brothers in arms! A team of heroes! What have I done to deserve it? A poetaster with a lute. A wild and lippy half-dryad, half-woman. A vampire, who's about to notch up his fifth century. And a bloody Nilfgaardian who insists he isn't a Nilfgaardian" (*Baptism of Fire* 234). Even though the White Wolf does not like being accompanied, he is reminded by Milva that he needs the others because "[w]olves don't hunt alone! Never!" (233).

In the *Miss Peregrine* series, the main character Jacob starts once again as a prototypical loner. The identity search is motivated by a sense of social isolation that the adolescent feels. The question asked is: "Is there some-body like me to share my experiences, ideas, or feelings with?" Jacob's identity as an American teenager in a small Florida town fails because of his grandfather's tall tales of an orphanage full of peculiar children he was once part of. The moment when Jacob stops believing in the stories marks the point when childhood yields to the confusion of adolescence: "We cling to our fairy tales until the price for believing them becomes too high, which for me was the day in second grade when Robbie Jensen pantsed me at lunch in front of a table of girls and announced I believed in fairies" (*Home for Peculiar Children* 20). He gets a chance to form his identity as a peculiar in another world not only by finding people like him but by forming a working group with them. When Miss Peregrine disappears, the peculiar children have to cooperate without a parental figure. As Ransom Riggs explains himself: "They have to find themselves as individuals [...] and negotiate their power structure and ask who's the leader, now that Miss Peregrine is not there, and deal with all these external stressors that they haven't had to face" ("A Book that Started with Its Pictures" n.p.). In the peculiar world Jacob finds his identity, he becomes a star when he defeats the wights, but he knows this identity will not be easily accepted in his real world.[2] He tries but is not successful as his parents consider him mentally ill. There is one more identity crisis that Jacob has to deal with. Since he has the same abilities as his grandfather who left the pecu-liar world for good, he may often be mistaken for him. Especially when it comes to his relationship with Emma, Jacob wonders whether she may actually still be in love with Abe and only projecting his image into Jacob. In Erikson's terms, Jacob does not know whether he can identify himself in Emma's eyes or whether it is his grandfather, who he also identifies with but at the same time knows he is different from.

As demonstrated above, identity search is motivated by a sense of social isolation. The feeling of being a misfit is a feature common to both YAL and classical fantasy. This convergence is further supported by the prev-alence of mentally or emotionally immature characters with adolescent

Growing Up in Fantasy 139

features in the comic book superhero genre. This is very well portrayed in the development of Marvel's Loki character. When *The Mighty Thor* comic series started in 1952, Loki was transformed from Odin's blood brother to Odin's adopted son competing with his brother Thor. This move to a younger generation and subjugation to parental supervision is significant. It transforms an independent individual playing mischief on anybody in the Norse world to an envy-ridden younger brother set against the elder one. The recent Marvel films take this development one step further – where in the old comic books Loki wanted to get the upper hand on Thor mostly by trying to steal his hammer, in the films Loki is "burdened with a glorious purpose" to rule the world. He is a solitary hero on a quest to assert his value. The fact that he finds along the way that being a ruler is not really his role is the bitter experience that most adolescents earn while pursuing their dreams. Loki then reinvents himself as a useful part of Thor's band of heroes saving the world in *Thor: Ragnarok* (2017); he finds his place in a social structure. Disney's latest series takes the approximation of Loki to an adolescent to an extreme. While fighting the TVA with his own female variant, we find out that Loki is falling in love for the first time in his life – with himself – which means he actually, through Sylvie's mirror, realises what he is like, learns to like himself, not hate his pitiful existence, value his and Sylvie's survival skills, and thus find a different purpose for his life rather than ruling the world.

Into the Possible Worlds

As the individual's quest for identity is a social one, it necessarily needs an inhabited world, a society to exercise it in. A narrative of any kind creates mental models of situations that are the topics of the particular narrative. These storyworlds, as David Herman (2009) refers to them, have a special quality of immersiveness:

> [T]he power of narrative to create worlds goes a long way towards explaining its immersiveness, its ability to transport interpreters into places and times they must occupy for the purposes of narrative comprehension [...] Interpreters of narrative do not merely reconstruct a sequence of events and a set of existents, but imaginatively (emotionally, viscerally) inhabit a world in which, besides happening and existing, things matter, agitate, exalt, repulse, provide grounds for laughter and grief, and so on – both for narrative agents and for interpreters working to make sense of their circumstances and (inter)actions (119).

Such an immersion in a fictional storyworld cannot go without consequences. Readers cannot simply shake off their feelings and forget their

140 *Martina Vránová*

experiences with the act of closing the book. This assumption serves as a basis for cognitive narratology, most famously advocated by Thomas Pavel. The issue that Pavel is trying to prove is that texts do have referential properties, that they can inform the readers about the world they live in. Unlike his structuralist predecessors, Pavel focuses on "[q]uestions such as literary truth, the nature of fictionality, distance and resemblance between literature and reality" (9). On the example of a religious myth sliding into fiction, as members of a particular community stop believing in the truth of the myth even though it retains a referential quality, Pavel shows that an individual can move between various domains of his or her life (reality). An individual can thus reconcile his or her religious beliefs, lived reality, and what one reads in fiction without too much trouble. This is the "consequence of the allowance for travel between domains, real and fictional" (42). Pavel then uses Kripke's theory to construct the possible or alternative world theory. A universe an individual inhabits is composed of an actual world (real reality) and a number of possible worlds (e.g., religious beliefs, folklore, and also unrealised possibilities). "For a world to be possible, it must be linked to the actual world by a relation of accessibility" ("Possible Worlds" n. p.). All possible worlds then have a relation to the actual world (an individual's reality), which means they inform the actual world in one way or another. Thus, an individual can derive experiences useful for his or her real life even from fiction. To support the relevance of this theory, we can look back to Tolkien's essay "On Fairy Stories" where he claims that fantasy "produces a Secondary World into which both designer and spectator can enter, to the satisfaction of their sense while they are inside" (49). It is exactly in the realm of literature and imagination in general where this theory becomes particularly productive. A work of fiction can be composed of its own possible worlds. Through immersion in possible worlds created by fiction, adolescents may be given a chance to resolve an identity crisis which is not possible to be resolved in their real lives. "In modernity, especially in Western society, rites of passage for children transitioning to adulthood have been weak, non-existent, or unhealthy" (Blumenkrantz n. p.). The whole process of maturation seems to be dragging on for years and years without any clear culmination or closure.[3] Adulthood does not really start with one's sexual activity, finishing secondary school, or even college. This may be the reason why nowadays young adults and new adults have an elevated need to reenact the rite of passage in a compressed manner in a novel/film/series/computer-game form (a new version of the old legend and myth) and to achieve a clear resolution at the end of these works of art together with their heroes. This idea is, however, not a new one. O'Neill in *The Individuated Hobbit* works from the same proposition defending Tolkien's works, and by extension the genre of fantasy, against accusations of creating an escape from reality: "it is the ill-health of our age which

Growing Up in Fantasy   141

creates the need for the special kind of fantasy that Middle-earth provides, and [...] the narrow view of 'reality' that the critics champion may be the beginning of what is really unhealthy" (2). In his view, Tolkien felt the same need for imaginative reenactment of the rite of passage that nowadays writers of fantasy and YAL do.

To adolescents, fictional worlds of whatever kind provide a safe space where they can experiment, be bold, and fail without actual consequences. In YAL, this mostly means the absence of parents as the direct source of authority. Even in realist YAL, the ultimate unbeatable source of authority is either missing or somehow incompetent (problem novels with abusive parents, alcoholics, etc.). The parent-child power struggle is repressed in the Freudian sense. Repression is a defensive mechanism which does not "arise until a sharp cleavage has occurred between conscious and unconscious mental activity – [...] *the essence of repression lies simply in turning something away, and keeping it at a distance, from the conscious"* (Freud 147). The parent-child relationship is left unresolved so that the growing adolescent can develop without the suffocating authority of the parent overseer, as if the success of maturity depended upon eliminating the parental supervision rather than dealing with it. However, when this repressed relationship surfaces, like in the problem novels, it becomes a source of immense problems.

The travel from a familiar world to a strange world full of adventures is also inherent to Campbell's monomyth. The self-defining experience has to be earned in a different world than the hero's home community. During the initiation stage on the road of trials, the hero encounters the Universal Mother and is atoned with the Father, but these two do not represent parents as such. Rather they represent the omnipresent cleft in the ideally monolithic human being. The hero meets the Queen Goddess, the Temptress, the Universal Mother in order to come to terms with his own physicality, corporeality, and sexuality. The "triumphant hero-soul" is united in a mystical marriage with the "Queen Goddess of the World" (91). Having dipped his toe in the vices, the hero must face the other extreme – the exclusively human characteristics of justice and grace. First, he faces the wrath of the Father while being backed up by the Goddess's protection and hope only to find out that even the terrible Father is capable of mercy and grace. The hero is then reborn in the realisation that "father and mother reflect each other, and are in essence the same" (110). As I will demonstrate further on, the Queen Goddess figure in YAL is often equalled with the complicated romantic and sexual encounter with the other sex, and the figure of the Father is represented by the mentor figure the hero is guided by, who is a source of authority yet different than the actual parental authority. The mentor does not only punish and praise; the mentor is also a friend, which is a position the parent is not capable of.

142 *Martina Vránová*

Going back to the possible worlds, the adolescent reader's mental travel to a possible universe constructed by fiction is reflected in the literary hero's journey outside the home community and back to prove that he or she is worthy of becoming an adult. One possible world is not enough though. It must fold upon itself and create a foul, but eventually cleansing, underworld for the purpose of the hero's quest – a Foucaultian heterotopia where one's otherness can be accommodated without public judgement. Foucault's heterotopia is invested with the inherent quality of revealing one's self to the person who enters it. Looking in the mirror, one enters the unreal space of heterotopia but at the same time the heterotopic self redirects its gaze back at the person in the real space: "I begin again to direct my eyes toward myself and to reconstitute myself where I am" (Foucault 24). The theme of travel into an unknown and dangerous space where, in the end, the hero succeeds and brings back self-knowledge is another feature where both YAL and fantasy collide.

In *Looking for Alaska*, Miles sheds the supervision of his parents, even though they do not present an example of a dysfunctional family, by his own decision. He decides to go to a boarding school which is, according to Foucault, a typical example of a crisis heterotopia. "[T]hey are privileged or sacred or forbidden places, reserved for individuals who are, in relation to society and to the human environment in which they live, in a state of crisis: adolescents, menstruating women, pregnant women, the elderly, etc." (24). As Miles' initiation into adulthood is taken elsewhere to be performed rather than at home, the reader follows him into an alternative possible universe with its own heterotopic world. The reader is thus twice hidden and protected from the parents' stifling protection. "In general, the heterotopic site is not freely accessible like a public place. Either entry is compulsory, as in case of barracks or a prison, or else the individual has to submit to rites and purifications" (Foucault 26). Such is also the nature of Miles's boarding school. Only those who are part of this community can enter the campus, and then they are subjected to rituals of pranking. Miles's boarding school has its own both written and, more importantly, unwritten rules. Being admitted to the community is symbolised by getting a nickname – a new identity. Thus Miles's roommate Chip, himself called the Colonel, invents the nickname Pudge for Miles and at the same time informs him that the Dean is called the Eagle. Miles also undergoes the initiation ritual on the night before his first classes start – he gets duct taped and thrown in the lake only in his underpants. Here, in this Foucaultian heterotopia, Miles meets his Temptress in the form of Alaska, and his Father in the form of the Dean and the comparative religion teacher Dr. Hyde. The dean is called the Eagle because he "lives in the dorm circle, and he sees all. He can smell a cigarette from like five miles" (*Alaska* 16). He has the all-seeing eye of God guarding the campus against all mischief.

After Alaska's death when Pudge and his friends play the Alaska Young Memorial Prank on the Speaker Day, the Dean is hugely entertained and impressed by the ingenuity of hiring a stripper to pose as a university professor studying adolescent sexuality. The moment when the Eagle lets the culprits go without punishment resembles what Campbell calls the "at-one-ment" with the Father which is "no more than the abandonment of the self-generated double monster – the dragon thought to be God (superego) and the dragon thought to be Sin (repressed id)" (107–110). The Dean then acts as the appropriate type of authority that makes the heroes/pranksters look within themselves. Facing the Father is to be the utmost horror for the hero, an abyss into which the hero sinks only to rise again and be reborn. Since meeting Alaska, Miles has been trying to solve the mystery of getting out of the labyrinth of suffering. Alaska's death is Tartarus of Miles's suffering and playing the memorial prank and facing the Dean is his, and the other pranksters', rebirth. The other Father figure in Green's novel is Dr. Hyde. In the view of Campbell's monomyth, this mentor figure is unsurprisingly a religion teacher whose classes focus on "the most important pursuit in history: the search for meaning" (*Alaska* 32). For Miles being dismissed from the class for not paying attention by a personality he considers a genius is the utmost punishment. Yet, Dr. Hyde's rules are not to be questioned: "For fifty minutes a day, five days a week, you abide by my rules. Or you fail. The choice is yours" (40). After Alaska's death, Dr. Hyde forces the students to face the emotional abyss they have sunk into. He puts on the board Alaska's question – "*How will we ever get out of this labyrinth of suffering? – A. Y.*" – makes them face their grief and make it meaningful (158). Bearing Alaska's question in mind the whole term, Dr. Hyde reminds his students that all the religious figures they studied – Muhammad, Jesus, and Buddha – "each brought a message of radical hope" (215) and assigns a question for the final essay: "What is your cause for hope?" (216). This essay is meaningful as it makes them rise of the abyss of grief.

In *The Witcher* series, we can come across an innumerable number of heterotopias: village festivals, military camps, the Brokilon forest, school at the Temple of Melitele, Aretuza, Kaer Morhen, etc. Lots of these serve as sanctuaries for the main characters. They are open to them but entering them once again requires certain conditions, e.g., Geralt's injuries to be healed by Neneke at Melitele's temple. They are places of learning and archives where the entire history of this alternative universe is "accessible in a sort of immediate knowledge" (Foucault 26). At the same time, the series is full of characters acting as mentors, thus exemplifying the relationship of Campbell's Father or protective Queen Goddess to the heroes: Vesemir to Geralt, Geralt to Ciri, Tissaia to Yennefer, Yennefer to Ciri, etc. A particularly illustrative example is, however, Fen Carn inhabited by

144 *Martina Vránová*

Emiel Regis. Fen Carn, or the Meadow of the Barrows, is an ancient elven cemetery that becomes a resting place for Geralt's company and refugee women and children travelling with them. Just as Foucault writes about the 19th-century removal of cemeteries from the churchyard to the outskirts of the city where they were "no longer the sacred and immortal heart of the city, but 'the other city', where each family possesses its dark resting place" (25), Fen Carn is a symbol of the downfall of the elven race in Geralt's times, situated in the middle of nowhere. This once stately memorial place has been claimed by the wild nature and reported to be haunted by "[g]houls, graveirs, spectres, wights, elven spirits, wraiths, apparitions, the works" (*Baptism of Fire* 116). It has the status of in-between not only because it is an entrance to the world of the dead but also to the world of the dying race that is despised by all other races. It is a metaphorical portal to other times – heterochrony (Foucault 26). The visitors are reminded of their own future dissolution into time and also the past glory of the elven race. Yet, it is this place that becomes an asylum for the night for the exhausted company. It becomes their choice only out of necessity as the women and children cannot continue, which is the condition to be fulfilled to enter it. In the end, its bleakness is subverted by encountering Emiel Regis. Regis is a god-like figure because he has power over life. As a vampire he can kill instantly, yet he chooses to live without blood and pose as a barber-surgeon. He can make an abortive concoction for pregnant Milva, yet in the end he saves her life by operating on her. He is a creature shrouded in myths which he likes to spin and spread himself. Geralt feels uneasy in his company, betrays his identity to the others, and chases him away. This scene is that of an older mythical creature being faced and defied by a younger but bolder progeny. Regis explains: "I'm a descendant of survivors, unfortunate beings imprisoned here after the cataclysm you call the conjunction of the spheres. I'm regarded, to put it mildly, as a monster. [...] And now I've encountered a witcher, who earns his living eliminating creatures such as I" (*Baptism of Fire* 219). Yet, Regis comes back as a healer and a mediator between Geralt and the remaining company. Despite their short acquaintance, Regis sees right through Geralt and explains to him that his wish to go through the ordeal alone is a desire for "a cleansing baptism of fire" and thus rebirth, which in real life is more complicated and never so straightforward and clear-cut as it is in legends (228). Regis than keeps this role of the voice of reason opposing Geralt's passion only to sacrifice himself in the battle against Vilgefortz, thus enabling Geralt to kill the mage.

Also in the *Miss Peregrine* series, Jacob and the other peculiar children have both mentors and enemies from which they learn and out of experience of encounters with which they grow. The truly peculiar ones are Miss Peregrine, Caul, and Myron Bentham. These three, being siblings,

Growing Up in Fantasy 145

make up the "holy trinity". Miss Peregrine is the Queen Goddess even though not in the sense of the temptress. As Campbell writes, as the hero "progresses in the slow initiation which is life, the form of the goddess undergoes for him a series of transfigurations: she can never be greater than himself, though she can always promise more than he is yet capable of understanding. She lures, she guides, she bids him burst his fetters. And if he can match her import, the two, the knower and the known, will be released from every limitation" (97). Miss Peregrine is indeed the knower. Being an ymbryne, gifted with manipulating time, she is a member of the superior class of peculiars whose duty is to create and maintain protective time loops for similar misfits. The subject of her profession, the known, is peculiar children like Jacob. The other part of Campbell's duality – Queen Goddess and Father – is split in between Miss Peregrine's brothers. Caul and Bentham work as representations of the dominant and the submissive where one cannot do without the other. Caul had the fervour, a gift in rhetoric and political manipulation to gather followers in order to shed the "infantilizing influence of ymbrynes" (*Library of Souls* 197). Betham was the creative genius who constructed the Panloopticon believing it could unite peculiars confined in their separate loops but Caul used it to search for the Library of Souls "mounting expedition after expedition [...] The goal of uniting peculiardom was forgotten. All along, my brother had cared only about ruling it, like the would-be peculiar gods of old" (195). When they eventually find the Library of Souls, Caul merges with a soul of a peculiar gifted with metal skin threatening to kill everybody opposing him and become the wrathful god. Yet, Bentham is there to stop him and begs Jacob to let him: "Listen to me [...] I've got to do this. I'm the only hope you have" (395). Hope matches destruction as the two brothers clash and cancel each other out. Also, Campbell's hero is to experience a rebirth at this moment, which Jacob does indeed: "I felt like I was coming back to life. The pain in my chest was receding" (393). In an attempt to get rid of the only tool to becoming a peculiar god, Jacob, the changed Caul shoots him but the bullet lodges in a scarf made of the bullet-proof wool of peculiar sheep.

When it comes to the representation of space, the *Miss Peregrine* series is composed of virtually nothing else but heterotopic places. Loops created by ymbrynes are such places in between which only the peculiar can enter and whose entrance is always guarded. In the first novel Jacob enters his grandfather's loop on Cairholm Island through an ancient tomb in a bog where the Cairholm man was found – a twenty-seven-hundred-year-old well-preserved corpse of a sixteen-year-old boy sacrificed in the bog because "people had once believed this foul-smelling wasteland was gateway to heaven" (*Home for Peculiar Children* 125). Similarly, in *Library of Souls* Jacob and Emma travel to the most notorious Victorian

146 *Martina Vránová*

London slums – Devil's Acre – with the help of Sharon, a boatman offering river tours who is "seven feet tall at least, his massive frame draped in a cloak and his face hidden beneath a dark hood" (50). This allusion to Charon transporting a Greek hero into the underworld to undergo his adventure is an explicit point where Campbell's and Foucault's theories collide. The culmination of the archetypal hero's adventures takes place in heterotopia – a place in between, which the hero enters and then comes back with the won boon. The place, even though often filthy, has a purifying effect on the hero. Jacob has his first talk with Miss Peregrine and Bentham in their libraries pointing towards the concept of temporality being preserved in them just like in the loops. According to Foucault, libraries are "heterotopias in which time never stops building up and topping its own summit" (26). Such is also the idea behind the Library of Souls – keeping spirits of long dead peculiars for further consultation in the future. However, Riggs goes further than just choosing heterotopias as settings. He thematises them. Ryan describes the thematisation of space in the following terms:

> An important aspect of the cognitive mapping of narrative texts is the attribution of symbolic meaning to the various regions and landmarks of the narrative world. [...] In the cosmology of archaic societies, space is ontologically divided into a profane world, the realm of everyday life, and a sacred world, inhabited by supernatural beings, with holy sites functioning as portals between the two. The narrative response to these cosmologies and topologies is a symbolic geography diversified into regions where different events and experiences take place – where life, in other words, is governed by different physical, psychological, social or cultural rules. In fairy tales or computer games, for instance, the symbolic map of the narrative world may associate the castle with power, mountain tops with confrontations between the forces of good and evil, open areas with danger, closed areas with security, etc. ("Space" n. p.).

The symbolic meaning attached to the notion of the library in the *Miss Peregrine* series is that of an access point to alternative possible worlds. The Library of Souls is presented as a living organism whose "[p]assage-ways branched off into the dark like veins" (*Library of Souls* 380), whose central cavern was "a huge, circular space like a beehive" (382) where "distinct and human sound moaning" could be heard (383). By opening a jar with a soul and partaking of the soul's knowledge, i.e., reading a book, one's real life is enriched. However, merging with the spirit, i.e., complete immersion in the possible world and refusal to return, results in the person's destruction, which is what happens to Caul and his bodyguard who try to absorb the peculiar souls. This image of travel into alternative possible worlds created by literature with the goal of informing one's own

Growing Up in Fantasy 147

real life is made explicit once again in the Panloopticon; Myron Bentham's home in the Devil's Acre houses a machine called Panloopticon, reminiscent of Jeremy Bentham's panopticon,[4] which creates entrances into loops. A hallway in the house features fifty doors with plaques on them leading into rooms which are second entrances into loops. As such, "the house becomes a central repository for all loops everywhere" (191). Bentham's house thus becomes the thematisation of the adolescent's mind undergoing adventurous journeys whenever venturing into a possible universe created by books, films, computer games, or just his or her imagination.

Conclusion

This chapter has shown that the genres of YAL and fantasy can inform each other with a wide range of ideas. Both these genres typically portray the Jungian archetype of a hero on a quest undergoing a rite of passage. Rising from an insignificant person not fitting into his or her home community, the hero sets out on a journey of trials, aided by a mentor figure and a band of brothers, sinking into a filthy heterotopia only to rise again with self-knowledge, a new identity formed. By the comparison of realist YAL and traditional fantasy, I did not only want to prove that these two genres have a lot in common but also that their union in YA fantasy intensifies these features. This is particularly visible in the thematisation of the mental travel to possible worlds created by fiction which, eventually, helps the reader overcome a developmental crisis and advance in identity formation. YAL, fantasy, and their union in YA fantasy have taken up a role of the disappearing cultural phenomenon of ritual, which is possibly one of the reasons for their immense marketing success.

Notes

1 So that the parallel between the inspected genres is more pronounced, I focus on the adult character of Geralt, not on Ciri.
2 Tackling an adult problem is a prerequisite to becoming an adult. In the Jungian view, we can see this as a rite of passage. In YAL, it is exactly the adult problem that is a significant source of genre variation. Apart from other features, genres vary with their subject matter. In *Miss Peregrine*, we can find elements of detective fiction as Jacob has to solve his grandfather's murder, fantasy because of the supernatural peculiar world, adventure when trying to find Miss Peregrine, horror or thriller when fighting hollowgast, romance with Emma, even a travel journal in the fourth part of the series where the children take a road trip of American loops.
3 This reality of maturation as a prolonged process without an actual closure is reflected in the current trend of writing that is basically YAL but for older audience. In 2009, St. Martin's Press coined the term "new adult" when announcing a contest for "fiction similar to YA that can be published and marketed as

148   *Martina Vránová*

adult" (McBride n. p.). Nowadays, we can still see an extensive discussion on YAL crossing lines of age resulting in the "crossover" fiction (see, for example, Naughton 2014, Summers 2020, Hershberger 2021).

4 Yet not in the disciplinary sense.

Works Cited

Blumenkrantz, David G. "Rites of Passage in a World That is Not Flat". *Systems Thinker* 20, 2018. https://thesystemsthinker.com/%ef%bb%bfrites-of-passage-in-a-world-that-is-not-flat/. Accessed 18 May 2022.

Breitmoser, Doris and Delphine Beccaria. "Literature for Children and Young Adults in Europe (Part One: Germany and France)". Czech Literary Centre. 18 November 2020. https://www.czechlit.cz/en/feature/literature-for-children-and-young-adults-in-europe-part-one-germany-and-france/. Accessed 19 February 2022.

Cadden, Mike. "Genre as Nexus: The Novel for Children and Young Adults". *Handbook for Research on Children's and Young Adult Literature*. Ed. Shelby A. Worlf, Karen Coats, Patricia Enciso, and Christine A. Jenkins. New York: Routledge: 2011. 302–313.

Campbell, Joseph. *The Hero with a Thousand Faces*. Novato: New World Library, 2008.

Cart, Michael. "Carte Blanche: A New Golden Age – YA in the First Decade of the 2000s". *Booklist*. 15 May 2017.

———. "Carte Blanche: The Present and the Prospective". *Booklist*. 1 and 15 June 2016.

Erikson, Erik H. *Identity: Youth and Crisis*. New York: Norton, 1968.

Foucault, Michel. "Of Other Spaces". *Diacritics* 16.1 (1968): 22–27.

Freud, Sigmund. *Repression*. London: Hogarth, 1915.

Gravemaster. "The *Witcher* Author on Netflix Adaptation: 'I don't care what is done to my character'". *Redanian Intelligence*, 2 November 2019. https://redanianintelligence.com/2019/11/02/the-witcher-author-on-the-netflix-adaptation-i-dont-care-what-is-done-to-my-character/. Accessed 19 February 2022.

Green, John. *Looking for Alaska*. New York: Speak, 2012.

Herman, David. *Basic Elements of Narrative*. Chichester: Wiley-Blackwell, 2009.

Hershberger, Katy. "YA Grows Up". *School Library Journal*. 14 April 2021.

Hunt, Jonathan. "Borderlands: Redefining the Young Adult Novel". *Horn Book Magazine*. March/April 2007.

Journey into Mystery. The Mighty Thor: The Vengeance of Loki. Marvel Comics. Issue 88, 1952.

McBride, Georgia. "St. Martin's New Adult Contest". 2009. http://sjaejones.com/blog/2009/st-martins-new-adult-contest/. Accessed 6 April 2022.

Melanson, Lisa Stapleton. *The Hero's Quest for Identity in Fantasy Literature: A Jungian Analysis*. University of Massachusetts, Amherst, 1994, PhD. thesis.

Naughton, Julie. "New Adult Matures". *Publishers Weekly*. 14 July 2014.

O'Neill, Timothy R. *The Individuated Hobbit: Jung, Tolkien, and the Archetypes of Middle-earth*. Boston: Houghton Mifflin, 1979.

Pavel, Thomas G. *Fictional Worlds*. Cambridge, MA: Harvard UP, 1986.

Pogue, Maurice. "Review of *The Last Wish* (*Witcher* Book Series), by Andrzej Sapkowski". *Geeks Under Grace*, 12 November 2018. https://www.geeksundergrace.com/books/review-the-last-wish-the-witcher-series/. Accessed 18 February 2022.

Riggs, Ransom. "A Book That Started with Its Pictures". Interview by Maria Russo. *New York Times*, 31 December 2013. https://www.nytimes.com/2013/12/31/books/ransom-riggs-is-inspired-by-vintage-snapshots.html?pagewanted=all&_r=1&). Accessed 20 February 2022.

———. *Library of Souls*. Philadelphia: Quirk Books, 2015.

———. *Miss Peregrine's Home for Peculiar Children*. Philadelphia: Quirk Books, 2016.

———. "Ransom Riggs". Interview by Becky Ohlsen. *Bookpage*, October 2016. https://www.bookpage.com/interviews/20444-ransom-riggs-fantasy/. Accessed 18 February 2022.

Ryan, Marie-Laure. "Possible Worlds". *The Living Handbook of Narratology*. 27 September 2013. http://www.lhn.uni-hamburg.de. Accessed 15 December 2021.

———. "Space". *The Living Handbook of Narratology*. 22 April 2014. http://www.lhn.uni-hamburg.de. Accessed 15 December 2021.

Sapkowski, Andrzej. *Baptism of Fire*. New York: Orbit Books, 2014.

———. *Blood of Elves*. London: Gollancz, 2012.

———. *The Last Wish*. New York: Orbit Books, 2017.

———. *The Sword of Destiny*. New York: Orbit Books, 2015.

Short, Kathy G., Carl M. Tomlinson, Carol Lynch-Brown, and Holly Johnson. *Essentials of Young Adult Literature*. Boston: Pearson, 2015.

Sims, Harley. "A Polish Tolkien? The Fantasy World of Andrzej Sapkowski". *Mercatornet*, 13 December 2016. https://mercatornet.com/a-polish-tolkien-the-fantasy-world-of-andrzej-sapkowski/10619/. Accessed 15 January 2022.

Smith, Scot. "The Death of the Genre: Why Best YA Fiction Often Defies Classification". *ALAN Review* 35.1 (2007): 43–50.

Stephens, Jonathan. "Young Adult: A Book by Any Other Name ... Defining the Genre". *ALAN Review* 35.1 (2007): 34–42.

Summers, Courtney. "Who Is a 'Crossover' for?" *Publishers Weekly*. 7 September 2020.

"The Problem of Fantasy Fiction". *University Wire*. 1 November 2013.

Tolkien, John Ronald Reuel "On Fairy Stories". *Tree and Leaf*. Boston: Houghton-Mifflin, 1988. 9–74.

Waititi, Taika. *Thor: Ragnarok*. Marvel Studios, 2017.

Waldron, Michael. *Loki*. Marvel Studios, 2021.

Yates, Jessica. "Tolkien, John Ronald Reuel". *St. James Guide to Young Adult Writers*. Ed. Tom Pendergast and Sara Pendergast. Detroit: St. James Press, 1999.

8 One Does Not Simply Teach Fantasy

How Students of English and American Studies in Hungary View the Genre and Tolkien's Legacy

Nikolett Sipos

Introduction

Fantasy has always been an integral part of our culture as the main mode for making sense of the world (Zipes 78), and in the last few decades, there has been a huge growth in its popularity in television, literature, and video games. In recent years, academic scholarship has become increasingly interested in the genre, however, when it comes to education, fantasy is still an underrepresented topic in classrooms. In Hungary, some primary school teachers are fighting for making J. K. Rowling's *Harry Potter and the Philosopher's Stone* required reading (Velkey n.p.), while in secondary school there is generally no room for talking about any of the classic fantastic works because they do not fit the national curriculum. As the genre plays a very important role in British and American culture (and even globally, as well), we can assume that a lot of young adult university students are fans of at least one fantasy narrative, be it a novel, a film, a series, or a video game – however, even when it comes to English and American studies, the genre is not usually discussed during lectures or seminars. Although fantasy is nowadays one of the most dominant modes in literature and television, and it plays a crucial part in popular culture, there are still only a few opportunities to discuss its significance in lectures and seminars; thus, instructors should pay more attention to discussing fantastic works. This study explores how Hungarian students of English and American studies view the fantasy genre and Tolkien's work in general, and whether there is a need for students to study fantastic works in a university setting.

Why Teach Fantasy?

As contemporary novels, television shows and games are gaining more and more popularity (Stephan), not only could fantastic texts be useful in primary or secondary education (Fredrickson; Robbins and Whitley) for critical literary examination (Thomas), but they could also be an integral

DOI: 10.4324/9781003407171-12

part of the curriculum in the humanities, especially in literary and cultural studies. This chapter concentrates on the importance of teaching fantasy in higher education, and how it should appear in the curricula of English and American studies.

The vast majority of the work on teaching fantasy has focused on primary and secondary education. One of the most prominent volumes on teaching fantasy is titled *Fantasy Media in the Classroom: Essays on Teaching with Film, Television, Literature, Graphic Novels, and Video Games* (2012). The essays introduce three ways of teaching fantastic works in the classroom: the first approach concentrates on how "fantasy material can enhance student learning about traditional texts, themes, and topics", while the second strategy "deals with similar classes, but treats the fantasy materials as important in their own right (not just for understanding the existing material)" (Ford 4). According to the authors, the third way of teaching the genre might be to narrow down the focus of these classes by only concentrating on fantastic works. If we apply this approach to the university setting, although the third solution is probably a bit far-fetched, as among the compulsory courses there may be little space left for literature or media courses that only deal with fantasy, providing an opportunity for an elective course or implementing more fantastic works in the general curriculum could widen the perspective of the students taking part in English and American studies, or even literary, cultural, and media programmes. Fantasy has undoubtedly become an important part of literary history: J.R.R. Tolkien's *The Lord of the Rings* and the works of C.S. Lewis opened the way to new fantastic works (George R.R. Martin's *A Song of Ice and Fire* [1996–], Philip Pullman's *His Dark Materials* [1995–2000] or Andrzej Sapkowski's *The Witcher* series [1986–2013], just to name a few), that had a profound impact on popular culture but are still not widely discussed at universities.

Although fantasy is still an underrepresented genre in literary courses, some traditional, canonised literary works that are closely connected to fantasy have an important role in education – these major works also had a great impact on the evolution of the genre. Jonathan Swift's *Gulliver's Travels* (1726), E.T.A. Hoffmann's *The Golden Pot: A Modern Fairytale* (1814), and Franz Kafka's *The Metamorphosis* (1915) are fantastical stories that are widely discussed in literary classes that deal with Central European literature. The importance of the different works of magical realism also cannot be denied: Gabriel García Márquez's *One Hundred Years of Solitude* (1967), Salman Rushdie's *Midnight's Children* (1981), or Toni Morrison's *Beloved* (1987) constitute an important part of literary classes. Although some of the aforementioned works are used to discuss general literary themes and topics in English and American studies, the focus is still on the *traditional*, and fantasy as a genre is still mostly regarded as a popular genre that has its own place outside the classroom.

152 *Nikolett Sipos*

Another important factor when it comes to the advantages of teaching fantasy can be the possible improvement of critical literacy skills (Fabrizi) and vocabulary building. The level of immersion in fantastic texts is generally very high, and as most students tend to be fans of at least two or three fantasy narratives, it is more likely that they are going to read texts that are similar to those they are attracted to. Both the improvement of critical thinking and language skills are important factors in teaching English and American studies to foreign learners; thus, implementing more texts from fantasy literature could help acquire better results.

However, the question arises: is fantasy *really* a popular genre among university students? Is the fandom present on university campuses, and if the answer is yes, are students interested in learning about fantasy in higher education? When focusing on the fantasy genre, one of the most logical decisions would be to include some classics in the curriculum, starting with J.R.R. Tolkien's works – however, the question is whether students would be interested in the Tolkienian mythology, or whether choosing a "classic" would destroy the experience, just like in the case of other traditional literary works, that students would prefer not to read.

In order to answer these questions, I have created an online survey that was distributed at the University of Pannonia, Veszprém, and Pázmány Péter Catholic University, Budapest. The survey was available for Hungarian BA and MA students taking part in an English programme. The main research questions were the following:

1 How do Hungarian students of English and American Studies view the fantasy genre?
2 Do they consume it in any form (be it literature, films, series, or games)?
3 What is their opinion about Tolkien's work?
4 Is Tolkien's legacy still alive amongst young adults, or do they think that it is outdated?
5 How does their opinion on Tolkien's fantasy differ from more modern fantasy narratives?
6 Is there a need for learning more about this genre at universities?

Methodology

My research included both quantitative and qualitative explorations of what students of English and American Studies think of the questions listed above. I have created a survey with 27 questions and distributed it online among the English and American studies students at the University of Pannonia, Veszprém, and Pázmány Péter Catholic University, Budapest. Anyone could have filled in the questionnaire who was a BA or MA student studying English, including teacher trainees who participate

One Does Not Simply Teach Fantasy   153

in an MEd programme. The questions were asked in Hungarian so that those who are not proficient enough in English could also give detailed answers to the questions that may need more elaboration. Although students were encouraged to answer the questions, we can assume that those who decided to contribute to this research are somewhat interested in this topic, as filling in the survey was not compulsory. As the questionnaire was only available at two Hungarian universities, this research is not a representative sample: its main aim is to give a possible answer to how Hungarian students think about fantasy, and whether there is a need to learn more about the genre within the confines of education.

Results

In total, 77 respondents completed the survey; the gender distribution was 33.8% men and 66.2% women. The average age of the respondents in total was around 25 years old: there were only 12 students who were aged 30 or above, which means that most of the respondents belong to the young adult generation. A total of 63 students were studying in a BA program, and there were 2 MA and 12 MEd (Master of Education) students. At the time of the research, 57.1% of them were studying at Pázmány Péter Catholic University, and the remaining 42.9% were studying at the University of Pannonia.

The survey had four main parts. The first section was about fantasy narratives in general, and all of the questions were compulsory to answer. The next three sections were called "Fantasy and Literature", "Fantasy and Film", and lastly, "Fantasy and Games". These questions should have only been answered if the respondents were familiar with at least one of these fantasy forms – in case they were not, they automatically moved on to the next section.

The first question of my research was how Hungarian students of English and American Studies view the fantasy genre. After asking for some general information about the respondents, the initial section of the survey examined whether the students are familiar with some of the most famous fantasy stories. The questionnaire introduced ten popular fantasy narratives, and participants were asked to rate their relationship to the examples. The possible answers were "I have not heard about it", "I have heard about it, but I do not know it", "I know it, and I think it is good", "I know it, and I think it is neutral", "I know it, and I think it is bad", and lastly, "I am a fan". When choosing the texts for this question, I have mainly picked narratives that are well-known in the fantasy community and are currently trending on streaming platforms – naming only the literary texts would have meant that participants who are only familiar with these narratives through the film or video game adaptation would have been excluded, even though the adaptations also play an important role in popular culture. Another reason for concentrating on the narrative universes was that by giving these examples, even if the students were not as informed about fantasy in general, I could still test their general familiarity with the genre. The question also had an extra purpose: without having to theoretically define fantasy, it served as a guiding star for the students so that answering the following questions would be easier by creating an overview of the genre, without having to come up with exact definitions.

The ten examples were *The Lord of the Rings, His Dark Materials, Harry Potter, The Witcher, Game of Thrones, The Chronicles of Narnia, The Wheel of Time, Mistborn, The Stormlight Archive,* and *Shadow and Bone.* The two best-known stories among the students were *The Lord of the Rings* and the *Harry Potter* series, which was not surprising, as these two examples have gained huge attention in the last two decades, thanks to their immensely popular film adaptations. While every respondent has at least heard about them, Tolkien's work was liked by 62 people, 34 of whom consider themselves to be fans and only one person who had a negative opinion about it. The *Harry Potter* series was also liked by the same amount of people but had 38 fans, and 3 people who did not like it at all. Interestingly, the third most popular narrative was *The Chronicles of Narnia* – 1 person had not heard about it, 14 did not know the storyline, but 47 students claimed that they liked the narrative, and 11 of them were fans. The fourth most popular example was *The Witcher*: 24 people did not know the story with 2 people who have not heard about it at all, and 45 students liked the story, from whom 28 considered themselves to be fans. There were only 2 students who were completely unfamiliar with the *Game of Thrones* – 20 respondents had not read the books or seen the television show, 19 people liked it, and 22 were fans of the narrative – and it was also the one with the largest number of haters, as 5 people stated that they did not like it at all. This particular result was quite surprising, as *Game of Thrones* has probably been the most famous high-profile fantasy story of the 21st century, becoming the most popular show of the 2010s (Hughes). Brandon Sanderson's *Mistborn* and *The Stormlight Archive* were known by the least number of students: these two examples were also the two series of novels that do not have an adaptation; thus, they are not as well-known as the other stories. The next three in line were *The Wheel of Time, Shadow and Bone,* and *His Dark Materials,* which is not surprising, as they did not get as big a media coverage as the more popular narratives. The answers given to the first question show that most of the respondents were familiar with at least two or three fantasy narratives to a certain degree, and they mostly had a positive opinion about it.

Students were also asked about what they think of fantasy literature in general – as it was an open-ended question, they had the opportunity to describe their opinions in detail. All the 51 people who answered this question agreed that the genre is very important – one of the most popular reasons behind that is that it opens up the mind and the imagination, supports creativity and serves as a kind of escapism from the real world. I have found it interesting that there were only four students who mentioned that fantasy is a great way to think about modern problems and issues in a fantastic environment, thus creating the illusion of something distant – for most students, fantasy rather serves as an opportunity to escape their own problems without having to think about them.

The second question of this research was whether students consume the genre in any form. According to the results of the survey, out of the 77 respondents 59 read fantasy novels, 72 watch films and/or series, and 41 play fantasy games either online or offline, so the cinematic experience was more popular than the other two mediums – however, literature still plays an important role amongst the participants. The result is not surprising, as several fantasy shows were born and gained worldwide popularity in the 21st century: Peter Jackson's *The Lord of the Rings* adaptations (2001–2003) opened up the possibilities for new narratives on screen, like *Game of Thrones* (HBO, 2011–2019), *Outlander* (Starz, 2014–), *The Witcher* (Netflix, 2019–), or *Shadow and Bone* (2021–), just to name a few. More than half of the participants also play fantasy games, which shows that the significance of the medium is undeniable.

Students were also asked to give examples for each category: the most popular fantasy books were the *Harry Potter* series (29 people), *The Lord of the Rings* (25 people), *The Hobbit* (18 people), *The Witcher* (14), and *A Song of Ice and Fire* (11). 49 students stated that they read fantasy novels in Hungarian, while 47 of them chose English as well – there were only two people who stated that they read fantasy books in other foreign languages (Italian and German). These answers show that the majority of the respondents are interested in reading fantasy as a recreational activity, thus discussing these books in seminars could be a fruitful experiment.

As for films and series, the most popular examples were *The Lord of the Rings, Harry Potter, Game of Thrones,* and *The Witcher.* Students also mentioned *The Hobbit* films, *The Chronicles of Narnia,* and the Marvel Cinematic Universe; four students only watch fantasy in Hungarian, while the other respondents mentioned English and other foreign languages (German, Korean, Japanese, etc.) as well. The most popular games amongst the player group were *The Witcher, World of Warcraft, The Elder Scrolls* series, *Harry Potter,* and *The Lord of the Rings* games. There was one student who only plays fantasy games in Hungarian; however, the other respondents marked English as a gaming language as well.

The third and fourth questions were about what students think about Tolkien's work, and whether his legacy is still alive amongst young adults or if they think that it is outdated: although there has been an upsurge in Tolkien's popularity at the beginning of the 21st century, when Peter Jackson's adaptations were released, today's fantasy narratives are differing from the Tolkienian legacy. If we think about *Game of Thrones* or *The Witcher*, two of the most influential fantasy narratives of the 21st century, there is no clear distinction between good and bad characters, and usually it is "the monster" who turns out to be the moral character. These stories are also focusing on sexuality and the lively description of brutal and aggressive scenes, and are maybe more action-based than Tolkien's works; thus, they are quite different from their predecessor.

In the "Fantasy and Literature" section, out of the 51 respondents, there were only 9 who had not read anything from the author; for the others, the most popular books were *The Hobbit, The Lord of the Rings,* and *The Silmarillion.* When asked whether they think that Tolkien's works are still relevant, out of 41 students 31 answered yes: they mostly supported their answers with the ideas that Tolkien's works are real classics about the fight between good and evil, and they introduce eternal struggles and topics. There were only five respondents who stated that Tolkien's books are not relevant today, but interestingly, none of them explained their answer; one person claimed that he has not even heard about the author, and 2 people could not give an answer because they did not know, while 2 students thought that Tolkien's works are definitely classics, but they are not relevant anymore. When asked about whether it is important that more and more people should get to know Tolkien's work, 5 respondents thought that it is not, because those who are interested in it would discover the books themselves, while 39 students stated that it is important to raise awareness of Tolkien and his fiction because not only are they exemplary literary pieces, but fantasy would not exist without him. The respondents also highlighted that besides being an essential part of our culture, Tolkien's books are great gateways to the genre. From these answers, it can be concluded that most students praise Tolkien's work, and they think about the Tolkienian oeuvre as classics.

When it comes to the film adaptations, out of 72 students there were only 14 people who had not seen a Tolkien adaptation before, which means that the respondents are more likely to go to the film versions then to read the books. As the survey was conducted at the beginning of 2022, there were two questions related to the upcoming Amazon Prime series called *The Lord of the Rings: The Rings of Power* – out of 71 participants 30 stated that they are planning to watch the show, 28 were unsure and 13 people said that they will not watch it. When asked about the importance of this initiative, 16 students formed a negative opinion about it: some of them were afraid that the show would be "too politically correct" because it would include people of colour, who are not the part of Tolkien's European mythology, while others were concerned that "it is all about money" and it would not live up to the standards of Peter Jackson's adaptations. These answers show that some students were concerned about the faithfulness of Tolkien's work, and they were afraid that the new adaptations would somehow deteriorate the quality of Tolkien's legacy. Those who were in favour of the series stated that it is a good idea, because the younger generation is more likely to watch the series than the original films, and they were interested in the details of the background story, while it would also help make *The Lord of the Rings* even more popular. These answers also suggest that students think about Tolkien's works as classics as most of them were concerned about the faithfulness of the adaptations.

The fifth question focused on whether students' opinion of Tolkien's fantasy differs from more modern fantasy narratives like *Harry Potter, Game of Thrones,* or *The Witcher.* In the "Fantasy and Literature" section, out of 46 respondents, 34% felt that Tolkien is more relevant, while 28% feel that it is the other way round, and the remaining 33% stated that there is no difference between modern narratives and Tolkien's masterpieces. Most of the answers to this question elaborated on how Tolkien's work is more "classic" and "timeless", while modern fantasy narratives were described as more subtle, with characters who resemble real-life people instead of black and white characters. Interestingly, in the "Fantasy and Film" section students generally agreed that the contemporary fantasy adaptations are enjoyable to the same degree; however, Peter Jackson's films are the standard that each fantasy adaptation has to live up to.

The last aim of the survey was to find out whether there is a need amongst Hungarian students of English and American Studies to learn more about the fantasy genre and fantastic texts in general. In the "Fantasy and Literature" section, all the 54 people who answered this question agreed that they would, and two of them (both students studying at Pázmány Péter Catholic University) stated that they had a course where they briefly dealt with the genre. The most popular reasons why they were interested in this idea were that it would make the classes more enjoyable and that it is on the same level as "high literature", and as fantasy is an important part of literary history, teachers should also focus on it. In the case of films, 60 students would have been eager to learn and talk about fantasy cinema at university; however, 5 students thought that it is not necessarily a good idea, and those who are interested in it should learn about it outside of school. In the last section, "Fantasy and Games", 36 out of 51 students would have liked to talk about fantasy games in lectures or seminars, while 15 would have preferred not to – most of them justified their answer by saying that they spend enough time playing computer games; thus, they do not want to talk about it at university as well.

158 Nikolett Sipos

Results of this research suggest that those students who filled in the survey are generally interested in fantasy literature, and most of them would be interested in learning more about the genre in a university setting. The majority of students consider Tolkienian stories "classics", thus introducing them in literary courses could raise student interest while also providing a broader picture about 20th century literary traditions. There is also a great interest in modern fantasy narratives like *Harry Potter, The Witcher* or *Game of Thrones* – introducing these works in lectures and seminars could also serve the same purposes as Tolkien's works, while they could be used to discuss contemporary issues in our culture and society.

Conclusion

The aim of this current study was to examine what Hungarian students of English and American Studies think about the fantasy genre and their relationship with Tolkien's legacy. As the survey was only filled out at two universities and we can suppose that the questions were only answered by those who show at least a slight interest in the genre, this research is not a representative sample: it is merely an overview that supports the idea that it is important to teach fantastic works to university students, because not only is it an influential part of our culture, but students are also open to explore this topic in an academic atmosphere.

The 77 respondents mostly agreed that fantasy is a very important genre, and the main arguments for why they like it were that it moves the imagination, helps creativity, and it also serves as a form of escapism. Although there were numerous fantastic narratives that students were familiar with (*Harry Potter, The Witcher, Chronicles of Narnia,* or *Game of Thrones*), *The Lord of the Rings* was definitely one of the most prominent stories mentioned by the majority of the participants, which shows that Tolkienian fantasy still plays an important part in our culture (even in the world of Generation Z). In terms of format, most students prefer films and series; however, 76% of the participants read fantasy novels, and more than half of them play fantasy games either in an online or an offline form, usually in English. The variety in the ways students consume fantasy shows that there is a great potential in using the genre as a means of improving their language skills: the deep immersion in the storyline can also help students improve their vocabulary and their general language competencies as well. By including fantastic works in seminars, students would also be more eager to participate in critical discussions and strengthen the feeling of belonging to a community.

When asked about their opinion on Tolkien's work, more than half of the students have already read something from the author, and most of them thought that these works are still relevant. Although the adaptations

One Does Not Simply Teach Fantasy   159

of Tolkien's books were more popular, and more than a third of the participants were interested in the (then) upcoming Amazon Prime series called *The Lord of the Rings: The Rings of Power*, it seems that even though the author's works are now falling into the category of "classic" fantasy, his legacy is still alive, as many young adults are still interested in Tolkien's mythology. Interestingly, when it comes to the relevancy of the Tolkienian stories and the more modern fantasy narratives like *Harry Potter*, *The Witcher* or *Game of Thrones*, the answers were diverse: roughly a third of the participants felt that Tolkien is more relevant than the fantasy stories of the late 20th and early 21st century, a third of them disagreed, and the remaining third felt that there was no difference between these two groups. Most of the students agreed that the stories of Middle-earth are important, classic and timeless pieces, and they became the standard that other fantastic texts have to live up to. Lastly, when it comes to talking about the genre in university lectures and seminars, most of the respondents would definitely want to discuss fantastic texts more in an academic setting, and they would be happy to learn about other fantasy narratives as well, be it films, series, or even video games.

The results of this survey demonstrate that students are open to talk about the genre in an academic setting. It is undeniable that fantasy is no longer a niche literary category and its impact on literature, television, and video gaming is getting bigger and bigger every day. Although this chapter mainly concentrated on students of English and American studies, and why it would be beneficial for them to talk about fantastic works in the classroom, opening the university curricula to fantastic works would be a great opportunity to widen the perspective of any student taking part in a literary or cultural university programme.

Works Cited

Fabrizi, Mark Anthony. *Teaching Critical Literacy Skills Through Fantasy Literature: Case Studies from Three Connecticut High Schools.* University of Hull, 2012, PhD. thesis.

Ford, Jim. Introduction. *Fantasy Media in the Classroom: Essays on Teaching with Film, Television, Literature, Graphic Novels, and Video Games.* Ed. Emily Dial Driver, Sally Emmons and Jim Ford. Jefferson: McFarland, 2012. 3–8.

Fredrickson, Nathan. "Designing a Course Integrating Critical Pedagogy, Fantasy Literature, and Religious Studies". *Fantasy Literature: Challenging Genres.* Ed. Mark A. Fabrizi. Rotterdam: Sense Publishers, 2016. 57–76.

Hughes, Sarah. "Game of Thrones: How It Dominated the Decade – Then Lost Its Way". *The Guardian*, 30 December 2019 http://www.theguardian.com/tv-and-radio/2019/dec/30/game-of-thrones-best-tv-2010s. Accessed 14 March 2022.

Robbins, Margaret A. and Jennifer Jackson Whitley. "From Fledgling to Buffy: Critical Literacy, Fantasy, and Engagement in Secondary ELA Classrooms".

160 *Nikolett Sipos*

Fantasy Literature: Challenging Genres. Ed. Mark A. Fabrizi. Rotterdam: Sense Publishers, 2016. 93–107.

Stephan, Matthias. "Do You Believe in Magic? The Potency of the Fantasy Genre". *Coolabah* 18 (2016): 3–15.

Thomas, Melissa. "Teaching Fantasy: Overcoming the Stigma of Fluff". *The English Journal* 92.5 (May 2003): 60–64.

Velkey, Robert. "New Ways of Education – We Should Give Harry Potter to the Children to Read". *Hungary Today,* 24 March 2017. https://hungarytoday. hu/new-ways-education-instead-classic-writings-children-read-harry-potter-compulsory-reading-school-45466/. Accessed 23 February 2022.

Zipes, Jack. "Why Fantasy Matters Too Much". *The Journal of Aesthetic Education* 43.2 (2009): 77–91.

9 From Niche to Mainstream? Screen Culture's Impact on Contemporary Perceptions of Fantasy

David Levente Palatinus

Introduction: Fantasy in the Context of Platform Logic

Streaming platforms have seen an unprecedented pace of proliferation over the past 10 years, and specifically during the pandemic. Subscriptions to Netflix, HBO, Prime, Apple TV, and most recently Disney, skyrocketed during the pandemic, even in Central Europe (Ádám; Mikos, "Film and Television"; Vlassis). In close connection to this, both the consumption and production of specific types of genre, including fantasy, also increased. Data from June 2021 (Medve) indicate that in Hungary alone, 81% of those people who were sampled showed familiarity with Netflix, while 59% of the respondents subscribed to the platform. In the case of HBO Max, as of 2022 March 70% was familiar with the service, and 37 subscribed, and Amazon Prime seems to have the lowest market share in this regard, with 20% familiarity, but only 4% of subscriptions (Ádám). Apple TV and Disney Plus only became available after the pandemic, so these services bear different relevance for the arguments presented here, but we have to acknowledge the growing number of subscriptions, especially in the case of Disney Plus – where apparently most subscribers are attracted to the platform not exclusively by popular mega-franchises like the original *Star Wars* films or the Marvel Cinematic Universe, but also, by association, by the related series as well (*The Mandalorian*, *Obi Wan Kenobi*, *The Book of Bobba Fett*, or *Loki*, *Wanda Vision*, *Legends*, *Hawkeye* – and a plethora of further upcoming series) that form an integral part of the (seemingly) ever-expanding narrative universe of each franchise. These productions, commonly dubbed as platform originals, prove to be an equally significant factor in propping up subscription numbers and are instrumental in the ways in which streaming platforms compete with each other and with broadcast and linear television networks (Szczepanik, "HBO Europe's original programming" 243).

It is also worth noting that with the introduction of COVID-related isolation measures, almost all platforms registered an increase in subscriptions

DOI: 10.4324/9781003407171-13

162   *David Levente Palatinus*

(Faughnder). The most noticeable growth was allegedly seen by Netflix, although the pertaining data to corroborate these claims remains difficult to access because of Netflix's very secretive data policies (van Es; Schanke Sundet "Talk to the Hand"). But even in the light of such fluctuating (in some cases dropping, in other cases stagnating) numbers, the global impact of streaming services on audiences' viewing habits remains considerable. The role of streaming platforms is particularly marked in a Central European context, especially when it comes to access to specific (niche) genres such as fantasy or science fiction. As it has been repeatedly argued, whilst streaming platforms provide a successful conduit for more locally relevant content to be produced (Szczepanik, "HBO Europe's original programming"; Barra and Scaglioni, "The Grounds for a Renaissance"; Carelli and Garogolo), they also facilitate access to global brands and "megaproductions" (Mikos "Transmedia Storytelling") via processes of acquisition and via platform originals. Thus, streaming services directly tap into the dynamics of fandom: as Brown argues, "streamability" offers fans a sense of "security" in the sense that they can return to (and repeatedly recontextualize) their programme (18). Similarly, the "binge-ability" of these programmes is also a contributing factor in governing audience engagement: by its close association with quality television programming (Wayne et al), it works to establish both the prestige of the particular content, and conversely, it lends legitimacy to the medium (Jenner, "Binge-watching"), and will be used as a central element to the service's own branding strategies (Wayne et al). As a consequence, local Central European audiences of fantasy and sci-fi are understood to integrate into a global fandom of the genres (Lotz), where they mobilize their viewing habits and practices of engagement as "a collective strategy to form interpretive communities" (Gray, Sandvoss, and Harrington 3). Therefore, contents falling into either category continue to be primarily accessible through streaming platforms to Central European audiences. This is partly due to the distribution arrangements through which these productions are marketed in the region, and partly due to the programming policies of linear television channels – which in this case would include both public service television as well as commercial channels (Varga).

These circumstances have considerable implications for the ways fantasy features in screen culture, and on the ways screen culture (that is, productions and distribution, aesthetics and narrative forms, as well as audience practices) has an impact on the cultural circulation of fantasy. On the one hand, the majority of screen fantasy productions, both film and television, continues to be available on streaming platforms, and on the other hand, audiences will find a plethora of fantasy series among the "platform originals".

These observations indicate a number of things: first, of course, they attest to the strategic centrality of scripted, original, premium content for

Screen Culture's Impact on Contemporary Perceptions of Fantasy 163

both production and distribution policies of streaming platforms. And fantasy as a form/mode proves to be particularly conducive to the kind of quality aesthetics and prestige content that is closely associated with high budgets and high production values – which, inversely, seems to have both a push and a pull effect on audiences' choices and preferences globally as well as in Central Europe (Szczepanik and Vonderau; Szczepanik, "Post-socialist producer"). On the other hand, if one looks at how fantasy shares on streaming platforms, one will notice that fantasy as a category (not necessarily as a genre, but rather as a type of programme that revolves around a specific set of contents), is frequently bundled together with science fiction, which might complicate demarcation and sampling in regards to audiences' preferences for specific instances of content, but can still be used to extrapolate access and penetration in terms the viewership that specific types of programmes and, more importantly, specific genres, can expect to have. Obviously, we're not only talking about "original" contents. Given the history of streaming, VOD and SVOD platforms, there will have been plenty of content available on them that they acquired from the original networks on which they were first introduced – and that feature as "imports" for local audiences (Carelli and Garofalo 61). With streaming services gaining increasingly larger segments of local markets as well (in Western contexts frequently at the expanse of public service broadcasting, but in Central Europe mostly because public and national television networks lack the funding to produce such large-scale premium contents on their own), there is now a growing number of "original" content available to audiences in regards to fantasy too. Such productions include contents that tap into and expand (transmedia) franchises that originated outside these platforms, like the Marvel or the Star Wars cinematic universes, adaptations from literary fiction or other media like *The Witcher* (Netflix), *The Wheel of Time* (Amazon Prime), or *His Dark Materials* (HBO Max), and productions that follow up on earlier flagship productions like *House of the Dragon* on HBO, or *The Rings of Power* on Amazon Prime, and that are themselves intended as flagship content used by the respective platforms as branding strategy and as a means to foster subscriber loyalty (Barra and Scaglioli, "The Grounds for a Renaissance" 14).

On top of that, players like HBO, Netflix, or Amazon play a significant role in determining what gets made: in many cases, certain networks, and even big film studios, would shy away from projects that they consider to be too risky. Streaming services frequently opt in on backing these productions either in cooperation or by taking them over completely (like Amazon Prime took over *The Expanse* after the original network, Syfy axed the production), or commissioning "high budget, high concept scripted products with supranational ambitions" (Barra and Scaglioli, "The Grounds for a Renaissance" 15). Last but not least, streaming services are also

164   David Levente Palatinus

able to provide global access to content that is produced locally (as with *Dark*, which was Netflix's first German-language original series), and through providing access, they also have a very significant impact on the mobilization of pertaining global fandoms. As I have already argued, the binge-ability of a programme is a decisive factor in terms of its popularity (Jenner, "Binge-watching") as well as in terms of the revenues that it might generate (see also Horeck).

The Ubiquity of Fantasy: Genre, (De)Convergence, and Adaptation

As regards the impact of the above circumstances on fantasy, the questions that keep haunting our discussion are those of convergence and (generic) hybridity. These two concepts will have determined a wide range of cultural ideas surrounding the production and consumption of fantasy, and understanding their significance will also provide insights for the ubiquity of the genre in contemporary literary fiction and media. They also help explain why contemporary audiences respond so strongly to these narratives. Whilst specific poetic and aesthetic traits are relatively easy to identify in the case of most programme texts in question, they're still characterized by a high level of hybridity. For instance, in spite of the clearly identifiable visual aesthetics that lends the Marvel Universe or the Star Wars franchise their trademark look, or the formulaic patterns of world-building (the missions, the conflicts and the character dynamics) in *The Rings of Power*, or the prominence of the juxtaposition of sex and violence in *Game of Thrones* or *House of The Dragon*, all of these programmes mobilize a wide range of registers, frequently blending not only elements of narrative mode (or visual aesthetics, for that matter) that cut across a variety of genres (an appeal to realism, for instance), but also features that are conventionally associated with specific subgenres (or categories) of fantasy. Writing about *Game of Thrones* "the network narrative", Haastrup observes that the production, whilst falling within the category of high fantasy and utilizing the "ontological break" (the appearance of an element that disrupts the audience's understanding of what "appears to be realistic representation" (132)), also subverts a central element of classical fantasy storytelling, the "Manichean battle between the forces of good and evil" (133). This, as Haastrup argues, is a clearly identifiable element in "adaptations of literature by J.R.R. Tolkien, or J.K. Rowling" (133). However, as it has been frequently discussed both in scholarly takes as well as in the pertaining fandom, the appeal of *Game of Thrones,* its peculiarly uncanny atmosphere, and, in close connection to these, its ability to glue audiences to the screen, derives precisely from its complication of this formula: good is not always only good, and evil is not irrevocably evil (Haastrup 134).

Screen Culture's Impact on Contemporary Perceptions of Fantasy 165

There are of course other film and television examples of fantasy that use the discrepancy between absolute notions of good and evil and their more fluid conceptualization as a source for conflict and a force that propels plots. The subversive representation of condemnable and redeemable qualities in their characters is precisely what gives many of these programmes their specificity, and what triggers acts of identification on the part of their respective audiences. The 'realism' of such fluid interpretations of a character's qualities (i.e. sympathy or resentment that is determined by the spatial and temporal constrains of the character's situation in the narrative) is perceived, even if unknowingly, as a gesture towards the lived experiences of the audience. Such narratives include earlier examples of urban (and young-adult) fantasy on television such as *Buffy the Vampire Slayer*, the *Vampire Diaries*, or more recently *Loki*. Certain films in the *X-Men* franchise also capitalize on the long form's ability to accommodate a more multifaceted presentation of specific characters by digging into their history or by placing them into different situations and allowing qualities not explored before to manifest (as is the case with Magneto or Mistique). And most recently, HBO's *House of the Dragon* or Amazon's *Rings of Power* also predicate construction of their respective storyworlds on such subversive representations of the dynamics of power. The season-finale of the *Rings of Power* allows audiences to believe that Galadriel is single-handedly responsible for the re-appearance of Sauron. *Game of Thrones* depicts Daenaerys' actions through the series (from Mirri's execution upon the death of Khal Drogo, to the destruction of King's Landing), both as justifiable responses to injustices and traumas suffered in the past, and as acts of a tyrant-in-the-making. In a similar vein, *House of the Dragon* frames Rhaenyra and Daemon's relationship precisely within the same context of intricacies stemming from their will to power which prove to be destructive not only for those around them but also for themselves.

Haastrup also observes that certain examples of urban fantasy adapted for the big and small screens mobilize various formulas, that is, imaginary structures and forms of identification that "feature both social and cultural historical perspectives" (133) to construct their narratives. Emblematic examples include the horror, the melodrama, the adventure, and the romance. *True Blood* and *The Vampire Diaries* are two examples that combine these traits with the haunting legacy of the urban Gothic and with the lure of uncanny monstrosity.

In actuality, the reason why it is difficult to find a single production that would be considered purely homogenous is due in great deal to the fact that contemporary media is predicated on convergence that predestines high-quality programmes to a hybridity that gives them a cutting edge – to which audiences respond well. The ubiquity of fantasy is closely connected both to the hybridity of this mode, and to its transmedia mode

166   David Levente Palatinus

of existence. Unpacking this correlation of transmediality and hybridity is a challenging enterprise and is not without its pitfalls. Johannes Fehrle and Schäfke-Zell Werner write about "productively bringing into contact" concepts of adaptation and convergence, but also emphasize that there will have been points where they're best "kept separate to retain their respective analytical strengths" (10). Arguing for a more inclusive interpretation of the underlying cultural logic of transmediality, Daniel Baker observes that "whatever the medium, fantastic narratives now dominate vast areas of popular imagination, so fantasy is obviously a pervasive phenomenon" (437). In a similar vein, Kathryn Hume also points out that the realist strategy is not too conducive to the level of audience engagement that fantasy can provide a platform for. Fantasy goes beyond reality and offers interesting, subversive perspectives (15). Therefore, it needs to be taken into consideration that fantasy, in today's media-saturated environment, operates, and exists primarily as a transmedia phenomenon. What this means in practice for the consumption (and by extension, the production) of fantasy is highlighted by the words of Henry Jenkins:

> A transmedia story unfolds across multiple media platforms, with each new text making a distinctive and valuable contribution to the whole. In the ideal form of transmedia storytelling, each medium does what it does best, and each franchise entry need to be self-contained so that the audience doesn't have to have seen the film, to enjoy the game and vice versa. Any given product is a point of entry into the franchise as a whole. (Jenkins 95–96).

Lothar Mikos replicates and elaborates further on these ideas, actually explaining how convergence plays a significant role in the transmediatization and proliferation of franchises. He, however, also calls attention to a trend that seems to be working against convergence as an all-encompassing governing principle, and he couples convergence with the process of deconvergence. To adopt his arguments to our purpose, we can say that while convergence explains how various media platforms interact with one another and how specific modes or forms or genres, in our case fantasy, develop and unfold across multiple platforms, the process of deconvergence implies that technological change leads to a multiplicity of channels and platforms that deliver audiovisual content, but it also generates fragmentation of both content as well as of the immersion of the audience ("Transmedia Storytelling"). The fragmentation of film and television leads to fragmented audiences because diverse audiences use different media platforms to get films and television shows whenever and wherever they want. Mikos contradicts Jenkins because he acknowledges the dispersal of audiences, and highlights that not everybody will be following the same contents on all the platforms on which they unfold.

On the other hand, the flux of convergence and deconvergence has an interesting result on how the resulting media products are constructed: they not only encompass various generic elements as we have seen before, but they also retain and integrate in themselves the characteristics of a multiplicity of media formats. In other words, transmediality does not just mean that each medium offers its own contribution whilst remaining self-contained. Rather, transmediality also implies one medium "imprinting" on the other in the sense that transmedia narratives encode in themselves the specificities of the multiple media through which they proliferate. For instance, Netflix's *The Witcher* is not simply an adaptation of the fantasy books written by Andrzej Sapkowski. The series deliberately and purposefully draws on the video game franchise as well. And while the video game may not have been the main inspiration for the series, it played a crucial role in the development of its visual aesthetics (Grimm). The series' narrative utilizes a hybrid structure (Gawronski and Bajorek), with a three-plot narrative that is supplemented by side-plots in the fashion of side missions known from video game narratives (although these side-plots are not adaptations of any of the video game narratives).

Consequently, in a convergent media environment, "these franchises, their formats are established as global brands" (Mikos "Transmedia Storytelling"). With streaming platforms joining the game and playing a significant role in establishing these global brands, fantasy universes are no longer created just by a single instance of literary fiction, film or TV show (in the case of original contents), nor does the situation boil down to questions of adaptation. Instead, all of the various offerings associated with the content in question contribute to the expansion, transformation, circulation and reception of that content. These trends are characterized by a dynamics of decentralization which breaks down generic as well as media boundaries, making them more fluid, and elements of a continuum, but they also suspend traditional hierarchies of genres and media, resulting in a rhizomatic proliferation of the pertaining narrative, aesthetic, and participatory dimensions of each fantasy universe.

Last but not least, these reconsiderations of transmediality and hybridity also necessitate a brief discussion of adaptation, especially in regards to audience engagement. The new convergent media environment disrupted a formerly accepted chronological logic that prioritized the text over the audiovisual adaptation, where the adaptation would programmatically be compared to the original, and the "success" and "merit" of the adaptation would depend on perceptions of fidelity and accuracy. Linda Hutcheon already rejects practices of fidelity criticism, shifting focus from the question of "proximity" (in a literal sense) to audiences' ability to relate to the

168   David Levente Palatinus

adaptation, to recognize the book in the film or television series in terms of setting, plot, character dynamics, and the overall ethos of the work that is being adapted (Fehrle and Werner 12). I would call this the priority of authenticity, rather than that of accuracy. In the fandom, however, the conceptualization of originality will remain a divisive factor: as long as the content in question continues to be delivered, what will be discussed in the fandom is the conceptual, narrative, aesthetic qualities of the adaptation, the degree of authenticity and, most importantly, the relatability of the programme in question. Seeing a reverse order of media chronology in the reception practices of audiences, one might argue that as a result of the shifting trends in the ways fiction (and in our case, fantasy) has come to be culturally perceived and consumed, the ways it has repositioned the question of adaptation, emancipating it to new levels of technical, aesthetic and even perhaps narrative originality, the hierarchical ordering of screen vs print texts was also called into question. This is no news for adaptations studies or for media scholarship. But what this consideration unmasks is a socio-cultural shift that we are witnessing in relation to practices of initiation and exposure to contents. There is now a vast body of audiences who were first initiated to these contents via the film adaptations, and then they went to the books. They were viewers before they became readers. As it is pointed out in the HBO Max television special *Harry Potter 20th Anniversary: Return to Hogwarts*, there's already a generation of adults in the process of introducing their own children to the films, and it suffices to remind of the power the Harry Potter studios have as an attraction, and the amount of visitors they can attract and the cultural impact they have on shaping the cultural status, understanding and conceptualizations of fantasy.

Technological Changes, Budgetary Constraints, and the Question of Quality

The adaptation boom was also greatly facilitated by the technological shifts in filmmaking that actually made it possible in the first place. Just to mention a few examples, the proliferation of CGI and digital technology, the green screen and motion capture are some of the most essential developments that one can think about. As Friedman points out, the processing power of computer animation technology proved to be a primary enabler for filmmakers and creators to "replace traditional special effects" and to "create unnatural landscapes, spectacular battles, and inhuman characters" that will blend "seamlessly [...] into the footage of real actors shot on physical sets" (5). He explains how "fantasy filmmakers take advantage of CGI technology to fill the screen with talking animals, self-aware plants, and landscapes that breathe with meaning" (15). These productions are

Screen Culture's Impact on Contemporary Perceptions of Fantasy   169

keen on paying heightened attention to detail also in terms of the film sets. Fantasy, whether on the big screen or the small, is particularly keen on the looks, in fact its specificity when adapted to the screen derives from the production's ability to successfully and convincingly capture visually that universe in which the narrative is set (Friedman 1). For that reason, these productions require very high budgets, and very complex sets. One of the most recent examples to quote here is the episode set in the "Blight" in *Wheel of Time* (Prime, 2021-), a rotten and bare land, created by the influence of the Dark One over the world. It is one of the most complex sets that was being used for the series that relied on physical props rather than CGI. According to behind-the-scenes commentaries available as bonus content on the platform, every single tree had to be constructed from plastic and other materials, and every single branch had to be separately and individually screwed to the trunk of the tree to create this maze-like structure.

In relation to this, the budgetary dimension has to be mentioned as well: as I pointed out before, streaming services have grown enough to be able to afford such production costs. To return to the publicity around the *Game of Thrones* prequel, *House of the Dragon* on HBO Max, and the publicity around *Rings of Power* on Amazon Prime, the numbers that circulate clearly indicate that these productions are in league with high budget Hollywood filmmaking: according to data published in *The Hollywood Reporter*, one episode of the *Rings of Power* costs approximately $60 million to make, with a total budget for the production's first season costing around 465 million dollars (Hibberd). The report says that by comparison, the per-season budget of *Game of Thrones* was "only" around 100 million dollars. Obviously, a lot of criticism has been directed at such mega-productions, and even in the fandom this has become very divisive information: in one Facebook fan group, such budgetary comparisons sparked heated debates about the expected quality of the production and how that would relate to the publicity and the promotion activities leading up to the premiere of the series (IGN). Both among critics and fans there was a lot of scepticism concerning the end-product. Commentators opined that whilst Amazon really has money to throw at the project, the question was – was it going to be good? In general terms, one can easily argue that while it can be overwhelming to hear and see such large numbers and see how much money is being spent on these productions, the question remains if this will not lead to a bubble effect, where the spectacle, the promotion and the publicity exceeds the scope of a truly compelling narrative that remains authentic and keeps the fans happy.

The risk is that these productions become enterprises with which the entertainment value is diminished at the expanse of the streaming platform trying to build its own brand solely on the basis of marketing considerations, and with the sole intention to expand rather than deliver content

170 David Levente Palatinus

that is true to the cultural categories and practices they tap into. Another emblematic example of such discrepancy comes from the Witcher fandom, where the Netflix series' reception (especially as regards the first season) was also characterized by controversies, and fans being divided over the question how much the series lived up to the expectations of fans of the literary fiction as well as those of the video games (Gawronski and Bajorek; Afilipoaie et al).

Even if a lot of questions are asked about the nexus between budget, success, and aesthetic quality in connection with these mega-productions, one cannot look past the fact that due to the streaming services' underlying business models and programming policies, fantasy continues to be a crucial form – because momentarily it sells well, and because there's obviously a popular demand for it. HBO very recently used *Game of Thrones* as part of a strategy to revamp itself and to reinvigorate its brand (McElroy and Noonan; McNutt). And streaming services, while competing with one another as well, are bound to follow established and proven-to-be-successful strategies to build their brand. As Wayne et al explain, Netflix, for instance, "largely followed HBO's model to establish its brand identity. For example, in giving creative and budgetary freedom to television 'showrunner-auteurs'" (Wayne et al). And in the present context, every platform that does fantasy actually aims at superseding somehow the success of *Game of Thrones*, which is commonly perceived (also by a significant proportion of audiences of televisual high fantasy) as the etalon against which everything else is measured. The question always seems to be "what is going to be the next *Game of Thrones* and who's going to make it?" Or "who's going to come up with something better than *Game of Thrones*?" There's definitely a lot of very high production values going into these projects, and it also shows that it's the platforms that have a real future with these productions, partly because of the serial format, and partly because of the budgetary constraints that public service broadcasters have, and partly because of the global reach to audiences.

Audience and Participation

When we look at the history of television and the history of fantasy on television, what we see is that the genre has been continuously present for both British and American television audiences. In Central Europe, fantasy programmes gained a more pronounced visibility in the 1990s when fantasy started to emerge, and programmes like *Buffy the Vampire Slayer*, *Xena: Warrior Princess*, *Charmed*, *Angel*, *Hercules: The Legendary Journeys*, and the likes garnered a considerable viewership, especially among young adult audiences. Many of these series were extremely popular and successful, but from today's point of view, they might come across as lacking, especially in terms of the visual aesthetics. This was in part due to the budgetary possibilities of the networks that produced them, but also in part to the fact that the emphasis fell on something other than spectacular visual effects. The melodramatic dimension featured more powerfully, and so did, from a narrative point of view, the question of how, via the dynamics between the different characters, the narrative could express and render the supernatural and the fantastic. Audience's responses primarily revolved around these instances. Audience engagement in the 90s, especially in Central Europe, was significantly different from what we are seeing in our contemporary times, partly because of the lack of social media, and partly because, as compared to the UK and the US, Central European audiences had (and to some extent still have) less access to the kind of televisual paraphernalia (Geraghty) that allows insight not only into the production processes of the programme (the "behind the scenes" contents), but also into the lives, activities and appearances of stars and celebrities outside of the context of filming.

Premium/subscription services quickly discovered the power of paraphernalia both for promotional purposes, and also to enhance the visibility of the fandom around specific programmes as well as around the brand the service or network embodies. HBO's flagship drama, *Game of Thrones,* was also surrounded by extensive televisual paraphernalia, and there continues to be a very extensive and multifaceted fandom around *Game of Thrones* (Barker et al). Various aspects of the fandom highlight transmediality: one of the most kind of emblematic examples of such paraphernalia is *Thronecast* (Sky Atlantic), which was an accompanying background programme and talk show that was broadcast on Sky Atlantic after each episode of *Game of Thrones.* The structure allowed hosts to invite either some of the actors and actresses or the showrunners to discuss the episode that just aired, the behind the scenes or details of the production, and in which direction the story was possibly going to go. It was a very interactive programme because it was also being broadcast online, and thus it was also possible for audiences to join in. The programme was accompanied and complemented by a Twitter feed, and by the impetus of social media dynamics, there were soon to be multiple Facebook fan groups established. In other words, the *Game of Thrones* fandom has always been characterized by transmediality due to a series of transmedia practices.

Another instance of participatory engagement derives from the heightened political and cultural attention directed at questions of casting. A lot of examples could be mentioned here, but I'll only highlight *The Wheel of Time,* and *The Expanse* (originally Syfy, then Amazon Prime), which were both critically acclaimed for going at length to promote and effectuate diversity casting. Both series have got one of the most diverse casts on television (Robinson; Augustus). The showrunners, however, managed

172   *David Levente Palatinus*

to avoid tokenism. Character choices come natural, they don't feel like they're there just so the programme can tick boxes on the political correctness board. These choices also gesture towards the political responsibility that fantasy, whether on paper or on the screen, will assume – not least by way of its proneness to extensive allegorization. In this regard, it's not so much a genre of escape or alternative universes, but a conduit to our contemporary lived experiences, fears, and anxieties, as well as hopes for a better, more inclusive, more livable, and sustainable future. Interestingly, these issues seem to be central to the ways in which the fandom engages with these programmes.

The third observation about the question of participation and audience behaviour has to do with platform choices. Converging media environments brought about an increased complexity that is partly the result of the types of contents produced, partly of the changing broadcasting and distribution practices service providers adapt. Consequently, audiences have to attune their viewing habits. These instances of audience behaviour are far from being homogenous, and will be influenced by a number of demographic factors. Barra and Scaglioli distinguish between "superficial" consumers, who will utilize convergent media only to some extent and use the Internet and social media to inform about specific contents ("Blurred Lines" 79), and those who will engage more deeply and will be drawn to digital practices associated with the acquisition of personal and group identities. Participatory fandom "is frequently expressed through such deep consumption practices" (81).

Audience behaviour in regard to fantasy too seems to corroborate what Webster describes as myths about digital media. First, users are not the only active agents in a converging media environment (354): agency unfolds as a synergy of pull media and push media, meaning that whilst people might be able to seek out media, media also find and act upon people – for instance via recommendation algorithm and targeted content. Therefore, people may not always be in the position to make informed decisions because of there are too many options and too many factors to consider. It would seem that for that reason, as Webster argues, users respond by "narrowing their choices to small 'repertoires', using heuristics and relying on recommender systems" (354), but such strategies are more frequently supplemented personal recommendations in users' social interactions (online or offline) within fan communities. These groups are prone to adopting forms of "herding behavior, information cascades, social contagions" which have the capacity to "shape cultural consumption" (355).

Like any fandom, fantasy fandom will also follow their preferred contents – somewhat irrespective of the network or platform on which they can access it. Non-representative samplings of social media discussions in fan groups[1] indicate that fans usually opt for a specific platform

Screen Culture's Impact on Contemporary Perceptions of Fantasy   173

not necessarily because of the recommendations platforms' algorithms may offer, but rather because of specific programmes that they will know about primarily from personal recommendations, social media discussions, or critiques and reviews they come across on the Internet or in print media (Burroughs). And whilst in the social media fandoms sampled for this study there was little discussion of linear versus streaming platforms, audiences tend to look at what is offered/available to them on which streaming service. It's not always the abundance of content enhanced by algorithmic governance that attracts audiences to specific platforms, not simply the drive to explore (yet again) the vastness of a service's repertoire. There's evidence suggesting that in specific cases, audiences actively seek out particular content – and will be driven to where that content is available. In other words, demand on the part of the audience, and audience's choices/preferences will impact back on the industry, as, among others, Vilde Shanke Sundet observe in her book *Television Drama in the Age of Streaming* (2021).

In addition, there's a great deal of intertextual contextualization on these social media forums, not necessarily in terms of comparing different fantasy programmes, but in terms of doing an indirect promotion for various programmes via personal recommendations. As a consequence, fandom incorporates very strong and self-conscious virtual communities. They don't consider streaming to be hyper individualistic because they see instead a virtual community that spreads across the streaming platforms as well as social media platforms where fans meet and communicate. These communities are not held together simply by the temporal and spatial constraints of the viewing experience. They are held together by an internalized awareness of belonging, that others are viewing too, simultaneously, and participating in ongoing discussions around the content.

These observations are inexorably linked with what Webster describes as users opting in and out of living in enclaves of preferred genres and ideologically agreeable content (356). According to Webster, while algorithmic governance "might be filtering our encounters with media in ways that are invisible to us" (356), whether it also leads to digital media filter bubbles that will have a direct influence on participatory agency remains unclear, especially upon observing fan behaviours.

It is important to acknowledge that the participatory dimension of fan communities manifests in a marked way around specific genres and forms, and streaming platforms have got a significant role to play in facilitating and channelling these processes, especially in times of crises. Conclusively, it can be argued that streaming services no longer target niche market groups, but rather construct their own global audiences for their own global brands that are constructed via transmedia practices, and Central European audiences are not significantly different in terms of global behaviours and consumer practices. Fantasy therefore will have been caught up

174   *David Levente Palatinus*

in a cyclical correlation between transmediality, the potentials of the serial format, hybridity, and the practices and preferences of global audiences. If we look closely, we recognize that we have witnessed shifting trends that gradually turned fantasy from a niche form into a multifaceted, mainstream narrative and cultural mode.

Note

1 The following fan communities on Facebook were sampled for the purposes of this study between 2021 January and 2022 December: The Expanse Geeks (https://www.facebook.com/groups/ExpanseGeeks/); Sci Fi and Fantasy: Everything Streaming and Movies (https://www.facebook.com/groups/SciFiandFantasy.TV.Everything.Streaming.Movies/); Everything The Wheel of Time (https://www.facebook.com/groups/609694296824689/); Game of Thrones Official (https://www.facebook.com/groups/1197450040384696/); Game of Thrones / House of Dragons (https://www.facebook.com/groups/449093012865771/); The Lord of the Rings: Rings of Power (https://www.facebook.com/groups/TheLOTR.Series/).

   The method comprised of qualitative and textual analyses of posts related to fantasy content, audience behaviour, audience choices and preferences, repostings of publicity items ranging from memes to social media and promotions, and content reviews in specialist online magazines (like *Screenrant* or *Entertainment Weekly*) to intertextual links to other related programmes and fandom-driven contents. Interpretative and evaluative discussions (in regard to narrative, visual aesthetics as well as instances of fidelity criticism were also observed.

Works Cited

Ádám, Rebeka Nóra: "Magyarország Netflixország – így törtek át a streaming filmszolgáltatók hazánkban is". https://mandiner.hu/cikk/20221028_streaming_magyarorszag. Accessed 23 December 2022.

Afilipoaie, Adelaida, Catalina Iordache and Tim Raats. "The 'Netflix Original' and What It Means for the Production of European Television Content". *Critical Studies in Television* 16.3 (2021): 304–325.

Augustus, Fenhua T. "Sci-fi needs to be more like The Expanse in its casting". *Space.com*, 19 October 2022. https://www.space.com/sci-fi-needs-to-be-more-like-the-expanse-in-its-casting. Accessed 23 January 2023.

Baker, Daniel. "Why We Need Dragons: The Progressive Potential of Fantasy". *Journal of the Fantastic in the Arts* 23.3 (2012): 437–459.

Barra, Luca and Massimo Scaglioni. "The Grounds for a Renaissance in European Fiction: Transnational Writing, Production and Distribution Approaches, and Strategies". *A European Television Fiction Renaissance*. Ed. Luca Barra and Massimo Scaglioni. New York: Routledge, 2021. 13–33.

——. "Blurred Lines, Distinct Forces: The Evolving Practices of Italian TV Audiences in a Convergent Scenario". *Media Convergence and Deconvergence*. Ed. Sergio Sparviero, Corinna Peil and Gabriele Balbi. Basingstoke: Palgrave, 2017. 159–176.

Screen Culture's Impact on Contemporary Perceptions of Fantasy   175

Barker, Martin, Clarissa Smith and Feona Attwood, eds. *Watching Game of Thrones: How Audiences Engage with Dark Television*. Manchester: Manchester UP, 2021.

Brown, Cameron Lynn. "Residual Fandom: Television Technologies, Industries, and Fans of Survivor". *The Velvet Light Trap* 90 (2022): 17–27.

Burroughs, Benjamin. "House of Netflix: Streaming Media and Digital Lore". *Popular Communication* 17.1 (2018): 1–17.

Carelli, Paolo and Damiano Garofalo. "Transnational Circulation of European TV Series". *A European Television Fiction Renaissance*. Ed. Luca Barra and Massimo Scaglioni. New York: Routledge, 2021. 56–68.

Faughnder, Ryan. "Streaming Milestone: Global Subscriptions Passed 1 Billion Last Year". *Los Angeles Times*, 18 March 2021. https://www.latimes.com/entertainment-arts/business/story/2021-03-18/streaming-milestone-global-subscriptions-passed-1-billion-last-year-mpa-theme-report. Accessed 24 March 2022.

Fehrle, Johannes and Werner Schäfke-Zell. *Transmedia: Participatory Culture and Media Convergence*. Amsterdam: Amsterdam UP, 2019.

Friedman, Ted. "The Politics of Magic: Fantasy Media, Technology, and Nature in the 21st Century". *Scope* 14 (2009). https://www.nottingham.ac.uk/scope/documents/2009/june-2009/friedman.pdf. Accessed 21 September 2022.

Gawronski, Slawomir and Kinga Bajorek. "A Real Witcher – Slavic or Universal; from a Book, a Game or a TV Series? In the Circle of Multimedia Adaptations of a Fantasy Series of Novels 'The Witcher' by A. Sapkowski". *Arts* 9.4 (2020). https://www.mdpi.com/2076-0752/9/4/102. Accessed 16 February 2023.

Geraghty, Christine. "Making Television Strange". *CSTOnline*, 15 May 2014. https://cstonline.net/making-television-strange-by-christine-geraghty/. Accessed 15 March 2022.

Gray, Jonathan, Cornel Sandvoss and C. Lee Harrington, eds. *Introduction to Fandom: Identities and Communities in a Mediated World*. New York: New York UP, 2017.

Grimm, Peter. "The Witcher Showrunner Reveals What the Show Took from the Games". *GameRant*, 9 February 2020. https://gamerant.com/witcher-showrunner-reveals-show-took-games/. Accessed 23 January 2023.

Haastrup, Helle Kannik. "Power Play and Family Ties: Hybrid Fantasy, Network Narrative and Female Characters". *Women of Ice and Fire: Gender, Game of Thrones and Multiple Media Engagements*. Ed. Anne Gjelsvik and Rikke Schubart. London: Bloomsbury, 2016. 131–151.

Hibberd, James. "Amazon's 'The Lord of the Rings' to Cost $465M for Just One Season". *The Hollywood Reporter*, 16 April 2021. https://www.hollywoodreporter.com/tv/tv-news/amazons-lord-of-the-rings-cost-465-million-one-season-4167791/. Accessed 23 January 2023.

Horeck, Tanya. "'Netflix and Heal': The Shifting Meanings of Binge-Watching during the COVID-19 Crisis". *Film Quarterly* 75.1 (September 2021): 35–40.

Hume, Kathryn. *Fantasy and Mimesis: Responses to Reality in Western Literature*. London: Routledge, 2015.

IGN. https://www.facebook.com/ign/photos/a.119104781632/101593310064616 33/?type=3). Accessed 16 February 2023.

Jenkins, Henry. *Convergence Culture*. New York: New York UP, 2006.

176   *David Levente Palatinus*

Jenner, Mareike. "Binge-watching: video-on-demand, quality TV and mainstreaming fandom". *International Journal of Cultural Studies* 20.3 (2015): 304–320.

———. *Binge-Watching and Contemporary Television Studies*. Edinburgh: Edinburgh UP, 2021.

Lotz, Amanda. "The Post-Network Era". *A Companion to the History of American Broadcasting*. Ed. Aniko Bodroghkozy. Oxford: Wiley, 2018. 153–167.

Medve, Flora. "Number of subscribers to video streaming services in Hungary 2022, by provider". Statista, 13 June 2022. https://www.statista.com/statistics/1313458/hungary-number-of-subscribers-to-video-streaming-services-by-provider/. Accessed 25 November 2022.

McElroy, Ruth and Caitriona Noonan. *Producing British Television Drama*. London: Palgrave Macmillan, 2019.

McNutt, Myles. "Distinction, Value and Fandom in Premium TV". *From Networks to Netflix: A Guide to Changing Channels*. Ed. Derek Johnson. New York: Routledge, 2023. 165–175.

Mikos, Lothar. "Film and Television Production and Consumption in Times of the COVID-19 Pandemic – The Case of Germany". *Baltic Screen Media Review* 8 (2020): 30–34.

———. "Transmedia Storytelling and Meganarration". *Media Convergence and Deconvergence*. Ed. Sergio Sparviero, Corinna Peil and Gabriele Balbi. Basingstoke: Palgrave, 2017. 159–176.

Robinson, Tasha. "How SyFy's The Expanse cast its multiracial future: Genre TV is relying on increasingly gender-balanced, multicultural casts to populate its far-flung worlds". *The Verge*, 25 February 2016. https://www.theverge.com/2016/2/25/11103434/syfy-the-expanse-series-diverse-cast. Accessed 23 January 2023.

Szczepanik, Petr. "HBO Europe's original programming in the era of streaming wars". *A European Television Fiction Renaissance*. Ed. Luca Barra and Massimo Scaglioni. New York: Routledge, 2021. 243–267.

———. "Post-socialist Producer: 'The Production Culture of a Small-nation Media Industry'". *Critical Studies in Television* 13.2 (2018): 207–226.

Szczepanik Petr and Patrick Vonderau, eds. *Behind the Screen: Inside European Production Cultures*. New York: Palgrave Macmillan, 2013.

Sundet, Vilde Schanke. *Television Drama in the Age of Streaming*. Cham: Palgrave Pivot, 2021.

———. "Talk to the Hand! Or Why I Want to Talk Television with Global Platform Representatives". *CSTOnline*, 12 February 2021. https://cstonline.net/talk-to-the-hand-or-why-i-want-to-talk-television-with-global-platform-representatives-by-vilde-schanke-sundet/. Accessed 15 January 2023.

van Es, Karin. "Netflix & Big Data: The Strategic Ambivalence of an Entertainment Company". *Television & New Media* (OnlineFirst, 26 September, 2022): 1–17. https://doi.org/10.1177/15274764221125745.

Varga, Balázs. "Familiar, Much Too Familiar… HBO's Hungarian Original Productions and the Question of Cultural Proximity". *A European Television Fiction Renaissance*. Eds. Luca Barra and Massimo Scaglioni. New York: Routledge, 2021. 275–295.

Vlassis, Antonios. "Global Online Platforms, COVID-19, and Culture: The Global Pandemic, an Accelerator Towards Which Direction?" *Media, Culture & Society* 43.5 (2021): 957–969.

Wayne, Michael L. and Ana C. Uribe Sandoval. "Netflix Original Series, Global Audiences and Discourses of Streaming Success". *Critical Studies in Television* 18.1 (2023): 81–100.

Index

Note: Page numbers followed by "n" denote endnotes.

Ábrahám, Zsófia 46, 48
Aczél, György 14
Adams, Douglas 25
Adams, Richard 68
Adams, Robert M. 17
adaptation 1, 5, 9, 124, 154; and
    convergence 166–168; and
    deconvergence 164–168; film
    2, 4, 34, 40, 66, 67, 74, 75,
    80, 84–87, 90–91, 98, 103,
    105, 107, 109–111, 155–158,
    168; radio 114; streaming
    and television 148; and
    transmediality 7, 163, 167;
    video game 153
adolescence 133–135, 138
Adventures of Tom Bombadil, The
    (Tolkien) 45, 46
Alakša, Ivan 96, 97, 114n4
Alaska Young (character) 136,
    142–143
Alice in Wonderland (Carroll) 76
allegory 8, 65, 78, 83, 105,
    108, 135
Amazon Prime 161; *Rings of Power*
    165; series 156, 159
Anderson, Douglas A. 27n9, 43
Annotated Hobbit (Anderson and
    Tolkien) 27n9, 43
anti-sociological novel 65
Apor, Péter 25
Apple TV 161
Aragorn 88
Arda 82, 83, 90
Arwen (character) 88

Athelas (fanzine) 96, 99, 99n8, 100,
    100n14, 103, 111, 112
Atlas of Middle-earth (Fonstad) 45, 49
Attebery, Brian 37
Aubron-Bülles, Marcel 42
audience 1, 4, 6, 8, 37, 76, 81, 119,
    131–133, 162–168; and
    participation 170–174
Aurin (fanzine) 24, 25
Avarossy, Éva 15, 17, 18, 54n17
Az ártatlan ország (Bényei) 37

Baker, Daniel 166
Baksai, Károly 54n9
Baptism of Fire (Sapkowski) 137
Barna, Bálinth 40, 53
Barthes, Roland 40
Bassham, Gregory 46
Battle of White Mountain (1620) 62
Baudrillard, Jean 49
Békési, József 46
Beloved (Morrison) 151
Benczik, Vera 40, 53
Bényei, Tamás 37, 38, 47, 53, 53n2,
    53n3
Beowulf: The Monsters and the Critics
    (Tolkien) 45, 47, 79, 110
Berecz, Adrián 101
Bethlenfalvy, Gábor 20
Bibiana (journal) 103, 106
Big Read, The 42
Bilbo Baggins (character) 16, 44, 67,
    76, 109, 121, 125, 126
Bitva Pána prstenů 80
Blood of the Elves (Sapkowski) 137

180   *Index*

Bobok, Jozef 108
Bodacz, Bohuš 99
Bokody, Péter 39, 49
Bombadil, Tom (character) 36, 86, 87
Bonácz, Ágnes 44, 45, 48, 49, 51, 53
Book of Lost Tales, The (Tolkien) 24, 43, 44, 47
Born, Adolf 67
Bronson, Eric 46
Brooke-Rose, Christine 49
Bucková, Martina 66, 96, 99
Buffy the Vampire Slayer 165, 170
Bujačková, Zuzana 63
Büki, Gabriella 45, 46, 48

Campbell, Joseph 135–137, 141, 143, 145, 146
Carpenter, Humphrey 37
Carroll, Lewis 16, 17
Cartaphilus (publisher) 44, 46
Carter, Lin 45
Cart, Michael 131
Caul (character) 144–145, 146
censorship 7, 62, 63
Central Europe 1–6, 9, 26, 69, 117, 151, 161–163, 170, 171, 173
Čermák, Jan 110
Čert, Jim 80
Chance, Jane 39, 42
character choices 172
Children of Húrin, The (Tolkien) 46, 93, 96, 99–101, 109
children's literature 7, 14, 16, 20, 21, 25–26, 34, 35, 41, 53, 68
Chronicles of Narnia, The (Lewis) 1, 132, 154, 158; film 155
Cicero (publishing house) 43, 45
Ciri (character) 137–138, 143, 147n1
Clarke, Arthur C. 18
classicisation process 14
Companion to J.R.R. Tolkien (Lee) 52
Complete Guide to Middle-earth, A (Foster) 45
communism 71n7, 89
Conan the Barbarian (Howard) 80
convergence 2, 5, 9, 138, 164–167
convergent media environment 167, 172
Corvina (publisher) 49, 50
Csányi, Vilmos 42
cultural transplantation 120

Curry, Patrick 37
Czechoslovakia, Tolkien and 61–63, 70–71; *Hobbit,* first adaptation of 66–67; literary magazines and Tolkien translated for first time 63–66; underground and dissident circles 68–69
Czech Republic 2, 3, 66, 67, 84
Czech translation 66, 95, 100–102, 123; proper nouns and geographical names 98; and Slovak translations 98–99; Tolkien's novel 75, 97

Daily Telegraph, The 17
Dark Mordor (heavy metal band) 111
Day, David 112, 113
Deák, Adrienn 53
"December Evening: The Second-Hand Bookshop", A 21
deconvergence 164–168
Dědinová, Tereza 8
Deitch, Gene 67
digital, formats 52; media 173; natives 74, 84; technology 89, 90, 92, 168, 172
Disney Plus 161
Dorůžka, Lubomír 66, 76
Drastich, Miloš 97, 107
Drout, Michael 42, 52
Dubs, Kathleen 40
Dungeons & Dragons (Dragon's Den) 80
Duriez, Colin 49

Eco, Umberto 21, 39
Elanor 22
Élet és Irodalom (journal) 23
Emiel Regis (character) 138, 144
Ende, Michael 20, 24, 25, 35, 77
environment 8, 63, 74, 75, 76, 108, 119; boarding school 136; convergent media 167, 172; cultural 61; fandom 97; fantastic 155; human 142; media-saturated 166; Slovak 109, 113; Slovak academic 105; Slovak literary 103
Eörsi, István 23
Éowyn (character) 19, 43, 54n16, 88
Erikson, Erik 134

Index   181

escape 8, 24, 76, 81, 85, 89, 90, 108, 136, 140, 155, 172
Esolen, Anthony 110
Európa (publishing house) 44, 45, 46, 47, 49
Expanse, The 163, 171

fairy-tale novel 16, 19, 21, 36
Falcsik, Mari 46
Fall of Gondolin, The (Tolkien) 47
fandom 1–3, 5, 6, 15, 22, 34, 35, 40, 80, 81, 93, 100, 103–106, 110, 111, 113, 119, 122, 152, 162, 164, 168–173
fantasy 2, 17–19, 119, 150; advantages of teaching 152; books 155; described 135; fandom 172–173; genre 152; genre in literary courses 151; literature 36, 154–155; narratives 153–154; platform logic, in context of 161–164; re-conceptualisation 5–6; on television 165; *see also* genre and Tolkien's legacy; Hungarian students of English and American Studies; YA fantasy
Fantasy Media in the Classroom: Essays on Teaching with Film, Television, Literature, Graphic Novels, and Video Games (Ford) 151
fantasy mode 7, 8
Fantázia (periodical) 97, 99, 100, 103, 106, 111, 113
fanzines 19, 22, 24, 25, 80, 93, 96, 99, 100, 103, 108
Farmer Giles of Ham (Tolkien) 20, 23, 46
Father Christmas Letters, The (Tolkien) 46
Fazekas, András 19
Fazekas, Gergely 46
Fehér, Viktória 48
Fehrle, Johannes 166
Fellowship of Friends of the Work of Mr J.R.R. Tolkien, The 80–81
Fellowship of Tolkien, The (Slovakia) 112
Fellowship of the Ring, The (Tolkien) see *Lord of the Rings*

Ferenčík, Ján 119
Ferko, Miloš 98, 100, 104–106, 105, 106
fictional worlds 19, 141
fidelity criticism 167–168, 174n1
Fighting Fantasy series 20
film 1–4, 6–8, 9, 14–15, 26, 34–36, 40–42, 45, 48, 53–54, 56, 67, 72–75, 80, 85–87, 91, 94–99, 105, 107–108, 112, 116, 139, 147, 151, 152, 153, 155, 158–159, 162–163, 166–169, 171; *see also* adaptation
Fimi, Dimitra 43
Finder, Jan Howard 15, 27n5, 27n6
Flieger, Verlyn 50, 51
Fónod, Zoltán 37
Fonstad, Karen Wynn 45, 49
Foster, Robert 45
Foucaultian heterotopia 142
Foucault, Michel 142, 144, 146
Friedman, Ted 168
Frišo, Peter 110
Frodo (character) 36, 44, 69, 71n2
Frye, Northrop 21
Füzessy, Tamás 27, 42, 43, 44, 45, 46, 50, 53, 54n9

Galadriel (character) 71n2, 88, 98, 112, 165
Galadriel (heavy metal band) 111, 112
Galaktika (magazine) 15, 16, 19, 20, 22, 23, 27n7, 28n17, 28n27
Galántai, Zoltán 23
Gálvölgyi, Judit 15, 22, 27, 42, 43, 45–47
Gandalf (character) 36, 67, 69, 71n2, 82, 120
Game of Thrones 154–156, 164, 170; films and series 155; HBO 171
Garth, John 49, 50, 51
Gáspár, András 22, 54n13
gender 2, 74, 89, 153
Gendiar, Michal 101, 102
genre and Tolkien's legacy: Hungarian students of English and American Studies 158–159; fantasy literature 154–155; fantasy narratives 153–154, 156; film adaptations 154–156; films and series 155; survey

182   Index

152–153; teaching fantasy 150–151; Tolkien's fantasy *vs.* modern fantasy narratives 157; Tolkien's work 155–156

genre fantasy 14, 18

genre of works in Slovak reception texts 103–110; academic literary criticism journals 104; approaches to the issue of 104–105; fantasy and 106; Harry Potter 109–110; online periodicals 103–104; schools and teachers 107; second wave of popularity of Tolkien's works 109

Geralt (character) 137, 143, 144, 147n1

Gimli (character) 36

global brand 162, 167, 173

Glorfindel (character) 36, 86

Golden Pot: A Modern Fairytale, The (Hoffmann) 151

Gollum (character) 16, 36, 67, 98, 122, 125–127

Göncz, Árpád 18–21, 22, 27n13, 34, 41, 43, 44

Gondolat (publishing house) 13, 15, 18

Gottweisová, Alena 98

G. Papp, Katalin 25

Green, John 132, 135, 143

Grunt, Jiří 80, 81, 83, 84

Grünwald, Mihály Erdei 15, 27n6

"Guide to the Names in *The Lord of the Rings*" (Tolkien) 18

Gulliver's Travels (Swift) 151

Gy. Horváth, László 44, 47

Gyuris, Norbert 39, 49, 50, 53

Gyűrű keresése, A (Tolkien) 23

Haastrup, Helle Kannik 164, 165

Halík, Tomáš 69

Hammond, Wayne G. 49, 120

Hargitai, Henrik 25, 28n24

Harry Potter (Rowling) 1, 34–36, 40, 108, 109; as book 155; film 155; narrative 154, 158

Harry Potter 20th Anniversary: Return to Hogwarts 168

Harry Potter and the Philosopher's Stone (Rowling) 150

Havel, Václav 69, 72n14

HBO Max 161; *Game of Thrones* 171; *His Dark Materials* 163; *House of the Dragon* 165

Hemingway, Ernest 18

Herec, Ondrej 104, 105

Herman, David 139

Heroes of Tolkien, The (Day) 112

heroic romance 13, 21

Hevier, Daniel 68, 95

high fantasy 2, 3, 20, 23, 164

His Dark Materials (Pullman) 132, 151, 154, 163

History (journal) 108

History of Middle-earth, The (Tolkien) 24, 35, 43, 47, 48, 52

Hobbit, The (Tolkien) 8; book 155, 156; in Czechoslovakia 64, 66, 67, 68, 70, 75–77, 80, 81, 82; Czech reception 86; first film adaptation of 66–67; in Hungary 13, 15–17, 21, 25, 26, 27n12, 28n18, 35, 36, 43, 44, 47, 49, 54n16; Krupa's translation of 94–96; in Slovakia 94–98, 102, 106, 108, 109, 111, 114n3, 117–127; Slovak translations 98–99; *see also* translation in *The Hobbit*

Hódosy, Annamária 39, 53

Hoffmann, E.T.A. 151

Holló és Társa (publisher) 24, 44

Hollywood Reporter, The 169

Honegger, Thomas 42, 51

House of the Dragon 163, 164, 165

Howard, Robert P. 25, 80

Hume, Kathryn 166

Hungarian Fantasy Club 19

Hungarian Society for the Study of English (HUSSE) 48

Hungarian Tolkien Society 7, 14, 26, 35, 40–41

Hungary, reading Tolkien in (20th century) 13–14; on to 21st Century 26; first wave of translations: *Hobbit and The Lord of the Rings* (1970s–1980s) 16–21; rumours: before first translations 14–15; second wave: 1990s 22–26

Index 183

Hungary, reading Tolkien in (21st century) 34–35; myth of many places 52–53; Peter Jackson and Hungarian Tolkien Society 40–43; revisions 43–45; third wave: new work by and about Tolkien 45–48; Tolkien as reference point: approaches in early 2000s 35–40; work on Tolkien, Popular, and Scholarly 48–52
Húrin gyermekei (Tolkien) 46, 47
Hutcheon, Linda 167
hybridity-hybridisation 1, 3, 9, 164, 165–167, 174
Hyžný, Matúš "Loki" 96, 99, 100, 111

Igen (periodical) 20
Imladris (fanzine) 80, 112
Impulz (magazine) 103, 109
Individuated Hobbit: Jung, Tolkien, and the Archetypes of Middle-earth, The (O'Neill) 135, 140
interdisciplinary character 5–6
Iser, Wolfgang 49
It Happened Tomorrow: The True History of Science Fiction (Lundwall) 19

Jackson, Peter 4, 7, 14, 26, 34, 40–43, 52, 87, 90, 95, 117, 155, 157
Jacob (character) 138, 144–145, 147n2
Janáček, Pavel 79
Jauss, Hans-Robert 49
Jenkins, Henry 113, 166
Josek, Jiří 77
J.R.R. Tolkien: Author of the Century (Shippey) 39
J.R.R. Tolkien Encyclopaedia, The (Drout) 52
J.R.R. Tolkien: Fantasy and Morality (conference) 50
J.R.R. Tolkien in Slovak Press (situation after 1990) 93; fandom in Tolkien's work 110–113; genre of works in Slovak reception texts

103–110; translation critique in Slovak academic and popular environment 97–103; unwanted Tolkien: on history of Slovak editions of Tolkien's works 93–97
Jungian psychoanalysis 131, 134
Juríčková, Eva 108
Juričková, Martina 101, 112, 113

Kádár, János 13
Kádár regime 13, 27n3
Kafka, Franz 151
Kalevala 47
Kampademie (Kampademy) 68, 69
Karpinský, Peter 95, 106, 107
Kascakova, Janka 8
Kazár, József 25, 53, 54n13
Kehoe, Jela 8
Kelemen, István 46
Kelemen, Zoltán 48, 50, 51, 54n10
Kemény, István 21, 27, 39
Kende B., Hanna 36
Kéry, László 21
Király, Teodóra 49
Kiss, Kincső 51
Kiss, Zoltán 40
Kiss, Zsuzsa N. 46, 47
Klimáček, Viliam 96, 98, 102
Klučariková, Daniela 101
Kľúčik, Peter 94, 95, 97
Knoll, L.H. 20
Koltai, Gábor 22, 23, 25, 27, 28n26, 42, 45, 53n8
Komáromi, Gabriella 25
Koncz, Éva 37
Könyvvilág 23
Kořínek, Otakar 95, 98–100, 102, 117, 118, 120–127
Kornya, Zsolt 25, 28n20, 28n31, 38, 39, 53n4, 54n16, 54n18
Kossuth 15
Kozák, Jan A. 74, 76
Kozmosz 14
Kranz, Gisbert 15
Kraviarová, Zuzana 102
Kripke's theory 140
Kritika prekladu 102
Kroupa, Daniel 69
Krupa, Viktor 63–66, 71n2, 94, 95, 98–100, 104, 117, 120–127

184 Index

Kuczka, Péter 14, 15, 19, 20, 22, 26, 27n4, 27n5
Kultúrny život (journal) 99, 103, 105
Kušnír, Jaroslav 99, 105

Lassi Laurië 42, 54n15
Lays of Beleriand, The (Tolkien) 47, 48
Leaf by Niggle (Tolkien) 46
Lear, Edward 17
Lee, Alan 95, 96
Lees, Nathaniel 43
legacy 1–6, 106, 107, 110, 112, 132, 155–159, 165
Legolas (character) 36
Lewis, C.S. 1, 27n4, 132, 135, 151
Library of Souls (Riggs) 145–146
Lihachova, Svetlana 42
Literárny týždenník (periodical) 103, 107
Live Action Role-Play (LARPs) 112
Lobová, Andrea 107
Looking for Alaska (Green) 132, 135, 142–143
Lord of the Rings, The (Tolkien) 1, 3, 8, 15, 131, 151; in Czechoslovakia 63–66, 68–70, 74, 77, 78, 80; in digital world 84–89; *Fellowship of the Ring, The* (Tolkien) 70, 79, 87, 95, 99; as films and series 26, 45, 46, 86, 87, 94, 99, 107, 117, 154, 155; in Hungary 13, 15–18, 20, 21, 23–26, 27n10, 27n14, 34, 36, 37, 38, 41–44, 48, 49, 51, 53n2; reception in the Czech republic 76, 78, 81–90; *Return of the King, The* 78, 95, 96; in Slovakia 93, 95, 96–99, 100, 106, 107, 108, 114n4; Slovak translation 115-, 120, 154, 155, 156
Lord of the Rings: The Rings of Power, The 156, 159
Lost Road and Other Writings, The (Tolkien) 48
Lovász, Andrea 25, 35
Lovecraft, H.P. 25
Lundwall, Sam J. 19, 53n2
Lyotard, Jean-François 39

Maár, Judit 36
Magvető (publishing house) 44, 46, 47
Magyar Ifjúság (periodical) 15
Magyar Névtani Dolgozatok (journal) 25
mainstream 7, 9, 94, 97, 101, 111–113, 174
Makai, Péter Kristóf 52
Malíček, Juraj 111
Marhoul, Václav 80
Márquez, Gabriel García 151
Martinez, Michael 45–46
Martin, George R.R. 151
Martinus Fantázia Award 104, 114n7
Marvel Cinematic Universe 124, 155, 161, 163, 164
medieval, chronicles 23; English literature 45; literature 14, 52; manuscripts 74; romance 135
mega-franchise 161
Mérleg 15, 27n8
Merry (character) 19, 43, 98, 54n16
meseregény (fairy-tale novel) 16
Mesterházi, Mónika 47
Metamorphosis, The (Kafka) 151
methodology and organising principle 6–7
Mező, Ferenc 17
Middle Ages, the 70, 77
Middle-earth 17, 22, 23, 37, 74, 75, 78, 79, 81, 82, 84, 88, 90, 93, 96, 100, 101, 108, 110, 112, 118, 120, 123, 141, 159
Midnight's Children (Rushdie) 151
Mighty Thor, The (comic series) 139
Miklya Luzsányi, Mónika 51
Mikos, Lothar 166
Miles (character) 135–136, 142–143
Miss Peregrine (character) 138, 145, 146
Miss Peregrine series (Rigg) 132, 138, 144–147
Mistborn 154
Mladá Fronta (publishing house) 77
Molnár, Gábor Tamás 53n3
Momo (Ende) 20
Monsters and the Critics, The (Tolkien) see *Beowulf: The Monsters and the Critics*
Móra (publishing house) 15, 16, 20, 28n18

Index   185

Morrison, Toni 151
Morse, Donald E. 40, 41, 53
Mr. Bliss (Tolkien) 46
mythology 16, 20, 38, 66, 69–70,
  86, 96, 105, 108, 112, 135,
  157; Celtic 50, 106; Germanic
  50, 106; Norse 36, 50, 103;
  Oriental 106; Slavic 103;
  Tolkienian 152, 159

Nagy, Andrea 47, 48, 50, 51, 53
Nagy, Gergely 7
Nagyvilág (periodical) 17, 21
Name of the Rose, The (Eco) 21
narratives, fantasy 153–154
Nasmith, Ted 42
Neff, Ondřej 76, 77
Németh, Anikó 23, 42, 49, 54n20
Netflix 161, 162
Neubauer, Zdeněk 69, 70, 82–83, 90
Neverending Story, The (Ende) 20, 24,
  25, 77
New York Review of Books, The 17
niche 2, 5, 7, 9, 159, 161, 162, 173,
  174
niche audiences 170–174
nonsense literature 17
Novák, Csanád 20, 22, 28n19, 28n28,
  54n13
Nováková, Luisa 83
Nyulászi, Zsolt 20

Oakenshield, Thorin (character) 122
O'Brien, Michael D. 109
One Hundred Years of Solitude
  (Márquez) 151
O'Neill, Timothy R. 135, 140
"On Fairy-Stories" 16, 23, 26, 35, 45,
  52, 81, 140
Orcs (fictional characters) 65, 89, 98,
  100, 102
Orkrist (heavy metal band) 111
Orthmayr, Flóra 53n
otherness 1, 4, 8, 74, 75, 83, 131, 142
*Out into the world to experience: On
  journeys there and back again*
  (Neubauer) 82–84
Outlander 155

Palantír (fanzine) 80
Palatinus, David 9

Palouš, Radim 69
Parker, Craig 43
participation 5, 170–174
Partvonal (publisher) 46
Pavel, Thomas G. 140
Pázmány Péter Catholic University 40,
  50–52, 152, 153, 157
Peoples of Middle-earth, The
  (Tolkien) 24
Peprník, Michal 68, 79
Pevčíková, Jozefa 8
platform, logic 161–164; originals 161,
  162; streaming platforms 9,
  153, 161–163, 170, 173; SVOD
  163; visual media 4, 166, 167,
  169, 172
Pődör, Dóra 50
Poetic fellowship 81
Poláček, Ivo 103
Polish Tolkien 132
politics 1, 27n8
Pollák, Tamás 54n13
Popovič, Anton 125
Pósa, Zoltán 20
Postoj (journal) 104, 109
post-socialist 2, 3, 69, 163
Pošustová-Menšíková, Stanislava 66,
  70, 77, 78, 100
Prague Spring 63, 64
Pratchett, Terry 25
Prekladateľské listy (journal)
  101, 103
press 2, 7, 8, 13, 15–17, 19, 22, 34,
  41, 63, 93, 97
Primusová, Hana 78–79
Prowse, David 43

Rabelais, François 136
race 85, 89, 144
racism 8, 75, 88
Rácz, Judit 25
Rappensbergerová, Naďa 66
*Reader, Come Home: The Reading
  Brain in a Digital World* (Wolf)
  84, 89
reception of Tolkien 1, 3, 5–9; in
  Czechoslovakia 62, 63, 67, 70,
  71, 74, 75, 79, 81, 82; in the
  Czech republic 85, 86, 89; in
  Hungary 14, 19, 26, 34–36, 49,
  52, 53; in Slovakia 93, 96, 97,

186   Index

99, 101–105, 108, 109, 111, 113
Reginae Mysterium 111
Regős, Pál 50, 54n9
remediation 2
repression 141
Return of the King, The (Tolkien) see *Lord of the Rings*
Return of the Shadow, The (Tolkien) 48
Revue svetovej literatúry 63, 64, 66, 71n2–n3
Réz, Ádám 18
Réz, András 53n8, 54n12
Rhys-Davies, John 43
Richter, Pavel 80
Riggs, Ransom 132, 138, 146
Rigó, Béla 19, 28n18, 41, 53n8, 54n10, 54n14
Rihák, Jaroslav 96
Rings of Power, The 35, 163, 164
rite of passage 8, 135, 136, 140, 141, 147
Road to Middle-earth, The (Shippey) 25
Roberts, Jon 41
Romboid (journal) 100, 103
Róna, Jaroslav 80
Rosebury, Brian 37
Roverandom (Tolkien) 46, 93, 96, 99, 106, 109
Rowling, J.K. 1, 34, 36, 151, 164
RPG 19, 22, 24, 26, 39, 41, 49
Rudé právo (communist daily) 65
Rushdie, Salman 28n27, 151

Šalamoun, Jiří 66
Sam(wise) Gamgee (character) 87
Sanderson, Brandon 154
Sapkowski, Andrzej 132, 136, 167
Saruman (character) 38, 44, 65
Saudek, Erik A. 66
Sauron (character) 38, 44, 88, 165
Savický, Nikolaj 78–79, 80, 81
science fiction 7, 14, 15, 17, 19, 20, 22, 26, 27n7, 28n23, 35, 39, 40, 53, 53n2, 76–77, 104, 108, 162, 163
screen culture 4, 7, 161–177
Scull, Christina 49, 120
Second World War 62, 66, 106, 107

Secular Scripture, The (Frye) 21
Selmeczi, Szonja 53n
serial, culture 140; format 170, 174
series: book 14, 19–20, 22, 24, 27n13, 28n25, 34, 38, 44, 47–48, 107, 109, 132, 136, 138, 143, 144, 146–147, 151, 154; comic 139; event 42, 50; film 95, 107, 154, 155, 158; television 35, 124, 136, 150, 152, 155, 156, 157, 158, 159, 161–162, 164, 165, 167–171, 174n1
Shadow and Bone 154, 155
Shaping of Middle-earth, The (Tolkien) 48
Shelley, Mary 18
Shippey, Tom 25, 28n26, 37, 39
Shire, The 65, 98, 120
Short, Kathy G. 131
Silmarillion, The (Tolkien) 14, 15, 17, 22, 23, 40, 42, 44–46, 52, 76, 82, 86, 93, 96, 110, 156
Sipos, Nikolett 8
Sir Gawain and the Green Knight 45
Skála, František 80
Skibniewská, Maria 100
Skoumal, Aloys 66
Slovak Hobbiton 98
Slovakia 2, 3, 5, 8, 17, 63, 66, 68, 95–98, 102, 111, 114n4, 125
Slovak translations: from 1973 and 2002 117–127; *Children of Húrin, The* 99; Czech translation and 98–99; *Fellowship of the Ring, The* 97; *Hobbit, The* 98–99, 102; Tolkien and 101; *see also* translation in *The Hobbit*
Slovart (publishing house) 95, 100
Slovenská fantastika do roku 2000 (Herec and Ferko) 105
Slovenské pohľady (journal) 99–100, 103
Slovenský jazyk a literatúra v škole (journal) 103, 107
Smith of Wooton Major (Tolkien) 23, 46
Smith, Scot 133
Snyder, William L. 67
socialist states 3
social media 171, 172, 173

Index 187

Sohár, Anikó 21, 22, 26, 27, 27n12, 28n23, 39, 40, 41, 51, 52, 53
Song of Ice and Fire, A (Martin) 151, 155
Spoločenstvo Tolkiena 103, 112
Star Wars 24, 40, 50, 51, 161, 163, 164
Stehlíková, Blanka 66
Stemler, Miklós 48, 49, 54n12
Stephens, Jonathan 132–133
Stormlight Archive, The (Sanderson) 154
Story of Kullervo, The (Flieger) 47
streaming platforms 9, 153, 161–164, 169, 173
Stryon 18
Suchý, Daniel 99, 105
Sundet, Vilde Shanke 173
Šuška, Čestmír 80
SVOD platform 163
Swift, Jonathan 17, 151
Sword of Destiny, The (Sapkowski) 137
Sýkora, Peter 108
Szabó, Csilla M. 46
Szamosi, Gertrúd 48, 51, 53
Szántai, Zsolt 45, 46
Szántó, Judit 23
Szász, Anna Mária 21
Szecskó, Tamás 16
Szentmihályi Szabó, Péter 13–16, 19, 21, 27n1, 27n7
Szobotka, Tibor 16, 17, 43, 44
Szőnyi, György Endre 41, 54n12
Szukits (publishing house) 23, 41, 44–46, 54n13

Takács, Ferenc 23, 28n27
Tallián, Balázs 45
Tandori, Dezső 18, 24, 44
Tarcsay, Tibor 40, 52
Tarjányi, Eszter 25
teaching (fantasy) 151, 152
television 6, 8, 42, 61, 124, 150, 151, 154, 159, 161–163, 165, 168, 170, 171
Television Drama in the Age of Streaming (Sundet) 173
Tézsla, Ervin 41, 45, 54n13
Theologiai Szemle 51

Thorin (fanzine) 80
Thor: Ragnarok (Waititi) 139
Tick, Péter 25, 53, 54n13
Todorov, Tzvetan 36, 49, 53n1
Tolkien Academy 50
Tolkien: A Look Behind The Lord of the Rings (Carter) 45
Tolkien and C.S. Lewis: The Gift of Friendship (Duriez) 49
Tolkien Book House (bookshop) 22
Tolkien, Christopher 46, 47, 109
Tolkien, J.R.R. 1; genre and Tolkien's legacy 152–159; Hungarian students of English and American Studies 9, 150, 152, 153, 157, 158; Hungary, reading Tolkien in (20th century) 13–28; Hungary, reading Tolkien in (21th century) 34–54; unwanted Tolkien: on history of Slovak editions of Tolkien's works 93–97; *see also* Czechoslovakia, Tolkien and; dynamics of J.R.R. Tolkien's work reception in Czechoslovakia; fantasy; genre and Tolkien's legacy; Hungary, reading Tolkien in (20th century); Hungary, reading Tolkien in (21st century)
Tolkien myth 110
Tolkien scholarship 46, 51
Tolkien Society (Hungary) 7, 14, 26, 35, 40–44, 47, 48, 50
Tolkien's Worlds (Garth) 49
Tótfalusi, István 16, 37, 46, 47
Tótisz, András (also T.O. Teas) 19, 27n15
translation: described 118; domesticating or foreignising 118–119; forms of 97; process of 118; strategies 118–120
translation in *The Hobbit*: Arkenstone 122–123; culture-specific concepts 124; foreign names 120; functional proper nouns 120–121; idiolect 126–127; inanimate objects 122; nomenclature 123–124; place names 123; standard English

188 *Index*

125–126; in standard English
125; surnames 121
transmediality 2, 7, 9, 166, 167, 171, 174
transmedia storytelling 166
Tree and Leaf (Tolkien) 23
True Blood 165
Turba, Ctibor 80
Turner, Allan 51
Tylšová, Lída 82
Tyšš, Igor 102

Uhrman, Iván 25, 27, 43, 45, 50, 53, 54n9, 54n11
Új Vénusz (magazine) 22
Unfinished Tales (Tolkien) 23, 43, 44, 46, 47, 93, 96, 101
Updike, John 18
urban fantasy 8, 165
Urbanová, Eva 8
Ürmössy, Zsuzsanna 43, 44

Vajda, Zsuzsanna 53n8
Valóság (periodical) 15
Vampire Diaries, The 165
Varga, Illés 25, 53, 53n6, 54n13
Varró, Attila 45n12
Varró, Dániel 36, 53
Végh, Dániel 49
Vekerdy, Tamás 16, 27n10
Velvet Revolution (1989) 68, 70, 80, 81, 84, 89
Vida, Győző 43
Visualising Middle-earth (Martinez) 46
Volná, Martina "Llewelyn" 113
Vonnegut, Kurt 89

Vránová, Martina 8
Vrba, František 66, 67, 70, 76, 100, 117, 118, 121, 122

Waldman, Milton 45
Warsaw pact 63
Watership Down (Adams) 68
Webster, James G. 172, 173
Werner, Schäfke-Zell 166
Wheel of Time, Shadow and Bone, The 154
Wheel of Time, The (series) 163, 169, 171
"Why Am I Fed Up with Tolkien?" (Kornya) 38
Winklerová, Lucia 100, 109
Witcher, The 132, 136, 143–144, 155; as book 155; narrative 154, 158; Netflix 163, 167
Wolf, Marianne 84, 89
worldbuilding 1, 2, 4, 8, 20, 23, 36, 37, 48, 53n3, 131, 164

YA fantasy/YA fiction 131, 132, 135, 147
Yennefer (character) 137, 143
young-adult 81, 132, 165
young adult literature (YAL) 131–132; adolescence meaning 133–134; defined 132–135; features of 133; fictional worlds 141; possible worlds 139–147; quest for identity 135–139; roles of 134

Zmeták, Igor 108
Zvelebil, Jan 80